POWER ANIMALS

Also by Steven D. Farmer, Ph.D.

Adult Children of Abusive Parents:
*A Healing Program for Those Who Have
Been Physically, Sexually, or Emotionally Abused*

Sacred Ceremony: *How to Create Ceremonies
for Healing, Transitions, and Celebrations*
(available from Hay House)

Please visit Hay House USA: **www.hayhouse.com**
Hay House Australia: **www.hayhouse.com.au**
Hay House UK: **www.hayhouse.co.uk**
Hay House South Africa: **orders@psdprom.co.za**

POWER ANIMALS
How to Connect with Your Animal Spirit Guide

Steven D. Farmer, Ph.D.

HAY HOUSE, INC.
Carlsbad, California
London • Sydney • Johannesburg
Vancouver • Hong Kong

Copyright © 2004 by Steven D. Farmer

Published and distributed in the United States by: Hay House, Inc., P.O. Box 5100, Carlsbad, CA 92018-5100 • *Phone:* (760) 431-7695 or (800) 654-5126 • *Fax:* (760) 431-6948 or (800) 650-5115 • www.hayhouse.com • *Published and distributed in Australia by:* Hay House Australia Pty. Ltd., 18/36 Ralph St., Alexandria NSW 2015 • *Phone:* 612-9669-4299 • *Fax:* 612-9669-4144 • www.hayhouse.com.au • *Published and distributed in the United Kingdom by:* Hay House UK, Ltd. • Unit 62, Canalot Studios • 222 Kensal Rd., London W10 5BN • *Phone:* 44-20-8962-1230 • *Fax:* 44-20-8962-1239 • www.hayhouse.co.uk • *Published and distributed in the Republic of South Africa by:* Hay House SA (Pty), Ltd., P.O. Box 990, Witkoppen 2068 • *Phone/Fax:* 27-11-706-6612 • orders@psdprom.co.za • *Distributed in Canada by:* Raincoast • 9050 Shaughnessy St., Vancouver, B.C. V6P 6E5 • *Phone:* (604) 323-7100 • *Fax:* (604) 323-2600

Design: Amy Rose Szalkiewicz
Front cover art and animal illustrations: Eric Nesmith: **www.nez-art.com**

Library of Congress Cataloging-in-Publication Data

Farmer, Steven.
  Power animals : how to connect with your animal spirit guide / Steven D. Farmer.
    p. cm.
  Includes bibliographical references.
  ISBN 1-4019-0332-0 (hardcover)
  1. Guides (Spiritualism) 2. Animals—Miscellanea. I. Title.
  BF1275.G85F37 2004
  133'.259—dc22
                                    2004000183

ISBN 13: 978-1-4019-0332-9
ISBN 10: 1-4019-0332-0

07 06 05 04   5 4 3 2
1st printing, August 2004
2nd printing, June 2005

Printed in the United States of America

For the animals

Contents

APPENDIX

Author's Note: Although animal spirit guides can be of either gender, in the text I've used the singular pronouns "she" and "her" (determined by the flip of a coin) in order to avoid the awkward "him/her, he/she" constructions.

"Ask the animals, and they will teach you, or the birds of the air, and they will tell you; or speak to the earth, and it will teach you, or let the fish of the sea inform you."

— Job 12:7–8

"Millennia before Charles Darwin, people in shamanic cultures were convinced that humans and animals were related. In their myths, for example, the animal characters were commonly portrayed as essentially human in physical form but individually distinguished by the particular personality characteristics possessed by the various types of animals as they exist in the wild today. . . . Then, according to various creation myths, the animals became physically differentiated into the forms in which they are found today."

— from *The Way of the Shaman* by Michael Harner

Introduction

YOU'RE ABOUT TO EMBARK ON A JOURNEY that could profoundly change your life. You may have a spirit guide already, or it may be a completely new concept to you. Either way, when you get to know your animal spirit guide and develop a close relationship with her, you'll open the door to a spiritual power that will serve to protect, guide, and heal you. A power animal is just that: an animal spirit guide that will empower you and help you deal with both the spiritual and the earthly realm.

Before we get started, please note that while you may discover only one power animal after reading this book, throughout I've sometimes referred to them in the plural. This is not only to avoid awkward sentence construction and make it easier for you to understand, but also because over time and with more experience, you may develop relationships with more than one power animal.

The idea of power animals reaches back to ancient times, when we humans had a more intimate and mutual relationship with the animals we shared the earth with. Although the concept is associated with shamanism, you needn't be a shaman or even be particularly interested in shamanism to benefit from having a relationship with a power animal. Also, the idea of animal spirit guides is not exclusive to any one culture, but is found in some form in nearly *all* cultures.

Meeting your power animals and working with them requires only your openness and willingness to explore this territory. By using this book and enclosed CD, I'll give you very specific instructions on how to meet, retrieve, and work with them.

Part I of the book explains what power animals are, how you can meet and retrieve your particular animal, and ways to develop the relationship once you do. Part II summarizes 36 different power animals. Here you'll find a communication from that animal spirit guide, characteristics you have in common if this is your power animal, challenges you may face where she can help, and things you can do to call on her. This is obviously not an exhaustive list, and whether or not your power animal appears in these pages, it's important that you learn how to communicate directly with her. This is where the enclosed CD comes in handy.

On the CD you'll find a guided meditation journey with specific instructions on how you can retrieve your power animal. On another track, there's a guided meditation journey that will be useful when you seek your animal spirit guide's counsel on questions and concerns you have. Additional tracks will support self-directed explorations with your power animal.

The best way to get started is to first read Part I in its entirety, and then peruse Part II, perhaps reading about some of your favorite animals. Then when you're ready, follow the instructions for the CD, starting with Track 1, as a way to find out who your specific power animal is. As you gain experience and feel more comfortable with journeying, you can use the additional tracks for further exploration.

Take your time with this material. After all, you're getting ready to set out on an adventure that will help you navigate through life with greater ease and confidence. May you be blessed along this path.

Author's note: You can also use this book as an oracle to find out which animal spirit guide is working with you or to get an answer to any questions you might have about your career, relationships, finances, and so on. Hold the book in your hands, take a couple of breaths, think of your question (such as "Which power animal is working with me?" or "What do I need to know right now?"), then flip through the last 80 percent of the pages.

When you get the sense to do so, stop and open the book to the page where you landed. Go to the opening page for that animal and read the message that responds to your question.

PART I
Discovering
Your Power Animal

1
What Are Power Animals?

POWER ANIMALS ARE SPIRIT GUIDES in animal form, valuable allies who can help you navigate through life's challenges and transitions. You can turn to these perceptive and trustworthy oracles for advice and counsel on any questions or concerns. They're exceptional teachers who will help you learn about both the spirit world and the natural world. Working with them on a regular basis will enhance your personal life and expand your spiritual capacities immensely.

Power animals can appear in meditations, visions, dreams, shamanic journeys, or on the earth in their physical forms. They can be mammals, birds, or reptiles. Even so-called mythical creatures such as unicorns or dragons can be power animals, although they have no physical representations in the material world. However, since a spirit animals' power is drawn from their instinctual and wild nature, it's uncommon for purely domesticated animals such as pets to be part of this group.

The source of power for your animal spirit guide isn't just a single animal, but the entire species. For instance, if your power animal is Bear, it's not just any particular bear, but an animal spirit guide that's representative of the entire species of bears.

Another positive effect of working with your power animal is that you'll develop a greater appreciation not only for that species, but also extend that care and respect to the animal kingdom as a whole. If Dolphin is your power animal, your love and appreciation will likely go out to all creatures of the sea and naturally expand to include those of the land and the air. Your animal spirit guide will also teach you to use this power compassionately, to heal and empower yourself and others.

2
Spirit Guides and Power Animals

THE TERM *SPIRIT GUIDES* (also known as *guardian spirits* or *helping spirits*) describes any spiritual beings that help us in a positive way. They protect us, guide us, and provide us with encouragement and inspiration. We may have any number of spirit guides throughout our life, whether or not we're consciously aware of them. Some have been with us since childhood, while others have appeared at various periods in our life, perhaps to help us through a difficult transition. Spirit guides can be religious figures, angels, ascended masters, ancestors, fairies, or, for our purposes, animal spirits.

Animal spirit guides, familiar to indigenous and shamanic cultures, are called either *power animals* or *totem animals*. Typically these terms are used interchangeably, although there are some subtle differences in meaning. *Totem animal* is the more widely used term, and this concept is universal to virtually all cultures.

Indigenous cultures typically have a tribal totem, another one for the "clan," and another for the family one is born into.

Contemporary cultures also have totem animals, such as those for clubs or societies like the Lions Club or the Loyal Order of Moose, or for sports teams such as the Chicago Bears or the Philadelphia Eagles. Even Christianity has the totems of the lamb and the fish.

Parents will often give their child a special totem animal, such as a teddy bear, for protection. Through the child's belief in the animal she holds in her hands, she's unwittingly calling in the spirit of that animal and its associated powers. The bear becomes a personal totem, or power animal, for the child, and this animal spirit guide may remain with her well into her adult life.

Power animals, rather than being associated with a family or a group, are specific and personal for each individual. Like totem animals, they are guardian spirits that empower us in our everyday lives. They also protect and guide us as we explore *non-ordinary reality*—the realm where spirits reside—just across the veil of our usual perceptions.

3
Your Power Animal and You

POWER ANIMALS AND TOTEM ANIMALS, as well as other spirit guides, are inhabitants of non-ordinary reality, and as mentioned, we can contact them through meditations, shamanic journeys, dreams, or visions to request their guidance, healing, and protection. Although the terms *power animals* and *totem animals* are often used interchangeably, the focus here will be on power animals because of the unique and highly personal relationship they develop with each of us.

Unlike other spirit guides, power animals (with the exception of mythical animals) can also appear in physical form in ordinary reality. When your power animal does make an appearance in ordinary reality, it may be an omen or sign from her, depending on the context, the frequency of the sightings, and the behavior of the animal (which I'll elaborate on later).

You may or may not be aware of who your power animal is. If not, you can use this book and the enclosed CD as a guide for finding out who she is. One of the tracks on the CD is a guided meditation journey to help you discover and retrieve your power animal; however, if you're already aware of who she is, the other tracks can help you further explore your relationship with this magnificent spiritual being. You can also use these other tracks to acquire additional power animals, although to start, I'd advise working with just one so that you get to know her more intimately.

You don't actually choose your power animal—you choose each other. Throughout your life you may have even had a number of favorite animals (including totem animals) as spirit guides, but it's entirely possible that none of them was your power animal. And once an animal spirit shows up in your life as a power animal, it's your choice to accept her in that role. In a sense, you make a conscious "soul agreement" with your power animal, one that's mutually beneficial. Your animal spirit guide finds great joy in working with you and experiencing ordinary reality through your physical senses, and you get an animal spirit guide that counsels, heals, and empowers you.

Throughout my life I've had relationships with a few different animal spirit guides. Some of them I've known about, while others have accompanied me at various times on my life's journey without my being aware of them. In the past several years since

I've followed a shamanic path, I've developed conscious relationships with various animal spirit guides, and presently I have four power animals. My first power animal came to me over 15 years ago in a dance, while others have gradually come on board since. I'm not at liberty to divulge who they are, as I strongly believe that these sacred relationships are highly personal and private and should be shared with discretion, if at all (besides, I checked in with them, and they agree!). It's important to treat these relationships with the utmost respect rather than casually or superficially, otherwise you risk diminishing the power you receive from them.

The alliance you form with your power animal isn't random or accidental—you choose each other in part because the personality characteristics possessed by this animal match up well with yours. In other words, you're a lot like your power animal. You may be aware of these attributes you have in common, or they might be hidden or obscured from your conscious self, remaining as shadow aspects of your personality. If these traits *have* been suppressed, you'll find that they will increasingly become a part of your self-expression as you develop the relationship with your power animal.

It's also important to take good care of this relationship, just as you would any significant friendship. Your power animal's assignment is to watch out for you and help you in a number of ways—in exchange, she gets to experience life as a human being through you. As long as you honor her and treat her right, she'll stick with you. In a subsequent chapter, I suggest some things you can do that will honor your power animal, and in doing so will help you cultivate your relationship with her.

Your animal spirit guide gives you power, while you show her gratitude and affection. It's a fair and reasonable exchange.

4
Connecting
with the Spirit World

BEFORE YOU BEGIN YOUR QUEST for your power animal, it's useful to know some ways to make a conscious connection with the spirit world. Three important components will open you up to a spiritual experience: *breath*, *clear intention*, and *receptive attention*.

1. Breath. As any student of meditation will tell you, conscious breathing helps you relax. It also helps you return more quickly to a relaxed and fluid state of functioning when you've been stressed. Being relaxed provides a critical foundation for spiritual work of any sort, and opens the way for contact with non-ordinary reality. To breathe consciously, exhale completely, then breathe in slowly as you silently say the words "I am . . ." Then exhale slowly as you say the word, " . . . relaxed." Repeat this pattern a few times, allowing your breathing to find a comfortable and steady rhythm. Silently repeating these words in coordination with your breathing helps you focus your attention on it.

2. Clear intention. When you do any kind of spiritual work, it's important to identify what your intention is. Your intention while meditating, for instance, may simply be to follow the breath with your attention, to focus on a mantra, or to just notice whatever transpires in your experience. Intention is what you want to have happen, and if it's in alignment with Spirit's desire it will happen. Once you've identified your intention, you're prepared for the next step.

3. Receptive attention. Once you're relaxed and have your intention clearly in mind, then it's just a matter of maintaining an attitude of receptive attention. Typically this is the result of a shift into an altered state of consciousness, a mild-to-moderate trance-like state in which you're paradoxically alert and relaxed at the same time. This state can be achieved through a variety of means, such as meditation, dancing, singing, chanting, drumming, rattling, or simply sitting in silence.

On the enclosed CD, you'll have the opportunity to experience some different shamanic methodologies for inducing this state of receptive attention, including drumming, rattling, and the unique rhythmic sound of the didgeridoo. These are all ancient techniques for inducing an altered state of consciousness that's useful for retrieving and working with your power animal.

5
Four Channels
of Spiritual Perception

YOUR PERCEPTION OF THE SPIRITUAL dimension of non-ordinary reality, including power animals, happens through one of four perceptual channels or a combination of them. Most of us have one or two channels that feel the most natural and that we tend to rely on. With practice, however, you can learn to receive spiritual input through the other pathways as well. Whatever channel you use, spiritual information can come to you as a result of setting your intention and being receptive, or at times will come to you unexpectedly.

The four channels through which your guardian spirit communicates with you are:

1. Clairvoyance. This is the *visual* channel through which you actually see spiritual beings, typically with your eyes closed (although it can happen with your eyes open). Some people have a natural gift for this type of vision, yet there's no need to force it if you tend to access Spirit through a different channel.

2. Clairaudience. This is when you hear the voice of your helping spirit through the *auditory* channel. Most often you'll hear it inside your head, although sometimes it will appear to originate from an outside source. You can distinguish the messages from your ego from those of your power animal by the quality of these communications. The messages from your helping spirit will be positive and empowering, whereas your ego (particularly your "inner critic") will be harsh, judgmental, and negative. The only exception is when you're in danger, in which case your guardian spirit will warn you in a loud and commanding voice, such as, "Stop the car now!"

3. Clairsentience. This is the *kinesthetic* pathway, where your power animal communicates through physical sensations, emotional feelings, and aromas. You literally sense the presence of your power animal, often through a "gut feeling."

4. Claircognizance. When you get a communication that comes through your *thoughts,* this is called claircognizance. These messages are typically called *insights* or *inspiration*.

A simple way of finding out what's typically your first choice is to imagine your living room at home. As you do, notice your first impression: Was it an image, sound, feeling, or thought? Whatever the first channel was that you used to access this memory is your primary channel for accessing spiritual communication. Another way is to imagine yourself on a tropical island, where all your needs are met. Again, notice what comes up first—the blue waters and white sand, the sounds of the surf, the sensation of the sun on your skin and how relaxed your body feels, or a thought, such as, *Hmm. I haven't taken a vacation like that for a long time!* Notice which channels you're more apt to use.

As you're discovering your power animal and developing a relationship with her, keep in mind which channels you rely on. It's also important that you don't try too hard to connect through any particular pathway. Putting a lot of effort into accessing the spiritual dimension usually inhibits or interferes with the perception of Spirit, no matter what channels you're using. Remember: It takes a receptive and relaxed focus for you to experience the messages and guidance of your power animal.

6
Power Animals and Shamanism

IN SHAMANIC CULTURES, nearly everyone has animal spirit guides; however, animal spirit guides and power animals in particular are not the exclusive domain of the shaman.

Shamans tend to have in-depth relationships with a few power animals, as these guardian spirits are critical for helping them do their spiritual work. In addition, shamans possess the unique gift of being able to intentionally send their soul (or consciousness) to non-ordinary reality and receive help from various spirit guides who reside there. The typical method they use is called the *shamanic journey*. Spirit guides assist shamans in bringing back healing and important information for an individual or the community. Shamans always travel with one or more of their power animals—and even when they aren't journeying, shamans continue to have an active relationship with their power animals in ordinary reality, as it helps empower and protect them in daily life.

Just about anyone can learn to use certain shamanic concepts and methodologies as an aspect of their spiritual path. One of these is the shamanic journey, and the other is to have a relationship with a power animal. Even those of us who've been raised in contemporary cultures can learn to take a shamanic journey and to work with power animals. You don't have to be a shaman for these to be a useful part of your spiritual repertoire.

Unlike the more traditional shamanic journey, later I'll show you how you can retrieve your power animal through a *guided-meditation journey* (provided on the enclosed CD). This is a synthesis of a guided meditation and a shamanic journey, one that will make it easier for you to connect with your power animal. Once you've established who your power animal is and have some experience with the guided meditation journey, you can advance to taking a self-directed journey with any of the CD tracks using shamanic drumming, rattling, or the didgeridoo. In addition, you can journey to your power animal to find answers to questions, looking to her as an oracle.

7
The Realms of Non-ordinary Reality

IN ANY SHAMANIC JOURNEY, YOU'LL SEND your soul or consciousness to one of three realms of non-ordinary reality:

1. The lower world is where you'll primarily find animal spirits. It's very important to distinguish the shamanic concept of this realm from the Western world's notion of what's commonly called "the underworld." The lower world definitely isn't the Judeo-Christian concept of hell, full of fire and damnation, a place you go when you die if you've been bad. Instead, it's a magical and wondrous place, and much of it looks like the natural world of ordinary reality. This is where you'll go to find and retrieve your power animal, to consult with her for teachings and guidance, or to simply visit and play with her. To get to the lower world in non-ordinary reality, you'll descend from an opening in the earth, such as a cave or tunnel. (I'll describe this in more detail in the following chapter.)

2. **The upper world,** sometimes called "the celestial realm," is mainly inhabited by spirit guides in human form, including archangels, ascended masters, ancestors, or other human-looking spirit guides. In journeying to the upper world, you'll travel there via something that reaches upward, such as a rainbow, a tree, or a whirlwind.

3. **The middle world** is the one we're most familiar with. In shamanic work you can send your soul or consciousness across time and space to some other geographic location on this planet. This may be to gather information, to bring healing to someone who is suffering, or simply to explore some other area of the middle world.

For our purposes, we won't concern ourselves with the upper or middle worlds, as we'll be focusing on the lower world, where power animals exist. However, if you choose to pursue further training in shamanic work, you'll have the opportunity to explore the upper world and middle world realms.

8

Finding and Retrieving Your Power Animal

AS YOU LISTEN TO THE FIRST TRACK on the enclosed CD, you'll be guided through a shamanic journey that will take you to the lower world. There you'll be given specific instructions on how to discover who your power animal is and how to bring her back with you.

Don't be discouraged if you don't find your animal the first time you try—many gifted shamanic practitioners have had to repeatedly attempt to journey before they were successful. Here, I'll give you a description of what you can look for and what to expect with this guided-meditation journey.

Before you begin, think of a place in the earth that leads down-ward. This will be the opening of your passageway into the lower world. It can be a place you're familiar with, or one that's in your imagination. It might be a knothole in a tree, a rabbit hole, the bottom of a lake or the ocean, a cave, or anything else that will lead you downward. Once you've identified this location, keep it in mind as you start your journey.

Find a comfortable place to lie down near your CD player's speakers or with some headphones. Cover your eyes with a soft, dark cloth that will shut out the light so that you can see better (in non-ordinary reality) as you journey. It's important not to fall asleep, which can be avoided if you raise one of your forearms at a 90-degree angle so that it's straight up in the air. That way, when the drumming starts, if you should nod off, your forearm will fall and wake you up.

If you have other spirit guides, invoke them before the jour-ney begins. If not, no worries—I invoked guardian spirits during the recording of the CD tracks, and they'll serve to protect you whenever you listen to them. As the shamanic drumming begins (a steady, monotonous rhythm of four to seven beats per second), see yourself going toward your predetermined point of entry. Once there, jump in. You'll find yourself going down a hollow tun-nel. Keep going, and soon you'll see light in the distance, as in the proverbial "light at the end of the tunnel."

This light is your exit from the tunnel and your entry into the lower world. As you step through the opening, you'll find yourself in an outdoor area that looks very much like some part of the natural world. In the guided meditation, it will be a forest, but it can also be a seashore or mountains. On the CD, as you step into the forest, you'll explore by walking around and observing whatever you see. You'll soon notice various animals crossing your path. Look out for repetitive appearances by any animal. Watch closely until an animal appears before you *four* times. This is your power animal.

Once an animal has shown up for the fourth time, communicate telepathically with her and ask if she'd be willing to return with you. Almost invariably she'll agree to do so. After you get her agreement, physically reach your left hand out, palm up. Your power animal will immediately come to you, and her etheric form will contract and become small enough to fit in the palm of your hand. Physically close your hand, bring it to your heart center, open it, and place your right hand over your left. Take three slow deep breaths; as you do, feel the energy of this power animal merge into your entire body, starting at your heart center and emanating outward.

Next, continue to explore the lower world until you hear the *callback* signal from the drum. This is when the shamanic drumming stops, followed by three sharp drumbeats. You'll then hear about 30 seconds of rapid drumming, during which you should be making your way back to where you entered the lower world, working your way back up the tunnel to the place you started. After the rapid drumming, there will be a slight pause, followed by three more sharp drumbeats. By this point, you should be returning to ordinary reality.

Slowly move various parts of your body, taking your time to do so. You've just been in a trance, so there's no need to hurry getting back to your body and to ordinary reality. When you're ready, slowly open your eyes and look around to orient yourself to the present moment. Get up when you're ready, still very slowly, and notice how you feel. Congratulations—you've just retrieved your power animal!

Next I'll describe some ways in which you can develop the relationship.

9
Honoring Your Power Animal

ONCE YOU'VE RETRIEVED YOUR POWER ANIMAL, there are several ways in which you can strengthen your bond and develop your relationship, resulting in greater access to the guardianship and spiritual power she has to offer. It's not enough to do only the power animal retrieval—it's a good start, but it merely *initiates* the relationship with your animal spirit. If you don't give her the regular attention she deserves, as with any relationship, she may end up moving on after a while.

Here are a few ways in which you can honor and develop the relationship:

1. Try additional journeys. Once you've retrieved your power animal, you can use other tracks on the CD for further shamanic journeying. For example, Track 2 is a guided meditation journey designed to help you consult your power animal as an oracle, so you can bring important life questions to her to receive guidance or answers. Once you've become familiar with journeying to the lower world, you can then take a self-directed journey for any purpose you choose by listening to Tracks 3, 4, or 5. By journeying with any of these tracks, you'll get to know your power animal in-depth. You can approach her anytime for advice on questions or concerns, to explore non-ordinary reality further, or to just "hang out" with her. Your power animal will be pleased and honored whenever you make the effort to visit and get to know her better.

2. **Dance your animal.** Stand for a few moments with your eyes closed, with music or drumming as a backdrop, and call on your power animal. Let her come to you and allow her spirit to enter your body. Then simply dance! By doing so, you'll serve as a vehicle for your animal's spirit to be expressed through your physical form. You may find yourself dancing slow or fast, corresponding to that particular animal's pace and rhythm. As you're dancing your power animal, you may even find yourself uttering her sound with your voice. Your power animal loves it when you dance with her!

3. **Find your power animal's song.** Go outdoors to a relatively isolated place, take a journal or a pad of paper with you, and find a comfortable spot to sit. Ask your power animal to teach you a song that honors her, then simply wait and listen to any tune that

comes to you. It may first appear as a melody that you can hum or whistle. Then you might notice words coming to you that fit the melody. Usually you'll receive a very simple melody and simple words, which will probably be in your primary language, however, the words may also manifest as an unfamiliar language, perhaps sounding like gibberish. Regardless of how the song shows up, write down the words or the sounds phonetically. Throughout the remainder of the day, periodically sing the song until it becomes familiar to you. Once you know this tune, you can use it to invoke the presence of your power animal.

4. Meditate on your power animal. Find a quiet place indoors or outdoors, close your eyes, and call on your power animal. Unlike journeying to the animal, here you're inviting her to come to you. Take note of the qualities of your animal spirit, such as her physical characteristics, her temperament, her personality, and so on. Ask your spirit animal if there's anything you can do for her.

5. Study and research. Find out more about your particular power animal by reading about her. You may find her represented in the power animal summaries (found in Part II of this book), in one of the books listed in the Recommended Readings section on page 341, on the Internet, or from programs on television, such as those on the Discovery Channel or Animal Planet.

6. Get active. Contribute your time, energy, or money to organizations that support animal rights or environmental causes, particularly ones that relate to your specific power animal. Doing so not only increases your bond with your power animal, but with the *entire* kingdom of animals. The animals will be grateful for any efforts you can make on their behalf.

10
Divinations and Omens from Animal Spirit Guides

YOUR POWER ANIMAL CAN SERVE AS AN ORACLE in a variety of ways, especially, as I previously described, when you have an important life question or you seek some guidance. You can use Track 2 on the CD to do a guided meditation journey, or use Tracks 3, 4, or 5 to do a self-directed journey to ask your power animal for advice. These are called *divination journeys*.

Animal spirit guides also teach you when they show up in your dreams, meditations, or ordinary reality. When they do, whether or not that animal is your power animal, they're attempting to give you a message. When an animal shows up in ordinary reality in an uncommon way or at unusual times—such as an owl in the day-time, a deer in your front yard, or a whale out of season—this is most definitely an omen. Pay close attention to whatever is going on and see if you can discern the message. You may have to meditate on the experience before gaining any insight on the meaning, it may also help to consult this book or other resources as to the significance of that particular animal.

Another powerful omen is when an animal shows herself to you frequently or persistently (at least three or more times) in a short period of time, such as over a few hours. It can be the actual animal, a symbol for the animal such as a carved figure or totem, or the printed word for the animal. Pay close attention to see if you can discern the meaning. If Deer shows up three times in relatively rapid succession, for example, is this a call for gentleness with yourself or someone else? If it's Hummingbird, are you missing the joy and sweet nectar of life as a result of your narrow focus? These signs don't tell you their precise meaning; they're merely trying to get your attention. The meaning is for you to determine.

11
The Power Animal Summaries

IN PART II, YOU'LL FIND INFORMATION on 36 different power animals. This grouping provides a broad representation drawn from the world of mammals, birds, reptiles, and even a couple of commonly known insects. These are provided as examples of various spirit animals; obviously, the list isn't exhaustive. But whether or not you find your particular power animal in these summaries, your best way of getting to know spirit animals, their characteristics, and the meaning they have in your life is to *journey to them and let them teach you!* They'll reveal more and more about themselves as you get to know them.

For each of the spirit animals listed, I've included one or two key words that describe the spiritual attributes or essence of that animal. For instance, Raccoon, who graces the cover of this book, carries the strong essence of resourcefulness. Of course there are other attributes properly belonging to Raccoon, but the term *resourcefulness* captures her most essential characteristic.

On each page you'll find four sections, broken down as follows:

1. A message for you. I received these messages from each of the spirit animals when I asked them what they wanted to communicate. You'll note that every one of them has a different style of communicating and a unique voice. As you get to know your individual animal, she'll give you additional information and ongoing guidance. If this isn't your power animal, the messages contained herein can still provide inspiration and guidance. I'll give you some suggestions in the next chapter on how to discover the messages that are most meaningful for you.

2. If this is your power animal. You'll find that you and your animal possess similar characteristics and idiosyncrasies, or else she'll draw forth those qualities that are inherent in you but lie dormant or that have been suppressed. You may acquire a power animal at a time in your life when you most need these particular qualities, and she'll help draw them out of you. A few of these characteristics have been described for each power animal, yet they're certainly not the only ones you share. Studying these can give you insight into both your power animal and yourself, and you'll discover more of these similarities as you get to know your power animal.

3. When to call on this animal spirit for help. This section suggests how this particular power animal can help you out with some troublesome situations. If you find yourself facing a difficult circumstance similar to those described in this section, you can call on this spirit guide to help you out, regardless of whether she's your power animal.

4. How to access the power of this spirit animal. Here you'll find some specific steps you can take to call on this spirit animal for help, whether she's your power animal or not. Most of these require you to take some sort of action that makes it easier for the spirit animal to respond to your call for help. You may even feel self-conscious doing some of these, but don't let that stop you. In fact, I suggest that you experiment with all of these ways. Then, once you and your power animal have bonded more deeply and you feel more confident in your relationship, you can simply call on her and she'll be there.

12
Other Uses for the Power Animal Summaries

AFTER YOU'VE RETRIEVED your power animal, if she's not represented in the summaries in Part II, use the CD to journey to her in order to get to know her better. (You can also refer to Chapter 9 and follow the suggestions there as a means of developing the relationship.) Whether or not your power animal is described in the following summaries, consider this information as a foundation for forming a relationship with her. Even if your power animal *is* depicted in these pages, it's still essential for you to spend time with her and honor her, particularly through journeying.

In the next chapter, I'll tell you how you can best use the various tracks on the CD. As for the power animal summaries, there are a few different ways you can use them. The most obvious is by finding your own power animal referenced in the summaries. Yet even though the information is definitive and captures the spiritual essence of the spirit animal, you'll still need to get to know her personally. The more you work with your power animals, the more they'll teach you about themselves . . . and about you.

You can also read about the characteristics of other power animals. For example, you may find an animal spirit guide from your past or one of your favorite totem animals that isn't necessarily your power animal. You may discover that one or more of these spirit animals has a particularly useful message for you at the time of your reading.

Yet another way is to use this book as an oracle. Simply think of a question, and then randomly open the book to one of the power animal summaries. Read the information on the page, especially the message from that particular animal spirit guide, and see how it resonates for you. It may directly answer your question, or you may need to meditate on the message to see how it applies to you. Another way to use the summaries as an oracle is when a particular animal shows itself to you in an unusual way or over a short period of time, as I detailed previously.

PART II
The Power Animals

Bear

Quality: Introspection

Bear's Message for You

"BE STRONG! Know what and where your boundaries are. You can love others, still disagree with their opinions, and say no to their requests. You don't have to justify your refusals. My power in making a stand is unparalleled, and you must also stand up for what you believe in and who you are. Neither do you need to fear criticism or defend yourself when it's offered. Treat others with respect, and demand the same from them. Trust your creative hunches—those urges to make music, write poetry, sculpt, or engage in any other forms of creative expression. Take action, with great care and love for what you're creating and expressing. Turn inward to the loving darkness of your soul's den to find the inspiration to birth such projects. Let them blossom in the cave of your creative mind and manifest as your heart's desire."

If Bear Is Your Power Animal . . .

- You tend to be quite assertive and confident, and you have such a strong presence that when you show up in a roomful of people, they know it!

- Your body has a certain bearish quality to it, and sometimes when you're upset, you may even sound as if you're growling.

- Your most creative periods are either during the winter months or during a cycle of extended solitude, and honoring these cycles rather than fighting them will bring out the best from your creative efforts.

- You're very protective of your family and friends, and will often defend them with fierce assertiveness.

Ask for Bear's Help When . . .

- You need some extra strength to stand up for yourself in a difficult relationship, or to set emotional, physical, or psychic boundaries with someone.

- You need some extra protection from unwarranted criticism or "psychic attacks," to shield you from such affronts.

- You're having difficulty with a creative project, either getting started or feeling blocked with what's already in progress.

- You need some quiet time to meditate or "hibernate," but external demands continue to tug at you.

How to Access Bear's Power

- Stand tall! To do so, lengthen your spine by simultaneously lifting the top of your head and slightly tilting the lower part of your pelvis forward, like Bear does when she stands on her hind feet and surveys her surroundings. Throughout the day, subtly shift into this posture and notice how much more powerful you feel.

- When you're alone, try saying, "No!" out loud, firmly and with conviction, bringing the sound up from your belly. Notice how this increases your sense of power even more.

- Follow through on doing one creative project that you've always wanted to do, whether it's making music, painting, sewing, or writing. Bring it forth with love and care, nurturing it along to its completion without concern for the outcome.

- Spend a day in the "cave" of your home, dedicating some of this time to being silent, turning off the phone, the stereo, and so on. Perhaps just sit and think for a while. Keep a journal during this time, writing down any insights, inspirations, or ideas you get.

Beaver

Quality: Productiveness

Beaver's Message for You

"YEP, IT'S TRUE WHAT THEY SAY: 'Busy as a beaver.' But don't get me wrong—I'm not just being busy so that I can *look* busy. Every move I make is purposeful. When I'm moving, I'm creating. So should your movements be purposeful. Don't keep busy just because you're anxious, you're afraid to slow down, or you want to impress your friends by telling them or showing them just how busy you are. You need downtime as well. Time for relaxation. Time with your family and friends. It's important. But if and when you've got a project to do, whether large or small, just get to it. Don't chew off more than you need, which is to say don't waste resources and use any unnecessary energy for the project at hand. When you go at something, always have a plan B, in case your initial efforts don't work out. Nice to know there's always another way to do something, even if it seems like there isn't at the time."

If Beaver Is Your Power Animal . . .

- You love to work and are a consummate "doer," whether the work is physical or mental, and you're willing to do whatever needs to be done without hesitation, procrastination, or complaints.

- You're a great team player, and understand the necessity of everyone working together harmoniously to complete a project.

- The type of work you're called to do typically benefits the larger community, the nation, or the world, yet you remain humble about your contribution.

- You're very resourceful with your creative projects, and in spite of any obstacles, you believe and act on the old adage, "Where there's a will, there's a way."

- You're extremely loyal to your friends and tend to make lifelong friendships.

Ask for Beaver's Help When . . .

- You feel trapped in some way, whether in a situation at work or in a relationship, and you don't know how to extricate yourself.

- There's something you've dreamed of doing or having, but you're not sure how to go about building, and thereby manifesting, your dreams.

- You're experiencing differences with your mate, your friends, or your co-workers, and you want to settle those differences in an amicable and peaceful way.

- You want to get rid of the clutter in your home so that you can have the kind of harmonious and peaceful surroundings you need.

How to Access Beaver's Power

- When faced with a project that you've been procrastinating about, just make yourself "do it" by removing any obstacles, turning away from all distractions, and forcing yourself to confront the project head-on.

- Get out into the woods or to a park where there's a stream. Put one foot in or near the water, and keep the other on land as you call on Beaver.

- Make a list of three significant goals for the coming year, then write out a plan as to what you're going to do and when you're going to do it in order to accomplish those goals.

- Whatever task you're faced with—be it an ordinary and mundane one such as washing the dishes or a more involved one such as writing a thesis—do it with gusto and enthusiasm.

Buffalo

Quality: Provisions

Buffalo's Message for You

"FOR MANY YEARS I was the bringer of sustenance and warmth, giving to the peoples through the sacrifice of my own body and breath. When called through strong prayer and right action, I'd come forth readily and willingly to fulfill my purpose. In exchange, the peoples honored spiritual law and continued to enact the ceremonies of their ancestors taught to them by White Buffalo Woman, most of which were to show appreciation and gratitude for nature's generosity. Through your own sincere prayers and right action, know that life will always supply whatever you need. To live in this natural state of abundance requires only faith, purposeful action, and gratitude.

"Since you often have more than what you need, be willing to share any surplus with others in your community, recycling all that you can and giving generously of your time and money. Rather than having a garage sale, have a garage *giveaway.* Demonstrate your confidence in life's abundance through your willingness to give away some of your more precious belongings. Express your gratitude to the Mother and Father of us all in as many ways as possible. And above all, know that you are now, always have been, and always will be provided for."

If Buffalo Is Your Power Animal . . .

- You never worry about having whatever you need, for you know deep in your heart and soul that you're always provided for.

- You're very generous with others, and you show this by giving of yourself.

- You have a very relaxed and confident way of achieving your goals, especially when you're clear about what you want.

- You do your best to accept anyone you come in contact with, always trying to see the good in them and doing your best not to judge them.

Ask for Buffalo's Help When . . .

- You have a project that you're about to start, but you're feeling a lack of confidence in your ability to achieve it.

- You lack faith in the natural abundance of life and instead feel needy and always worried about paying your bills or having enough money.

- You're so focused on struggling to fulfill even your basic needs of food, water, and shelter that you've forgotten to express gratitude for all that you do have.

- You're feeling sorry for yourself, and you're complaining out loud (or even quietly) about all the things in life that you don't have.

How to Access Buffalo's Power

- Sponsor a giveaway ceremony, in which you and several other friends gather, each bringing something that's personal, precious, and meaningful to them, which they then donate to the circle such that someone else in the group will receive it.

- For the next seven days, make every one of your daily prayers those of *affirmation* (in which you thank the Creator—or whomever you thank) instead of prayers of *supplication* (in which you ask the Creator for something).

- Study and meditate on the Lakota story of White Buffalo Woman, as told by the Oglala Sioux.

- Stand upright, holding your hands out, palms up, and fists closed for a minute or so. Then slowly open your hands as you breathe in. Notice the life force pulsating through your hands and how it feels to be in this posture of surrender and acceptance.

Butterfly

Quality: Transformation

Butterfly's Message for You

"EVERY ONE OF US EMERGES from the chrysalis of darkness and gestation, in which we enter as one self and come out as another. We grow wings, and as we stretch them, they eventually break down the confining walls of the cocoon, allowing us to enter into this present life form. Throughout each stage of this transformative process, I remain aware and fully present. So must you. Whatever part of the cycle you're in—be it the larva phase, the cocoon stage, or the emergent phase, where you spread your wings and float into your new life—know that you're safe and that this is part of a natural movement.

"You may not know exactly what's going on at any particular stage, but have faith. After a period of exertion, your soul will find its way through the darkness. Count on it. Then you will emerge into the next expression of 'you.' From this incarnation, you'll eventually move through other cycles of transformation, in this lifetime and into the next, each new form of 'you' building on the old. Throughout these cycles, faith, love, and intention will be your guiding light. Keep the faith, share the love, and set crystal clear intentions. You have absolutely nothing to fear!"

If Butterfly Is Your Power Animal . . .

- You have a profound appreciation of the seasonal nature of life, continually noticing the cycles of life-death-rebirth (corresponding to the stages of larva-cocoon-butterfly) that occur within and around you.

- You're a very spirited individual, full of vitality, with exotic, beautiful, and colorful tastes in your choices of clothing, décor, art, music, and even friends.

- You can't live in a harsh or toxic environment because it drains your life force, so you must reside in surroundings where the air and water are clean. To stay healthy, you have to eat lots of raw and organic foods and associate with sincere, loving people.

- You're a visionary. When you meditate in the silence of nature or in that private space in your home, you're able to see what lies ahead and what you need to do to achieve your vision.

- You tend to go through life changes very smoothly, accepting these transitions with gentleness and joy and welcoming that which lies just ahead. You're very willing to make the necessary changes when opportunities present themselves, even though others may be disappointed or resist what you're doing.

Ask for Butterfly's Help When . . .

- You need help in organizing a project, detailing the sequence of steps necessary to take in order to complete it to your satisfaction.

- You know that it's time for a change, whether it's in your relationships or in your career, and you need the courage to break out of your "cocoon."

- You're going through a major life change, such as a divorce, the loss of a friendship, or a career change, and you need help in discovering what lies ahead.

- You're having trouble "going with the flow" of the cycle you're in. For example, you're hurrying too much at a time when your body wants to slow down and rest, or else you're trying to stay quiet when you sense the need for activity.

- You need to lighten up and not take things quite so seriously.

How to Access Butterfly's Power

- Notice what colors you're drawn to, and attempt to discern what they mean for you.

- Choose a bad habit that you no longer want, develop a plan for changing it, and then implement it.

- Whenever the weather is right, wander around a park or somewhere in nature and simply observe butterflies in their natural environment. Note what you're thinking whenever one pops directly into your field of vision, then sit in silence to contemplate what that visitation might mean.

- Create a cocoon of sorts by wrapping yourself in a blanket for a few minutes as tightly as possible, then slowly unravel it and emerge. See if this experience is a metaphor for anything going on in your life right now.

- Dance. It doesn't matter how or to what kind of music (if any at all)—just dance for a few minutes, whether in solitude or in the presence of others.

Cougar
(Mountain Lion/Puma)

Quality: **Leadership**

Cougar's Message for You

"WHEN I HUNT AND TAKE LIFE, I'm only performing my role according to the laws of nature. I just take what my family and I need to survive—no less and no more. I'm very economical in that way. Once I know my prey, or goal, I'm clear and direct about my purpose at that moment. It's done with God's mercy and compassion, quickly and efficiently.

"You also need to set your purpose clearly and concisely—write it out if necessary—and then design everything in your life to support and conform to that goal. There's no need to equivocate, hesitate, or procrastinate. Understand that by doing so, you may meet others' disapproval and even rejection. Still, don't be alarmed, and don't hesitate. I'd be in a heap of trouble if I hesitated while I was in midair, thinking, *Hmm, I'm not sure if this is what I want.*

"So move forward with faith and courage and keep your eyes on the goal, and you can never go wrong. Love that way, too—full on and openhearted—and never let judgment or fear stop you."

If Cougar Is Your Power Animal . . .

- You tend to take charge, especially when others don't or can't, which sometimes leaves you open to criticism, blame, and resentment.

- You make your choices very quickly and decisively, and don't look back once you've made them.

- You're able to balance your personal power and strength with gracefulness and clear intention, particularly as you use your natural capacity for leadership for the greatest good.

- There's a part of you that's wild, untamed, and primitive, yet it's housed in a relatively domesticated persona. This side of you must be acknowledged and expressed, ideally by spending some time in the wilderness on a regular basis.

- You're quite sensitive and sometimes react to others' disapproval or rejection by lashing out aggressively, only to later have to make amends for your reaction.

Ask for Cougar's Help When . . .

- You're faced with a situation that requires you to be assertive and direct with others, especially when others are demanding that you change or alter your course of action.

- You've been unexpectedly handed a position of leadership that you don't feel quite prepared to take on yet, and you're feeling afraid.

- You feel overwhelmed and not up to the tasks before you, no matter if they're simple or complex, and you aren't sure how to go about accomplishing them.

- You're called on to give a speech and you need to bolster your self-confidence, especially if you have little experience talking in front of groups of people.

How to Access Cougar's Power

- Growl! When you're by yourself, express various emotions through this type of utterance. As you do, feel the sensation of power in your gut.

- Move around with stealth, whether at home or outdoors. Do so slowly and deliberately, pretending that you're stalking prey.

- Find a place that's as quiet as possible, sit in a comfortable position, and simply notice any smells or sounds that come to you without trying to name them or categorize them.

- Join a group or a class that teaches leadership and/or communication skills, such as Toast-masters International.

Coyote

Quality: **Paradox**

Coyote's Message for You

"SURPRISE, IT'S ME! Full of life, not always sure why I do the things I do; sometimes befuddled and chagrined, but I keep on trying. Sometimes I stubbornly and willfully try to solve problems by doing the same thing that didn't work before, but no matter— I'm a survivor. So are you. How many times in your life has something seemed to go wrong, only for you to find out later that it was an important lesson, simply a step on your spiritual path? When you really get that life is one big paradox, then you know the true secret of life. There are no negatives except as they complement the positives. Light and dark, masculine and feminine, yes and no, and most of all when it concerns me, wisdom and folly.

"Never take any of this too seriously, particularly those times you seem to only blunder along from one error to the next. Laugh about it, cry about it, but let the tears be those of relief rather than despair. It's only life. No big deal!"

If Coyote Is Your Power Animal . . .

- No matter how seemingly difficult or challenging a situation is, or when things don't go according to plan, you're always able to see the humor in it and also help those around you to lighten up.

- You're always looking for the hidden lessons in difficult situations. Usually you find something that has some immediate relevance and meaning for you or those around you, typically something which ordinarily would have been overlooked.

- You're remarkably resourceful, with an amazing capacity to adapt to any situation.

- You're a teacher, whether it's your actual profession or simply the way you are with others. You often teach through stories that illustrate life lessons, rather than rattling off facts or principles.

Ask for Coyote's Help When . . .

- You're faced with a choice whereby it's unclear whether your next move would be a smart one or one that would create chaos.

- You're confused about a dream, vision, or recent experience, and you want to understand its deeper and subtler meanings.

- You have the blues and have lost your sense of humor, failing to see the "cosmic joke" in life.

- You've got a seemingly insurmountable problem to solve and want to generate some creative solutions.

- You're bored with the repetitive routines of your life and find yourself resorting to compulsive and addictive behaviors to cope with the monotony, yet you're yearning for fresh and healthy kinds of stimulation.

How to Access Coyote's Power

- Play: Have fun in a spontaneous, frivolous way. Do a silly dance for no rhyme or reason. Sing a song as you're walking down the street. Find a grassy hill and roll down it. Walk up the down escalator (carefully!). And so on. . . .

- Journal about the different ways you try to fool others through the disguises you put on, whether by playing dumb, being tough, using self-effacing humor, always seeking others' approval, or whatever. Be ruthlessly honest with yourself without shame or judgment by bringing these characteristics into the light of your awareness.

- During the twilight hour—the "betwixt and between" just after sunset—spend some time in a park or in the woods, preferably when there are few or no people, and simply walk around calling on Coyote.

- Whenever you've been through a challenging life event, see if you can identify any gifts or positive outcomes that resulted from that experience.

Deer

Quality: Gentleness

Deer's Message for You

"NEVER UNDERESTIMATE THE POWER of gentleness and sensitivity! These qualities will help you navigate the forest of your life, and are expressions of powerful instinctual energies that not only help you survive, but also help you thrive. I can help you identify aggressive situations and sort them out before you get too close or too involved, and can also direct you to those elements and situations that will nurture and nourish you. Trust your instincts, your gut reactions, and heed them! They'll tell you when to flee and when to fight. When you can unconditionally trust your instincts, you can unconditionally love *all* of life. As you do, there's no need for worry or anxiety, since your body will alert you to any real danger, rather to reacting to false signals that are the result of prior conditioning of your natural instinctual responses."

If Deer Is Your Power Animal . . .

- You're very sensitive, and if there is the slightest scent of predator energy coming from others, you become very vigilant until you determine whether it's safe or not. If you determine that it's not, then rather than fighting back, you typically take flight from the situation, or find refuge in the forest of your inner self.

- You love life itself in all its varied forms and expressions—so much so that you willingly give of yourself, sometimes sacrificing so that others may continue on. You've likely had at least one or two near-death experiences, and following each you were reborn into a new cycle of life, just as the fawn is birthed from the doe.

- Your gentleness and tender nature are unparalleled, yet you may alternate between the stag's powerful and confident assertiveness and the doe's subtle and vulnerable power.

- You love the woods and the forest and actually feel safer there than in the city. When you're feeling overdosed and overwhelmed with city life, it's imperative that you spend time in nature to recharge and regenerate.

Ask for Deer's Help When . . .

- You're working on a creative project of any sort and you need to explore the forest of your imagination. Deer knows what to find in the forest that will nourish your creativity and what to bypass that could harm your efforts.

- You're in a situation that requires extra vigilance, one in which the wrong move can mean possible damaging consequences, and you need to trust your natural instincts in order to make the right move.

- You're holding on to a grudge or resentment toward someone in your life, and you want to release these feelings and judgments.

- You've been walking around with some shame or guilt about a perceived transgression from the past, and you're ready to let go of these self-judgments.

How to Access Deer's Power

- Spend some time in the woods or forest, walking around, paying close attention to the sights, sounds, and especially the smells. Take your shoes off, and go off the paths you normally tread.

- For just a few minutes, try experimenting with becoming more vigilant. Open your eyes slightly wider, really observe your surroundings, and listen closely to whatever sounds you're aware of.

- Be especially gentle with yourself and others, speaking in a slightly softer tone than usual. When you touch someone, do so gently. Observe any harshness or negativity you have with others, and as soon you're aware of it, release it and find compassion for them.

- Run! Whether you jog or sprint, run! Feel the breeze and the sense of freedom as you go.

Dolphin

Quality: Communication

Dolphin's Message for You

"WITHIN YOUR BREATH, you will find answers to all the mysteries of life—answers that come as feelings and sensations rather than as mere intellectual concepts. Know that by calling on me you can safely and comfortably play in the world of invisible realities, as well as in the material world, where these invisible realities manifest. Conscious breathing is a bridge between worlds.

"Don't make it work to play, just simply and naturally play in both of these worlds *and* in the betwixt and between. In actuality, they're seamlessly united realities, so once you really get that, it's possible to go back and forth between these worlds rather easily, and it's even easier to communicate between them. Also know that communication has many layers and textures, and human words are only a small part of it. In fact, you cannot *not* communicate. I also encourage you to try new waterways, to swim out to sea if you've been staying close to the shore, or to take a deep breath and dive in to new adventures. And remember to breathe!"

If Dolphin Is Your Power Animal . . .

- You play *in* life and *with* life, yet when something requires focus, you're able to quickly and efficiently bring your entire awareness and attention to the circumstances in front of you. You're someone who very much lives in the now.

- You have a unique capacity to naturally and easily enter into altered states of consciousness (such as meditative states and shamanic journeys), often by simply taking a deep and conscious breath. You can remain alert and present even as you glide between the two worlds.

- You're an instinctive and inspiring leader. You know how to provide strong and wise leadership because you're aware that the best leaders are good followers, able to intuitively tune in to the will and wisdom of the community consciousness.

- When you're happy, everyone around you is, too, no matter what state of mind or mood they were in prior to connecting with you. You affect people more than you think you do!

- You're highly intuitive and even telepathic with those you're closest to, and often have the experience of simultaneous thoughts with your loved ones.

Ask for Dolphin's Help When . . .

- Things have gotten too predictable and monotonous and you need to breathe new life into your surroundings.

- You're feeling overwhelmed with your emotional state and your life circumstances, perhaps taking it way too seriously. You know you need to breathe more easily, lighten up, and be more playful.

- You need to break the habit of restricting your breathing, thereby constricting your life force. You can use Dolphin breathing (described below) to gently release pent-up emotions and help you find more calm and tranquil waters.

- You feel stuck in some relationship. Dolphin can help you reach out, even at the risk of rejection, and help you communicate only positive thoughts and feelings to the other person, including admiration and respect.

How to Access Dolphin's Power

- Try *Dolphin breathing:* Close your eyes, sit or stand comfortably, and take a deep breath as follows: First exhale completely, then inhale, filling first your belly and then your chest. Hold your breath as long as you can without straining. Release your breath with a *"Puh!"* sound, and let your body relax as you do. Repeat two to four times. As you exhale, let go of any and all disturbing emotions, worries, cares, or fears.

- Dolphin's natural smile is an effective model for changing your somber mood to one of lightness and playfulness. A few times each day, curl the outer edge of your lips slightly upward in a smile, as if you have a "happy little secret." Note how you feel while doing this and how others respond to you.

- Make it a point today to tell others, from the clerk at the grocery store to your closest friends, what you specifically appreciate about them, or else simply thank them when they do something for you. Express your love through your actions, such as small favors.

Dove

Quality: **Serenity**

Dove's Message for You

"MY POWER IS OBVIOUSLY not in my diminutive stature, shyness, or silly walk—neither is yours. Yet it's a type of power that surpasses the illusory power of anger, aggression, vengeance, greed, competition, and spitefulness. Even though it's quieter, gentler, and not always immediately apparent, it's the most potent force that any human being can experience. Yeah, you got it. Love. It's much simpler to love than most humans imagine, what with your ways of complicating what's true, right, and natural. You just do it. Let your love shine, and—don't forget this part—*let others love you.*

"A lot of humans forget that to complete a circle you need something coming back to you, which love will. You just have to be ready to receive it. In order to be able to do so, you have to open your heart and empty out any thoughts or feelings of blame, shame, or judgment. I'll help you release whatever prevents you from feeling the serenity and joy that results from making peace and harmony your number one priority. Please acknowledge and even appreciate the shadows, but don't lose yourself in them or act them out. Shine the light of the Holy Spirit on them, and know all is well. I love you. We *all* love you."

If Dove Is Your Power Animal . . .

- You've dedicated your life to bringing peace and harmony to the world, and others can feel your calming presence as soon as you enter a room.

- You present somewhat of a paradox in that you're not only evolved spiritually, but you're also very grounded and down-to-earth.

- You're gentle yet passionate, and you express this passion in a variety of ways, not the least of which is as a lover.

- Whether you're male or female, your maternal instincts are very strong. You're very nurturing to children, as well as to others you're close to.

Ask for Dove's Help When . . .

- You feel troubled, worried, distraught, anxious, or upset, and you need to bring peace and calmness into your life.

- You're having difficulty with your mate, and you want to infuse a greater feeling of security into the relationship concerning your love for each other.

- You've lost touch with your faith and feel as if your spirit has been zapped of its vitality, or you find yourself searching for more substantial meaning in life.

- You've lost someone dear to you through death, and you'd like to find some comfort and a way to connect with his or her spirit on the other side.

How to Access Dove's Power

- Listen closely to Dove's mourning call, which typically takes place following sunrise or prior to sunset.

As you do, breathe it in and notice what sensations and emotions it evokes.

- Volunteer your time with an organization, such as a seniors' association or child-care center, where you have the opportunity to experience doing something for someone without any financial or material compensation.

- Do your best to mimic Dove's song—her soft, low, throaty cooing—and pay attention to what this evokes in you.

- Make a list of your deceased loved ones and add a short sentence describing a characteristic of each person. Read each name and statement while meditating on Dove, allowing any feelings to flow through you and to be released into the earth. This will make more room for serenity in your heart.

Dragonfly

Quality: Light

Dragonfly's Message for You

"I DANCE AND FLIT, born of the waters and always connected to them, yet as I mature, I live in the air and on the land. I've managed to not only survive on this incredibly rich planet for millions of years, but to also bring beauty to it, even as I've enjoyed the beauty that surrounds me all the while. Look! See my body's pure colors. See my wings, reflecting and refracting light in all their majestic splendor, dancing with me whether I'm at rest or zigzagging through the air.

"You too are a master of light and color. You're able to use these skills to create illusions while seeing the truth behind the falsehoods of others. Paramount to nurturing these gifts is your relationship with the realm of the nature spirits—the fairies, devas, and leprechauns who were at one time physical beings. Now they remain invisible to the unimaginative, yet for those who believe, they're accessible just across the veil. Your openheartedness and acceptance will allow you to hear, see, and feel them.

"Let them be your allies. Let them teach you. They're pleading with anyone with this consciousness to pay attention, and to help them restore the balance on the planet. They want to help humans reestablish right relations with all other beings on this earth, especially the plant kingdom, and to know the beauty and power of the master energies of the trees. Let me guide you through this realm. Let me help you get to know these spirits. Don't get caught in the illusion that these beings don't exist. They love humans, and where there is willingness to believe, they will appear."

If Dragonfly Is Your Power Animal . . .

- You've been an emotionally intense and very passionate individual since childhood, yet as you've aged you've learned to balance these tendencies with intellectual detachment and emotional containment.

- You have a strong connection to the elemental world (the world of nature spirits), and are at your best when you consistently work directly with plants or gardening.

- You have to spend time outdoors in the light every day, or else you become easily depressed and morose.

- You're a master of breaking down illusions, whether they're yours or another's—typically by shining the light of awareness on them.

- You have a deep and ancient connection to divine magic and mysticism, with a particular gift for color magic (the art of shifting and changing others' perception through the use of light).

Ask for Dragonfly's Help When . . .

- You're emotionally shut down, largely as a result of early emotional trauma, and you want to free up your expression.

- Your life feels stagnant and you know it's time for a change of some sort, but you're not sure what to do to make the necessary adjustments.

- A situation or relationship has become shrouded in illusions and falsehood, and you want to clearly see the truth of what's going on.

- You're involved in a number of different activities, to the point of feeling fragmented, and you need to balance your time and energy with respect to these various endeavors.

How to Access Dragonfly's Power

- Make a list of all the things in your life that you want to change. Choose the three most important, develop a strategy of how you'll make the adjustments, commit to the strategy, and then follow through.

- For one week, make it a point to spend at least 30 minutes each day outdoors bathing yourself in the light. Note how this makes you feel.

- Pick a day to wear the brightest and most colorful clothes you can find, even if you have to borrow or buy some.

- Play with prisms. Observe how they refract the light, noting the color sequence, and how they blend so readily from one color to the next.

Eagle

Quality: Spirit

Eagle's Message for You

"WHETHER OR NOT YOU'RE AWARE OF IT, you have complete access to an awesome spiritual power! When your vision has become too narrow or limited and you can't find solutions to any of your problems or challenges, take a look from where I can see. Come with me and I'll take you to the sun and stars. You must have the courage to relinquish stale and comfortable habits and beliefs and soar into unknown realms and new realities, continually expanding your view. Now is the time to take full responsibility for your life and to be prepared for instant karma. As your spiritual awareness increases, so will positive and negative repercussions become more immediate and have greater force.

"When you have to make a choice, no matter how large or small, first hover above all the possibilities laid out before you. Then choose one, and go for it wholeheartedly and without equivocation. Don't let material concerns keep you from soaring!"

If Eagle Is Your Power Animal . . .

- You're fascinated by altered states of perception and consciousness, and are drawn to shamanic realities. Your spiritual practice and discipline is of an independent nature, and you don't do well with overly structured or dogmatic religious or spiritual practices.

- The lives you've lived before have led to this present existence, now with a considerably evolved state of consciousness. You've come to this lifetime to fully accomplish your soul's purpose—this time with no interruptions or distractions.

- Even though you're an old soul, you must still go through a number of initiations before coming fully into the spiritually directed life. If you're relatively young in years, you have plenty of time to work into it, but be prepared for spiritual tests along the way.

- You need to work with one or more of the four-leggeds as an animal spirit guide to help you stay grounded with your lofty perspective. If you tend to be emotionally disconnected, then work with one of the water creatures as a spirit guide as well.

Ask for Eagle's Help When . . .

- You're so caught up in the minutiae and details of day-to-day living that you feel weighed down and have lost sight of the larger perspective.

- You're faced with a number of tough choices, whether concerning your work, your relationships, or which direction to go during major life transitions.

- You've had some recent spiritual insights, or even a spiritual awakening, and you're not sure how to best integrate these new revelations into your day-to-day life.

- You feel as if you're expending way too much energy trying to make a buck, and you need to learn how to conserve energy while still getting the job done.

How to Access Eagle's Power

- Be patient. Meditate, journey, sing, or dance to call Eagle, but know that this animal spirit guide does not come easily or immediately.

- Notice any judgments you have about others, and be completely honest with yourself. Write these down, then note how these are projections of some similar aspects or traits in yourself, often ones you deny are even part of you.

- Every evening before you retire, write down a list of ten things that happened that day for which you're grateful. Do this every evening for at least 21 days and watch what happens.

- Go to an area where you can carefully look down. This can be on a cliff, a mountaintop, or at the top of a tall building. As you observe all that is below, take in as much as you can, taking several slow, deep breaths as you do.

Elephant

Quality: **Resolve**

Elephant's Message for You

"IT'S YOUR SACRED TASK TO HONOR, PROTECT, and defend the part of you that's connected to the divine, which we may call your inner king or queen. This sovereign aspect is rooted in deep and ancient wisdom, not only of the human species, but of all forms of life. One of my assignments is to help you with this task, to be your warrior and guardian. You need not take on airs about your role, but simply accept it with grace and humility, with your heart open, your feet firmly planted on the ground, and your head held high. You need not let any of life's challenges and difficulties bring you down—I'll take care of those as well. While staying aware of your connection with the divine, also stay down-to-earth, enjoying the pleasures of your senses and appreciating the richness of your family, friends, and community. Whenever called, be of service to the old, the young, and those less fortunate, and do so with an attitude of holy equality. Let nothing stand in the way of accomplishing your sacred mission."

If Elephant Is Your Power Animal . . .

- You're very intelligent and have an insatiable thirst for knowledge, seeking it through formal education, life experiences, and especially the wisdom of elders.

- You're a natural problem solver, using your keen intelligence coupled with your intuitive capacities to resolve seemingly intractable dilemmas for yourself or others.

- You're most fulfilled and on purpose doing some kind of social or political work, or engaging in public service. You often assume a role of considerable responsibility in these realms, whether in your immediate community or in the world at large.

- You enjoy your sexuality, and are a caring, uninhibited, and passionate lover, with a strong libido and an inordinate ability to satisfy and please your partner.

Ask for Elephant's Help When . . .

- You have a clear idea of what your immediate and long-term goals are, but you're not sure how to conquer any apparent obstacles. These obstacles can be mental (negative beliefs), emotional (fear, doubt, or shame), or physical (other people or things).

- You're feeling lonely and isolated, as if you haven't a friend in the world, and you need some strength and fortitude to pull you out of your self-pity.

- You feel the need for greater confidence and more patience in tackling a new job, relationship, or educational pursuit, or in those instances where you're placed in a position of greater power and responsibility.

- You're feeling weak, small, or tired, and want to feel stronger, bigger, and more energized so that you can greet each moment with complete confidence.

How to Access Elephant's Power

- Volunteer your time helping others in need, such as at a hospice, children's hospital, or retirement home.

- Burn Nag Champa or sandalwood incense while you're meditating in your favorite way or simply sitting in silence for a few moments. Play some soft classical music in the background.

- Once you've identified a specific goal, write down all the possible roadblocks that might hinder you, and ceremonially burn the paper as you watch all these obstacles go up in smoke.

- Make a study of Tantric or Taoist practices, doing so with respect for the sacredness of these sensual arts.

Fox

Quality: Shape-Shifting

Fox's Message for You

"'SLY AS A FOX'? I don't think I'm particularly sly or cunning, although these qualities have been attributed to me. You see, it comes quite naturally to me, and I don't think it's any big deal. But then telling you it's not a big deal may be part of my charm and cunning, right? So it is when we work together. You may not even be aware that I'm around, but you'll know I'm near by how easy it is for you to slip away at a party, or how effortlessly you blend in with the people around you, or how others don't even notice you when you don't want them to. I can help you through just about any kind of predicament. Just don't get lazy or let your ego run rampant with these abilities, or try to trick people, because you'll just trip yourself up and get caught in a trap of your own making.

"If you think you're smart and try to act smart, people will be on to you in the blink of an eye. It's not about acting dumb either, because you're not—although sometimes acting that way just may get you out of scrapes or help you through unpleasant situations.

"Trust in your innate intelligence, and let your senses be your guide in all that you do. And remember: You don't have to prove a thing to anybody—period! Besides, if you try to do so, you give too much of yourself away. Always keep your privacy to yourself, and always keep a part of yourself private."

If Fox Is Your Power Animal . . .

- The slyness that was born as a way of surviving significant trauma in your earliest years has evolved into a wily instinctual intelligence and very sharpened senses that work in your favor, giving you great confidence in dealing with worldly affairs.

- Although you're already a night person, you'll likely become even more nocturnal, getting especially activated on nights of the full moon.

- You're an astute observer, undetected by others, who hears what isn't being said and sees what isn't being seen, to the point that you can know instantly what's about to happen. This gift allows you to be one step ahead of everyone else.

- Not only can you blend in with your environment to the point of being invisible, but you can also shape-shift into different identities by adjusting your body language and vocal characteristics so that even people who know you may not recognize you at first.

Ask for Fox's Help When . . .

- You're faced with a seemingly insurmountable problem in which subtlety and discretion are called for—as opposed to directness and confrontation, which would only make things worse.

- You feel as if you've been too visible for your own well-being (or else you're in the public eye a lot), and you need a break from the scrutiny and want to simply blend in without drawing so much attention to yourself.

- You're in a situation that requires you to think on your feet and make some quick decisions and act on them.

- You've learned to camouflage yourself with low self-esteem due to earlier conditioning, and you now want to change your beliefs about yourself and develop other strategies that are more satisfying and that bring you greater pleasure.

How to Access Fox's Power

- Practice being invisible by noticing the colors and textures of your immediate surroundings, then visualizing your body as being part of these surroundings, covered with these same colors and textures.

- When you're in a social situation, such as a party or gathering, experiment with adjusting the intensity and size of your aura (the energy field around your body) to match the energy fields of those with whom you're socializing.

- Go jogging outdoors two or three times a week. Occasionally break into a faster trot for a few moments, preferably along soft earth or sand.

- Whenever there's an opportunity, simply sit back and observe others closely, paying particular attention to the details of their body language and the tone and inflection of their voices. If possible, do so without their being aware of it.

Frog

Quality: Purification

Frog's Message for You

"SING! LET YOUR VOICE BE KNOWN! It will clear and refresh you, seep into your bones and your soul, cleanse and heal your surroundings, and bathe yourself and others in the vibrations of ancient rhythms and eternal chants. Be still and listen to my chant. It brings the rains, the rains that clean the land and clear away the mud and debris, replacing the stagnant waters with clear, refreshing H_2O. Call on the rains to help clear emotional and mental toxins that have accumulated, those that contaminate your heart, mind, and body and prevent you from being fully *you*. Like a container filled with dark, muddy liquid in which you pour rainwater, the showers from above will flush and purify any negativity, thereby opening the way to greater clarity of purpose and direction. This clearing will help you recognize a more profound sense of your true identity and give you a greater sense of your destiny. You need not fear this purification, because the waters are gentle. Trust in the waters. Trust in your song."

If Frog Is Your Power Animal . . .

- You're sensitive to the emotional states of others, and you very readily express your care with compassion and empathy. You always seem to know what to say—and what *not* to say.

- Your singing is very sweet and powerful. It can arouse emotions and at the same time soothe and heal the heart and soul of anyone listening. You can use your voice to clear any spiritual toxins and negative energy.

- Abundance is second nature to you. You never feel lack in your life, and you always have everything you need available.

- When people first meet you, their impression is that you're just an ordinary person, until they get

to know you and discover the depth and nobility of
your character.

Ask for Frog's Help When . . .

- You need to cleanse your life of people, places,
  or things that no longer fit your lifestyle or your
  increasing desire for peace and serenity.

- You're feeling weak, hassled, irritable, overwhelmed, empty, tired, or frustrated, and you want
  to clear away this negative debris.

- You need to do a clearing and blessing of your
  home or office, or you need to clear a specific room
  in those places.

- You feel like you've lost your voice or you're hesi-
  tant to state the truth for fear of others' reactions,
  yet you know it's important to speak up.

How to Access Frog's Power

- Sit like Frog for a few moments, then hop around
  and see how that feels.

- Sing or chant, alone or with a partner or group, a melodic, rhythmic tune that's pleasantly repetitive.

- Do a physical cleanse and detoxification for three to seven days, consulting an expert as to the most appropriate type of diet for this purpose.

- Take a cleansing sea-salt bath, placing candles around the tub and your favorite aromatherapy oil in the water. Play some soft music, all the while quietly repeating this declaration: "I now release any and all negativity from my body, mind, and soul."

- Contribute your time, efforts, and/or money toward any reputable organization whose objective is to clean up the pollution in the waters of the earth.

Giraffe

Quality: Foresight

Giraffe's Message for You

"SOME SAY THAT WITH ME it's about reaching upward for the heavens or grasping for something that's just out of reach, but that's not the case. I have no trouble doing this. Instead, I actually have trouble reaching down when I need a drink or to get some tasty morsel near the ground. When I do, I lose my sense of what's on the horizon. It's then I feel the most vulnerable. I'm sure it's the same for you. That is, when you get your head too low and too close to the earth, the dust of the ground obscures your sense of perspective and vision. Yet I still have to get close to the ground once in a while to take care of my needs, and it's a very different kind of perspective. It also helps so I don't become exclusively focused on what lies beyond the immediate. Nice to keep your sights on the road ahead, but once in a while it's important to get down and see what's happening a little closer to the earth.

"You don't need binoculars to have my kind of vision, this way of looking at the beyond. Simply be open to the foresight that naturally occurs when you open your eyes and look out at the horizon. Keep your balance as you do so. Your friends will help you with that, so stay close to them. They'll let you know when you've gotten a bit too airy and out of balance.

"You've also got to be clear in your communications, especially with friends and family. No need to fear letting them know who you really are. And no need slump. Stand tall! Your feet are always gonna touch the ground. Just remember where they are."

If Giraffe Is Your Power Animal . . .

- You have the remarkable ability to see what lies ahead, whether this knowledge comes through dreams, visions, or ideas, or as signs from your environment.

- You're very easygoing, laid back, and friendly, enjoying casual get-togethers more than formal occasions. And once you've made friends with someone, you stick with them for a long time.

- Since one of your major strengths is communicating, you're quite articulate in getting your thoughts and feelings across. You also encourage others to be clear and straightforward in their communication.

- You have your head in the heavens and your feet on the earth, resulting in a balance with your spiritual and material life.

Ask for Giraffe's Help When . . .

- You have some concerns about the specific outcome of an event, project, or relationship, and would like to get a sense of what the future will bring.

- You've found that you're tense and uptight in your personal and professional relationships—perhaps focused on tasks at the expense of social needs—and you want to relax and become friendlier with others in your world.

- You feel as if your life has become stagnant and you've become complacent, to the point that you're having difficulty seeing ahead or you're avoiding acting on what you do see before you.

- You're having trouble communicating your ideas in your professional relationships, or expressing your more intimate feelings with those you're closest to.

- You have your sights set on a clearly defined goal, yet are feeling some fear about moving forward toward that aim.

How to Access Giraffe's Power

- Make it a point to socialize more. Call up friends just to say hello, do a favor for someone, or spend more time with your mate and family. Express your care through these kinds of simple yet loving actions, rather than by just using words or empty promises.

- Stand tall. Slightly stretch your neck and spine upward, with your feet spread slightly apart. As you do, look around you, then look at the most distant point you can see. While you're doing so, be aware of the sensations of your feet on the ground.

- While sitting comfortably, gently place the palm of your hand over your third eye (the area in the middle of your forehead that's considered to be the seat of your intuition), and rest it there for a few moments. Notice any thoughts, visions, or other impressions that occur while doing so (or a few moments after you remove your hand) and write them down.

Hawk

Quality: Perspective

Hawk's Message for You

"I'M A CREATURE OF THE AIR, and I'm fascinated by what I can see from up here. I'm not always hunting when you see me. Much of the time I'm just cruising, riding with the currents, and enjoying the vast landscape before me. It provides such an awesome and beautiful perspective. And that's what you need: perspective. You're too caught up in the mundane aspects of your life, and that's fertile ground for worrying. You're too close to your concerns, so take a break from them. Fly away for a while. It will help. Don't get so hung up in the details of your life and instead trust in the power you can generate by moving with the currents of life. Stop trying to change others or the situation, and accept things as they are. Take some time out to just *be,* perhaps by sitting high up on some rocks or taking a walk through the forest or in the mountains. You're at your best when you maintain your spiritual perspective, and it's really not that difficult to do. You have experience and wisdom that you too quickly turn away from or deny. Trust that, and you'll *see* the fundamental truth in all this."

If Hawk Is Your Power Animal . . .

- You tend to see the bigger picture and have a very broad perspective. Within this panorama you also have a keen ability to zero in on details that attract your attention.

- You possess deep spiritual awareness, and when you express your true spirit, you soar! When you do so, you affect others positively, so don't hold back!

- You're a master of going with the flow, particularly sensitive to the emotional currents that ebb and flow through human-kind. You ride these currents effortlessly and gracefully, and possess this keen ability to not get your feathers ruffled.

- You're quite good at interpreting signs and omens from the natural world that tell you to pay close attention, particularly those that will somehow affect the bigger picture. Whether these indicators come as a blessing or a warning, you know that they serve a higher purpose.

Ask for Hawk's Help When . . .

- Your emotions—whether fear, anger, guilt, depression, or all of the above—are so overwhelming that you've lost your perspective and misplaced your faith.

- Your plans have gone awry, twisting and turning in unanticipated ways, and you're having difficulty reconciling this with your expectations and willful insistence that things go your way.

- You're in a period of intense mental activity, such as an educational pursuit or training, and you need to maintain a greater level of vigilance and alertness for a stretch of time to accomplish the task at hand.

- You feel heavy or even depressed, and you find yourself slumping and looking downward a lot.

How to Connect with Hawk's Power

- Spend some time on a mountainside. Sit or lie down, close your eyes, and let your mind soar high above the treetops, imagining what it would be like to be able to see from this perspective.

- Close your eyes and take a few minutes to imagine your life one year from today, in as much detail as possible. When you've done so, jot down what you envisioned, read it aloud, then close your eyes and see how that feels in your body. Then write down the specific steps you'll take today, tomorrow, this week, and this month that will lead you to manifest all that you've visualized.

- While standing, spread your arms out wide, lift yourself up, look outward with your head raised, and imagine the wind surging beneath you. Observe what comes across your visual field as you breathe and soar.

- Practice soft focus: Look at an object in the distance, and as you do so, soften your gaze by allowing your vision to expand to the perimeters of your eyesight. Notice other elements in your visual field while keeping the center of your vision on the original object you started with.

Horse

Quality: Freedom

Horse's Message for You

"WHEN WE JOINED IN PARTNERSHIP and friendship with humans, distances became shorter, the land that seemed so vast began to shrink, and the horizon that appeared to be unobtainable was only a day's ride away. We're good together. Really good! And we want to continue that relationship in its many forms, but please let our relationship be based in love. Many of us have been willing to compromise our deep-rooted need for the freedom to roam the Great Plains and hills of the land to be at your side as your companions and helpers. All we ask is that you treat us kindly and let us run free now and again, like our brothers and sisters who haven't been willing to compromise.

"Know that *your* freedom isn't necessarily something granted or earned, nor is it just a physical freedom. It's a state of heart and soul, one of autonomy from the cultural and societal conditioning that tries to restrict you from expressing yourself, from being who you truly are. No trauma can be so harsh as that of self-denial and self-repression. It restricts breathing and causes one's heart to ache and one's soul to wither.

"First, find compassion for yourself, and then extend it to others, especially those who trigger you, those whom you reactively judge in a false attempt to protect yourself. When you extend this heartfelt compassion to others, it will come back to you tenfold. Let *that* be the source of your freedom and your power. Then, as we ride together, whether in spirit or in form, melded into one being, feel the wind streaming through your hair, the graceful, rhythmic, and coordinated movement, and the continually shifting panorama unfolding around us as we roam together through this adventure called life."

If Horse Is Your Power Animal . . .

- You value your autonomy and your freedom and are willing to do whatever it takes to maintain these attributes.

- You're adept at traveling to other dimensions of awareness and alternate realities, while at the same time being quite capable of dealing with the physical world.

- You're drawn to either shamanic work or some form of metaphysical endeavor, such as being a professional psychic or medium.

- You're friendly and adventurous, very comfortable with yourself in social situations, yet impatient with others whenever you feel that they're trying to stifle you in some way.

- You love to explore just for the sake of exploration, whether it's wandering around a shopping mall or blazing a trail through the forest.

Ask for Horse's Help When . . .

- You're feeling constricted, either by physical circumstances or by habitual, ingrained beliefs about your limitations.

- You're feeling the urge to travel and explore, but you have some fears and worries about doing so.

- Your energy level is down and you need to recharge in order to deal with a situation or task that will require both strength and endurance, or to tackle a vast number of seemingly impossible duties in a short time frame.

- You're being prompted to explore shamanic or meta-physical work, but you're not sure how to go about following these urgings.

How to Access Horse's Power

- Since it's relatively easy to find domesticated horses, make it a point to spend some time around them. As you do so, pay close attention to their behavior and to any intuitive impressions that come to mind.

- With some of your favorite soft music playing in the background, meditate on a white horse (which cross-culturally represents the balance of wisdom and power). Note what you feel, as well as what else the white horse signifies for you.

- Take a journey or trip somewhere by foot or in a vehicle, one where you have no specific destination in mind.

- Whether outdoors or in your living room, trot, gallop, run, and whinny every so often while you're doing so, noticing sensations and feelings that come up as you do.

Hummingbird

Quality: Joy

Hummingbird's Message for You

"I LOVE LIFE! It's such a treat to be able to fly backward, forward, up, down, and sideways. Lots of flexibility as to which direction I go. I'm especially sensitive and careful about who I let close to me, so if something seems at all scary or intimidating, I'm outta there! Life's too precious to stay around anything that doesn't feel right. I much prefer the flowers and the trees. Speaking of the flowers, not only do I get to see all the pretty flowers, but I get to smell and drink from them, too.

"As for you, say yes to life! Taste the sweet nectar that's always nearby, even if you have to fly around for a while until you find it. Know that the only true prison you have is your belief in your limitations.

Let them go, and experience the abundance of love and opportunity that's all around. It only takes a willingness to see it, taste it, and feel it. Also know that you are perfectly capable of handling any debilitating negativity by flying away to safer grounds. Whether by physically removing yourself or detaching from the situation mentally and emotionally, you don't have to just hang around because you don't want people to think bad things about you. You always have the freedom to choose love and joy!"

If Hummingbird Is Your Power Animal . . .

- You're so full of joy and have such a positive attitude that whenever you find yourself around negativity or harsh energies, you're so sensitive that you may have to fly away to avoid becoming affected.

- Your freedom is critical to your health and well-being. A job or a relationship that's physically or spiritually confining or assaultive will eat away at your soul.

- Your very best choice for work is self-employment, preferably that which allows you to be outdoors.

- Because of your quietness and subtle presence, others may mistake you for being fragile, but this is definitely not the case. You're very powerful, which comes from your gentleness and loving behavior toward others.

Ask for Hummingbird's Help When . . .

- You're feeling depressed or overwhelmed and would like to add a bit of lightness to your life.

- You're around any negativity or emotional harshness and feel the need to protect yourself.

- You're distracted and unable to focus on the present moment.

- You're feeling guilt, shame, or anger about something in the past. Hummingbird will help you free yourself of the emotional debris of any guilt, shame, or anger associated with these memories so that you can forgive yourself and others and move on.

How to Access Hummingbird's Power

- Go outside somewhere where you can be surrounded by flowers, or gather some to place throughout your home. Make it a point to pause and smell them, appreciating their beauty and noticing how the different types of flowers, along with their colors and aromas, make you feel.

- The basis for joy is love, and the best way to receive love is to give it. To experience joy, do one loving, selfless act each day for the next couple of weeks without concern for the outcome. Do it for the pure act of giving, whether you give money to a homeless person, pick up trash at your local park or beach, or express your appreciation or admiration to a friend or family member.

- Release yourself from the weight of guilt and shame by taking a piece of notebook paper and writing at the top, "I now and immediately forgive myself for . . . " Then list at least six to eight things from your past that still haunt you. Be brutally honest. Next, read the list out loud and as you do, notice the sensations and emotions in

your body. Breathe consciously with each statement, and when you're done, either ceremonially
bury this paper or burn it, noting how this feels.

Kangaroo

Quality: Abundance

Kangaroo's Message for You

"I HAVE A VAST PLAYGROUND that I take full advantage of, enjoying the fruits of the land and playing with friends. I'm able to find whatever I need at a moment's notice. I'm completely grateful for this opportunity to exist, and have no need to worry or wonder where the next meal is coming from. I'm comfortable with periods of drought as well, although sometimes sacrifices need to be made. Actually, no drought exists when friends and family are around.

"You're much more blessed and cared for than you might think. Stop spending so much time in your head, worrying about this or that and getting bugged by every little thing that seems to go wrong.

It will go much better once you cast off those shackles of mistrust and negativity. You'll get a lot more done, too, and then you get to play more. The abundant life is really a lot simpler than you make it.

"So take a look around you and find out who you love and who loves you. Roam around a bit, but stop searching for what you need and just let it manifest before you. This is how life works; or at least, that's how it works if you just *let it* work without hanging on to old stuff that drags you down and keeps you from moving ahead.

"Stop and take a look directly down your nose. What do you see? You see what's ahead of you, and that's always the direction you should go. Follow your nose, and where your nose goes, so do you! Cherish each and every experience, and trust, deeply trust. Don't try to figure it out. Just pray, listen, and do what Spirit tells you. There's really no other way."

If Kangaroo Is Your Power Animal . . .

- You tend to focus on the immediate moment and the future, with very little attention to what's already passed. You're able to quickly let go of any and all emotional attachments to what's already occured.

- You're a very social individual, comfortable and competent in the company of larger groups of friends or family. You occasionally need periods of solitude to balance yourself, and find that this need increases as you get older.

- You continually live in a state of true abundance, trusting that life always provides and that your needs are somehow always met.

- You're very patient and giving with others, especially children and family members. If necessary, you're willing to put your own needs on hold so that others' can be met.

Ask for Kangaroo's Help When . . .

- You find yourself continually obsessing and ruminating about the past, such that it's difficult to move forward in your life.

- You feel off balance in your work or in your relationships because of too much focus on one or the other, and you're not sure how to regain your equilibrium.

- You have a tendency to think in terms of lack or "not enough," and you want to experience greater abundance in your life.

- You've moved into a position of greater responsibility—particularly one in which you're in charge of a number of people—and you need to bolster your confidence in dealing with this new phase of your life.

How to Access Kangaroo's Power

- Try hopping around on both legs at the same time, holding your hands a few inches in front of your solar plexus, mimicking Kangaroo's movement.

- Whenever you find yourself interacting in a group, make it a point to do whatever you can to maintain harmony and balance within it.

- Make a list of everything you can think of that's right in your life and for which you feel appreciative, then go down the list and focus on gratitude for these things.

- Choose a day when you put your own needs aside, eliminate complaining, and focus on giving to others. You can do this through giving compliments, helping with some task, or offering some other sincere gesture.

Lion

Quality: Nobility

Lion's Message for You

"MY BEING EXUDES DIGNITY, divinity, and nobility. It's not so much my roar that everybody fears—my mere presence demands respect and deference. I don't qualify this with false humility, self-degradation, or apology; nor, in spite of what you've heard, do I feel any sense of pride whatsoever in who I am. I don't need to. I'm just very clear. If *you* need to roar to clear the way for your own self-acceptance, then please do so. Once you've done this, listen closely to your heart. It sings of your purpose, even though your purpose may change and shift with time and age. That's where you'll find the courage to be who you are. Not in your mind, not in the world around you, but in the center of your body and being. Life will enfold and support you, as long as you honor and follow your heart. There truly is no other way.

"Although you may be tempted and swayed by externals, especially others' opinions and judgments about you, sit quietly in the savannah of your personal sanctuary and simply listen. Listen with all of you. Tune in to the knowingness that resides in your bones and in your soul to help you go forward in life. Once you hear the call, move ahead without second thoughts or doubts of any kind.

"Know that you're protected, that absolutely nothing can harm you as long as you're listening and operating from that most precious of founts, your heart of hearts."

If Lion Is Your Power Animal . . .

- You carry yourself in a stately manner, with a strong presence and air of nobility that makes people notice you whenever you walk into a room.

- You're capable of a great deal of compassion, yet when your anger is triggered—which isn't easily done—everyone else backs off in the face of your roar.

- You're quite courageous, possess a great deal of physical and emotional strength, and are a natural leader and organizer. You're often called to take on tasks that require the application of these gifts.

- You function best as part of a group or community rather than alone, and are frequently asked to take an active role in the group.

- You enjoy taking risks by going into situations that will stretch your capabilities and expand your knowledge.

Ask for Lion's Help When . . .

- You feel beaten down by difficult life circumstances and need an extra boost to continue facing these challenges.

- Your dignity has been assaulted and your integrity has been questioned, and you need to recapture a sense of self-respect and poise.

- Your family, group, or community has called on you to assume a position of authority and leadership.

- You've taken on a task or project that seems beyond your talents and capabilities, yet something inside you knows that you can do it, even though it requires you to stretch yourself.

How to Access Lion's Power

- When you're walking about, lift your chin and head up, straightening and stretching your spine so that the effect is one of feeling taller and more dignified.

- *Roar!* Yes, go ahead and find out what it feels like to do so, whether quietly or with full force, noticing as you do how it feels in your gut and your heart.

- Close your eyes and pretend that you're a king or queen. Breathe slowly and deeply, and see if you can feel that sense of nobility, dignity, and connection to the divine in your body.

- If there's someone close to you from whom you're withholding some feelings, speak your truth lovingly and assertively, without apprehension about his or her response.

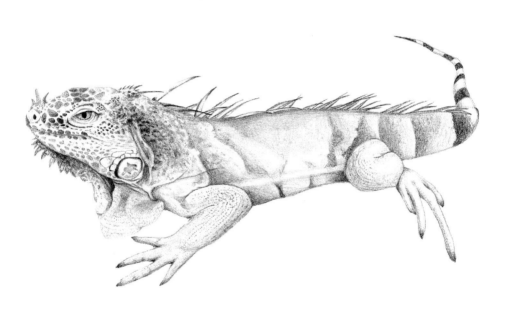

Lizard

Quality: Dreamtime

Lizard's Message for You

"I REACH BACK IN TIME, yet I'm with you even as you read this. I'm an ancient and fundamental part of you, operating just below your usual level of awareness. I'm your reptilian consciousness, which has survived through eons of time, ever since the great dinosaurs roamed the earth. I've survived through the ages largely due to my extraordinary perceptive and sensing capacities. I can hear what's not being said, see what others don't, and sense others' intentions and movements before they're even aware of them. When someone tries to grab me, I may lose my tail, but I walk away with my life. I'm sure that's happened to you a couple of times, hasn't it? The gift in this is that I easily grow another one and continue on my merry way. So if you 'lose your tail,' or you're afraid that you might, no worries! You'll grow another one and go on about your life, perhaps in a new way—a little worn, but a lot wiser.

"I'm an ancient being, the source of your instinctual reasoning. Even though life on this planet has evolved into hundreds of thousands of different forms, it all remains physically and etherically interwoven and interdependent. Many of us are connected through the core of the reptilian self, and all of us are connected through our DNA, which is the source and substance of all animate life. You may philosophically believe that we're all one, but you can only *know* that unity through the reptilian, instinctual sensing of that fact through your bodily sensations. I'll help you in your waking state, but most definitely in your sleep and in your dreams. Just ask me, and I'll connect with you in the dreamtime."

If Lizard Is Your Power Animal . . .

- You're usually in a state of relaxed attentiveness, yet you're also acutely aware of what's going on around you at all times. You're sensitive to even the subtlest of cues from your environment.

- You're a dreamer and you pay close attention to the details and symbolism of your dreams, often basing your life's course on their meanings.

- You instinctively know when to stay still and when to move. And when you move, you do so quickly and purposefully.

- You're able to detach from fear and personal bias, basing your decisions on instinctually knowing the right thing to do, rather than making emotionally and impulsively determined choices.

- You're primarily clairsentient, having strong and accurate gut feelings about other people and situations, knowing without knowing how you know.

Ask for Lizard's Help When . . .

- You're having difficulty remembering your dreams, or you're having trouble understanding the cryptic messages contained therein.

- You feel somewhat numb or depressed, and want to reawaken your senses and restore your vitality.

- You feel overly involved or enmeshed in some relationship or situation, and you need to detach so that you can listen to what your instincts are telling you.

- You've been getting a lot of advice, solicited and unsolicited, and it has become difficult to hear your own intuitive voice.

How to Access Lizard's Power

- Keep a dream journal, recording your dreams by writing them down as soon as possible and noting any meanings that jump out at you. Be especially aware of any recurring themes.

- *Lizard meditation:* Take yourself to a place in nature that's warm and sunny, where there's little or no extraneous noise. Lie on a rock if possible, and breathe slowly and deeply, focusing your awareness on your senses. Listen to the sounds around you, look at your surroundings, smell the aromas, and notice the sensations in your body as you do so.

- Write down your goals and desires for the future, being as specific as possible. Place this list under your pillow for several nights, asking for Lizard's help in dreaming this future into manifestation.

- List any reservations associated with achieving your dreams. Then ceremonially burn this paper. In so doing, you'll release these fears and watch them go up in smoke.

Lynx
(Bobcat)

Quality: **Secrets and Confidentiality**

Lynx's Message for You

"THERE'S A GREAT DECEIT that many hold that we're somehow simple beings locked into a very dense collection of matter known as a body. These illusions are sometimes necessary in order to cope with the intensity that we have to deal with in the world the way it is these days. I beseech you to go further than your eyes usually do and listen more closely than you've ever listened before. Find a quiet spot, lie on the earth on a warm summer day, and listen to her heartbeat. Feel her breathing. Perhaps you can even hear a low tonal vibration—a slight, quiet, but steady rumbling. Then let your mind drift into the cosmos, into the stars and sun and sky. As you do so, pay attention to the less than obvious. Note those elements of being that are typically unseen and unheard, especially amid the flashiness and the clamor of this world.

"Go into the silence. Really go into it, not as an exercise or an assignment, but to get ahold of what's even greater than the stillness you find there, that which serves as the conduit into the Great Mystery. It's far past the time for humans to do this, but it's not just for humans that I ask. It's for *all* our brothers and sisters, for all our children and their children. Go into this quiet and stillness as often as possible, and carry what you find there into every interaction in which you engage. There's a deep compassion in silence that can't be discovered when you're in the midst of the noise of civilization. Know that in this blessed silence you'll find the true Source of all. Don't try to find it; let it find you. Let it *know* you."

If Lynx Is Your Power Animal . . .

- You have a remarkable ability to see those elements in others that they either keep hidden or aren't aware of, including fears, falsehoods, secrets, and even untapped abilities.

- You're a person of few words, preferring solitude and solitary activities, yet you feel relaxed and confident when you're in social situations, always listening closely as you quietly observe others.

- Others see you as trustworthy, and in fact, you're excellent at keeping confidences and avoiding gossip. When people come to you, they disclose things about themselves that even their good friends may not know.

- You have a keen awareness and understanding of ancient mysticism and divine magic, as if you were born knowing these secrets and mysteries.

Ask for Lynx's Help When . . .

- You're involved with someone either personally or professionally and your gut is telling you to be cautious with this person, although you don't yet know why.

- You notice that you've been talking too much at the expense of really listening.

- Someone has shared something highly personal with you and has asked that you keep it confidential.

- You've recently been introduced to any of the mystery schools or ancient mystical readings, and you want to explore these in greater depth.

How to Access Lynx's Power

- Sit back and observe how people act and what they say in social situations. As you do, notice what impressions and images come to you that are probably not obvious to those you're observing.

- For one entire day, speak only when absolutely necessary; otherwise, remain silent.

- When you're with someone, make it a point to be really interested in their stories, ideas, or feelings, without talking at all about yourself.

- Make a study of any mystical spiritual disciplines, such as the Gnostic Gospels, the Kabbalah, or Sufism.

Opossum

Quality: Strategy

Opossum's Message for You

"ALL THIS FUSS AND BOTHER about my playing dead, or that I somehow make myself play dead, is poppycock! I'm really very easily scared, even though it may not look like it when I'm laid out on the ground. The truth is that whenever someone threatens me, I get so overwhelmed that I just freeze and fall over. It's a pretty good talent that the Creator gifted me with, wouldn't you say? I even *smell* like I'm dead at those times, so everyone leaves me alone. Of course, with a skill like this, it's natural to want to cultivate it to a fine art, so I've gotten very good at it. Yeah, I know it's a bit extreme, but it works!

"You don't have to play dead, but do whatever you have to when you feel threatened. There are a lot of variations on that theme. You can act tired, make up a story that allows you to leave, pretend you're not feeling well, act like you're not afraid even if you're terrified, or act afraid even if you're not—any of these actions and more will help you out in uncomfortable situations. They don't have to be life-threatening situations for these strategies to work in your favor. Just don't fool yourself. A nice perk is that when you get really good at this, you start seeing through others' facades without feeling the need to expose them."

If Opossum Is Your Power Animal . . .

- You have the remarkable ability to put up a front, all the while knowing who you really are within the guise that's required for the circumstance.

- You're able to see through others' false fronts and deceptions. Yet even though you see through these masks, you accept others for who they are and deal with them accordingly.

- You're a natural and gifted actor, whether or not you've pursued this craft as a career or hobby, or simply use these gifts in social situations.

- You're quite capable of pretending to be unafraid in the face of threatening situations, or of showing indifference in order to deal with a conflict that requires this strategy.

Ask for Opossum's Help When . . .

- You feel trapped in a challenging predicament and don't know how to get out of it gracefully.

- You find yourself playing out habitual self-defeating strategies—such as martyr/victim, "Poor me," "I'm not enough," and so on—that interfere with your achieving your potential and living out your soul's destiny.

- The circumstances you're in require you to portray the opposite of what you're really feeling, such as a fearful situation where others look to you for leadership and you must act fearless, or a disagreement where you think you're right but must act as if you're wrong in order to create harmony.

- You're faced with a complex situation that requires you to strategize in order to navigate your way through it.

How to Access Opossum's Power

- Study either Tai Chi or Aikido, which are martial-art disciplines that teach you how to protect yourself through strategies of nonresistance and nondefensiveness.

- Take an acting class or a course in improvisational theater, or perhaps even audition for a role in a local play.

- Find an area outdoors where you can lie down and pretend that you're dead for a few minutes.

- Identify and write out the various physical, mental, psychological, and spiritual strategies you use that allow you to escape unpleasant or threatening situations.

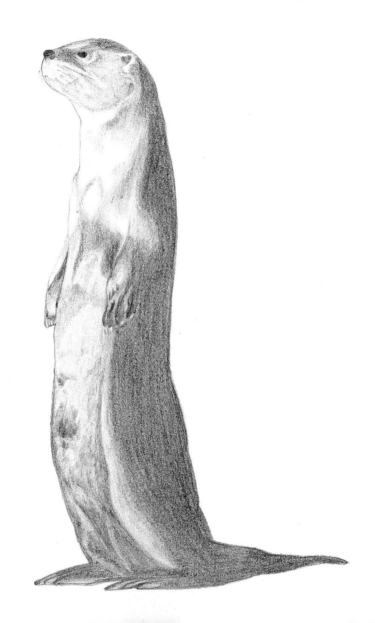

Otter

Quality: Inner Feminine

Otter's Message for You

"I'M LONG, SLIM, SLEEK, graceful, sensual, caring, and loving, with virtually no enemies—and you thought I was just an odd, skinny little runt of an animal, eh? It's my destiny to bring joy, love, and playfulness wherever I am or to whoever I'm with, and to gloriously receive all that Mother Nature gives to me and my family and friends. It's not about worrying or trying to control life. It's not even about letting go, because in truth there's really nothing to let go of, since it's an illusion that you were in control in the first place! I do want to comfort you somehow, to give you whatever you truly need, and when you call on me I'll do my best to be a loving and supportive guide.

"This requires something else to really make it work: You must call on the goddess within each of us, whether you're male or female. And just to remind you, you don't have to do anything you really don't want to do. There's always a choice, even when at those darker moments it doesn't seem like there is. You can always find an alternative to whatever your present situation is. If you don't believe that, then go out and spend some time walking in the woods or just playing with friends. When you do, it's only afterwards that you'll realize that while you were walking or playing you weren't worrying or trying to control anything.

"Again, there's no need to let go—just be still, let that tranquility emanate from you, and allow your being to determine what action to take, rather than that silly mind of yours that thinks it's oh-so-smart!"

If Otter Is Your Power Animal . . .

- You're extremely curious, friendly, and enjoy being around other people. You assume that others are friendly and safe—until proven otherwise.

- You're very active and adventurous—you're always on the move and find it hard to sit still for long.

- You have a nicely balanced and positive feminine energy (whether you're a man or woman). This manifests itself as an openness and receptivity to others without preconceived judgments, a generosity of support and happiness for others' accomplishments, and a glow of love and joy wherever you go.

- You're quite fun and playful, bringing this in attitude and action to nearly every aspect of your life.

Ask for Otter's Help When . . .

- You find yourself addicted to worrying, constantly thinking in terms of *"What if . . . ?"* and dwelling on the most catastrophic of possible outcomes.

- You've been feeling lethargic, staying indoors too much, and taking life much too seriously.

- You're fragmented and scattered, going around and around from idea to idea, unable to clearly focus on any one idea or project.

- You've been getting powerful messages from the universe, but you've been resisting by blocking or denying them. However, at some level you recognize the validity of these communications.

How to Access Otter's Power

- While outdoors, stand comfortably straight and tall, holding your arms up and out from your side, palms up, as you repeat either silently or aloud a few times: "I now receive all good things from life."

- Find a creative activity to pursue, perhaps one you've been considering for a while, and do it in the spirit of joy and playfulness without concern as to whether or not you're any good at it.

- Spend some time with children, or take yourself and your inner child to a playground of some sort and simply play, without concern about outcome or others' judgments.

- If you're a woman, spend some quality time with a circle of female friends, sharing your cares and concerns. If you're a man, make it a point to really *listen and hear* what others are telling you, especially your mate.

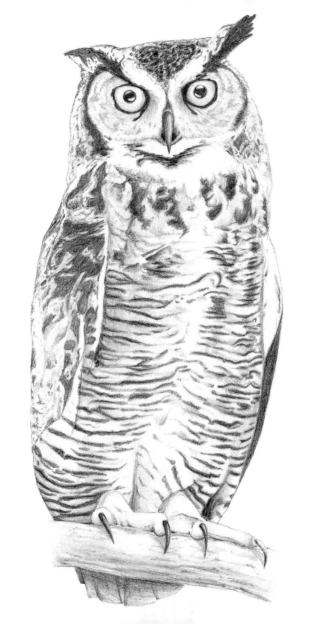

Owl

Quality: Wisdom

Owl's Message for You

"I LIVE IN THE NIGHT, but not for fear of the light. All my senses are geared to the world of shadows. Some say that I'm a portent of death, but that's not necessarily so. Death is only one aspect of darkness. The shadowy realms can be kind of scary, yet there really isn't anything to fear. The darkness is just as sacred as the light, and in it there is magic, mystery, and ancient knowledge. You can't have one without the other, and light will always dissipate the darkness.

"You have the ability to be aware of your own shadows and see the shadows of others, which is truly a powerful gift—so powerful that it can be intimidating to others. Use this ability with compassion, discretion, and sensitivity. With your heightened powers of perception, you're able to see through appearances and illusions without judgment. Notice also any darknesses in yourself that inhibit the full expression of your heart and soul's destiny. Just observe these without shame or judgment. Clear that darkness by first sitting with it for a brief time, illuminating it with the inner light of your awareness. Then call on me to remove it and I'll carry it into the night and transform it. No need to live in darkness and shadow; simply heal any shadows with the Light."

If Owl Is Your Power Animal . . .

- You have a great deal of wisdom, but you may not always accept it. Your gift is actually "soul wisdom" more than intellectual knowledge. A wise person doesn't always have to speak up or show off their insights and knowledge; the real trick is to know when to share and when to simply listen.

- You have very finely tuned awareness. You keep your eyes and ears wide open, looking and listening closely to subtleties of communication, both verbal and nonverbal. This acute sensitivity, coupled with compassion, is very healing to those you're associated with.

- You pay close attention to signs and omens, particularly when you're in the dark about some important situation or relationship. It's important to trust these signs.

- You have very powerful clairvoyant and intuitive skills, and you need to accept and nurture them. You may even have the gift of prophecy, foretelling events before they happen.

Ask for Owl's Help When . . .

- You're faced with difficult decisions, no matter how large or small. Pay close attention to signs and omens that will help you make the right choice.

- You've having trouble in a relationship with someone discerning what is truth and what is illusion about that person.

- Circumstances of your life have taken a sudden and dramatic turn (such as a divorce or job loss), and you need help navigating through this dark period.

- You've undertaken a new, challenging course of study, and you're feeling a lack of confidence with respect to this task.

How to Access Owl's Power

- Spend some time in silence in nature—perhaps in a forest, on a beach, or in your own backyard. As you sit and observe, pay close attention to the smallest details. Listen closely to the sounds around you. Notice each passing experience, not only just what you see and hear, but also whatever sensations you feel in your body. Try this during the day and also at night.

- Who are you? Respond to this simple question by repeating out loud, *"I AM!"* softly but firmly as you look around at your environment, breathing deeply and steadily. Do this for a few minutes each day for a week. Notice how it makes you feel.

- Move like Owl with stealth, without making a sound. Try this indoors and out. Keep your eyes open as you do so, listening closely to the sounds around you. Breathe steadily as you move.

- For the next two weeks, read from books of universal wisdom, such as those by Krishnamurti, Yogananda, Sogyal Rinpoche, or any texts by or about spiritual masters.

Panther
(Leopard/Jaguar)

Quality: **Passion**

Panther's Message for You

"YES, I'M A GREAT HUNTER, and I stalk my prey with the greatest of stealth and with the greatest of tenderness. Even at the moment I strike, I appreciate that the soul of this being who has surrendered itself has agreed to do so. They've made their choice—not out of fear, as you might assume—but out of love. Love not just for me and my family, but a love that allows life to perpetuate itself in the grand cycle of death and birth. For you, it's necessary to stalk only those parts of your ego and consciousness that are weakened, old, infirm, and no longer useful to the overall totality of who you are.

As you harvest these aspects through your willingness to hunt them down with the light of your awareness, you provide for the perpetuation and renewal of what needs to be birthed in you that serves your own growth cycle. By doing so you create more room and support for fulfilling your soul's destiny and purpose.

"You need very little time for the hunt, as there are always abundant resources available to feed your body and your soul. Between the moments you're meeting your basic needs, there are long stretches of time when you can enjoy the earthly and sensual passions, passions that ignite your soul and turn you on. No, not just sexual passions, but also the passionate appreciation of the breeze against your skin, the beauty of the sunrise, the sounds of your children singing, the steady beat of your heart, or the sweet aroma of your lover's skin. It's a mistake to limit passion to the confines of the sexual act. Instead, let it be in each breath you take, in every moment you exist. Let passion live through your very being and express itself through you, as you."

If Panther Is Your Power Animal . . .

- You do your best work under the pressure of a deadline or a time-limited goal, yet you maintain balance by pacing yourself, allowing time for rest and play.

- When you have a dream or a goal, you maintain a quiet intention about it as you work toward its realization, knowing that if you talk too much about it, it will dissipate motivation and endanger its full manifestation.

- You're very tactile and sensual, often communicating through touch, yet you're so sensitive that the wrong kind of touch can irritate you. On the other hand, pleasant touch can revitalize and reenergize you.

- You were born with a gift of extraordinary "in-sight," a unique gift of inner knowing that has made you feel different from others much of your life.

Ask for Panther's Help When . . .

- You're feeling frightened or threatened and need a strong sense of protection and guardianship.

- You've gone through or are going through a period of suffering (or even a metaphorical death), and you need support in moving into the rebirth part of the cycle, in which you reclaim your true power.

- You've been wounded in some way physically or emotionally, and you need help in your healing and recovery.

- You've been confronted with some aspect of your life or your character that has been denied, avoided, or has remained in shadow because of its seeming unpleasantness, and you're ready and prepared to face this aspect, no matter what the consequences.

How to Access Panther's Power

- Spend time touching and caressing your romantic partner, just enjoying the pure sensuality of the experience without it necessarily leading to or culminating in sexual intercourse.

- In your journal or on a separate sheet of paper, at the top write, "I am now ready to let go of . . ." and list all the situations, people, and aspects of your own character that you're prepared to release.

- Do a *stealth walk:* While barefoot, walk as slowly and quietly as possible on the earth, with feet turned slightly inward, letting the outer edge of each foot touch the ground first.

- Pay close attention to the sensations in your solar plexus (also known as the third chakra) periodically throughout the day—these are your gut instincts. Notice when this area tightens up; as you do, be aware of any thoughts or immediate circumstances that may be triggering this sensation.

Rabbit

Quality: Fertility

Rabbit's Message for You

"SOME PEOPLE THINK that all there is to being a bunny is fear, but don't let that fool you. We *do* look and act skittish sometimes, but there's so much more to us than fear. For one, we produce a lot of little ones. That's because there are so many of our brothers and sisters that need food, and we're willing to sacrifice some of our lot so that life can go on. Not a big deal. I don't hate those who use my body for food. I'm not capable of that. It's just the way it is, and I accept that. For you, this kind of fertility is more than fertility of the body, solely for the reproduction of the species. It's about fertility of the mind and heart. Fertility of the mind— that's about dreaming and creating, leaping at the possibilities of generating fine works of artistic expression, from the child's clay bowl to the incredible masterpieces that you humans are capable of turning out. Then there's fertility of the heart, letting your heart be open and loving to all forms of life, showing it in so many different and creative ways.

"You can't always measure your success by how much you're leaping and jumping around; you also have to pause for those still, quiet moments. That's when you can smell what's in the wind, feel the sun on your body, and outwit those who want more from you than you're truly willing to give. Our lives are short; so is yours. Enjoy it to the fullest—let yourself jump, leap, and hop, knowing that you're as protected as you need to be. Trust that when you get very still, you'll always hear your own soul's heartbeat."

If Rabbit Is Your Power Animal . . .

- You're quick-witted and nimble in your speech and actions, able to triumph over adversaries and get yourself out of uncomfortable situations by using your intelligence, common sense, and wit.

- You always have a Plan B, and are so flexible with your agenda that you're prepared for any contingency. You can readily shift plans as the need demands, even in highly stressful or scary situations.

- You tend to have cycles in your personal and work life in which stretches of inactivity and relative stillness follow periods of intense activity, where progress is made in leaps and bounds.

- You're sensitive, artistic, and articulate, with a philosophical depth that sometimes surprises others until they get to know you.

- You're optimistic and positive and find it difficult to tolerate gloominess and pessimism.

Ask for Rabbit's Help When . . .

- A great opportunity presents itself—but to take advantage of it, you need to act swiftly.

- You're working on a project that's coming along very slowly, and you want to speed things up.

- You're trying to make a baby, and although you'd still like to get pregnant, you want to stop trying so hard and return to enjoying the pleasure, delight, and playfulness in making love with your sweetheart, without attachment to any outcome.

- You've tried unsuccessfully to accomplish a project or a venture, and have been met with frustration at the seeming blocks that so far have prevented you from achieving your goal so far.

How to Access Rabbit's Power

- The next time you're outdoors, find an unobtrusive spot and stand there for a few moments, staying as still as possible.

- Cover yourself with some blankets and pillows, enough to make you feel cozy and comfortable, and let this be your burrow for a few minutes.

- Try a vegetarian diet for a few days, with lots of fruit and salad.

- Grow a vegetable garden and ceremonially set aside a certain section that welcomes small animals (including rabbits) to come and eat directly from it.

- Hop—that's right, hop, just like when you were a child—for at least a minute, changing direction and speed frequently as you do.

Raccoon

Quality: Resourcefulness

Raccoon's Message for You

"YES, I ADMIT IT—I'm a scavenger. You have to make a living somehow! Plus, with kids to feed and all. But I'll tell you what: I can live just about anywhere, from the woods to your neighborhood, and still make a go of it. I'm just not too fussy. But I *am* a bit curious, and I find what I need in places you wouldn't even think of.

"As for you, you're a lot smarter and a lot more resourceful than you think you are. You can use your innate intelligence to discover all sorts of things about yourself, others, and your world that you didn't even realize, and you never have to worry about finding solutions to problems and challenges. You also don't have to be so open with everyone, letting them know all about you. Keep some of yourself in reserve and private, sharing certain aspects only with those you can completely trust. Don't do this out of shame about these traits, but out of intelligent discretion. Much of your creative output takes place in the dark and at night, so honor that and do the work you need to at these times. Trust your instincts as much as you humanly can. They'll serve you well."

If Raccoon Is Your Power Animal . . .

- Because of your gift of manual dexterity, you express yourself best with your hands, whether through sculpting, painting, writing, or some other endeavor. You *must* honor and express that characteristic in some creative way, no matter what else you do in your life.

- You have a number of different personalities, some of which you openly express, while others remain hidden behind your public persona. Just remember who you are at the core, and allow yourself to play out these different identities with sincerity and compassion, and without taking any of them too seriously.

- You're at home whether you live in the city, suburbs, a rural area, or the wilderness. You're very adaptable and flexible, and can make a nest just about anywhere you stay.

- You're a forager, incredibly resourceful at finding just what you need at any given time. When faced with difficult situations or problems, you can use this resourcefulness to discover creative solutions.

Ask for Raccoon's Help When . . .

- You're feeling pressured to shape up and conform to someone else's expectations, and you want to maintain your autonomy and be okay with the diversity in your personalities and expressions.

- You're faced with a task that requires you to use your hands with refinement and agility.

- You're itchy for adventure and exploration, either due to feeling stuck in your work or your relationship, or for no logical reason at all.

- You find yourself in a new situation that's been both challenging and frustrating, and you need to approach it with flexibility and adapt to these circumstances without compromising your personal integrity.

How to Access Raccoon's Power

- Play with masks. Either attend a mask-making workshop or purchase one or two and try them out, noting how it makes you feel to do so.

- Dress differently than you ordinarily do. If you usually dress up, dress down, and vice versa. Then go to a public place where you can remain relatively anonymous, and experiment with your body posture, way of walking, and facial expressions. Note how it affects you to disguise yourself like this.

- Make an exhaustive list of your resources. Include your personal idiosyncrasies, talents, and skills; memories of successes and triumphs; people in your life; and spiritual and community resources. Keep this list available to remind you whenever you're faced with a challenging or seemingly overwhelming situation.

- Instead of preparing a meal, forage through either your refrigerator and cupboards or the grocery store, looking for small portions of different kinds of foods that you proceed to eat.

Raven
(Crow)

Quality: **Magic**

Raven's Message for You

"RELAX YOUR BODY! There's nothing to fear now that I'm here. I've returned from the realm of the dark and mysterious, the Eternal Subconscious, the Great Unknown, where all creation is initiated. I hearken you to attend to whatever is happening in your life right now. At this very moment! Pay close attention. This is a particularly auspicious time for you, a time to consolidate all that you've learned up to this point and to really, truly *know* it and trust what you know, with no apologies and no pretentiousness or arrogance. Just realize your strengths and your limitations, yet don't let either be limiting. You're a magician. A wizard. You have the gift of being able to go back and forth from that shadowy realm of creation's initiation to this realm of light and materiality. You can be completely comfortable in both worlds—and in the worlds betwixt and between the dark and the light. That's the essence of magic: to be able to traverse these worlds with ease and grace and bring back teachings and healings from the darkness into this reality. Yet it's only when this magic is performed with love and humility that one can survive the power and intensity of that which is accessed in the void. Let me help you come out of the darkness with your wings full and your call strong."

If Raven Is Your Power Animal . . .

- You're very social, vivacious, and somewhat moody, yet you're quite flexible in your approach to life. You readily and easily adapt to any new circumstances or environments.

- Through deep meditation and clear intention, you know how to work with the fertile and creative energies of the void to bring forth whatever you need into material reality.

- As you age and mature, your knowledge of altered states of spiritual consciousness grows, and the realms beyond the veil become increasingly accessible to you.

- You have a knack with all animals, from the tiniest to the largest, and you have a particular talent for communicating with them.

- You're supremely confident and not easily intimidated, yet you have an underlying cautiousness and alertness, especially with those who behave aggressively. You always seem to know what to do, and you do so quickly and decisively.

Ask for Raven's Help When . . .

- You've had a particularly traumatic childhood and are ready to recover and reclaim the innocence and joy that were lost.

- You've lost touch with the magic in your life and want to learn how to recapture it.

- You're in need of physical or emotional healing, and you've tried just about everything. Now you're ready to support your healing by praying regularly and putting your faith in divine intervention and miracles.

- You have a loved one in need of healing who is geographically distant. Raven will be the courier of your prayers and healing energy from any healing ceremonies you do on behalf of this loved one.

How to Access Raven's Power

- Organize and facilitate a healing circle to send prayers and healing to anyone or anything in need of this sort of spiritual treatment and care.

- Spend some time in the darkness (in a way that's safe) and let it enfold you as you breathe, sending any fear that surfaces down through your body and grounding it into the earth beneath you.

- Write a poem or a short piece on all the associations you have with Raven, especially noting what you admire about her.

- Learn Raven's call by sitting near a group of them in the early morning to hear their calls. Listen for the variation and the commonality of each, and practice these calls each day.

- Create a calling ceremony on the winter solstice by asking Raven to carry forth your prayers, your requests, and your dreams from the dark to the light.

Seal
(Sea Lion)

Quality: **Imagination**

Seal's Message for You

"I'M A CREATURE OF THE OCEAN, yet I love the land as well. Although I can spend days out at sea, there are times when I just have to bring myself onto the land. It's also your prerogative to swim in the ocean of your imagination, and while you may not spend days there, there's no need to come ashore too quickly. There's plenty of time to materialize that which has gestated in this fertile and fluid playground. Remember, all life begins in the ocean. *All* life. That's why we must treat the waters with great respect and care. So must you treat your own creative imagination. Allow yourself to swim in this vast reservoir of creativity and bring forth onto terra firma that which is ready to birth.

"No need to rush or hurry. Too many people doing that these days as it is, so don't join that crowd. Where do you start? Well, you know that stuff you've got hidden away in a closet or storage area somewhere? Those are the materials with which you can express your imaginative and creative side in new and different ways. So get it out of the closet and let it be the medium for manifestation.

"Let your consciousness flow in the direction that instinct and wisdom take you, and nurture this soul medicine from your imagination into physical existence. Release all your self-imposed limitations, and go for it! Just know you can do it, and have fun in the process. And please: Take good care of the waters."

If Seal Is Your Power Animal . . .

- You're very adaptable and have faced a number of situations in your life where many would have given up, yet you continue to rebound with even greater strength and resolve.

- You're incredibly imaginative and creative, and you must have a few different ways in which to channel and direct these gifts or else your life force will greatly diminish.

- You can live just about anywhere, from temperate to cold climates, as long as you're near a body of water.

- You're outgoing and sociable, love to play with friends and family, and are able to brighten up any social situation.

Ask for Seal's Help When . . .

- Your creative imagination and expression is blocked or stagnant, and you need a strong dose of inspiration and motivation.

- You're going through a major life change, such as a separation or divorce, and you feel the need for extra strength and protection.

- You're experiencing such a creative surge that it's keeping you off balance and ungrounded and you need to get a bit more down-to-earth so you can take care of the more mundane realities and responsibilities.

- You feel emotionally void or stuck in some self-defeating emotional turmoil, and you need to take a break and get out and have some fun.

How to Access Seal's Power

- Become involved by donating your time or money to an organization dedicated to stopping pollution and cleaning up the oceans, lakes, and rivers.

- For the next month, keep a notebook with you at all times, writing in it whenever you're moved to do so. Be sure to include any dreams that you recall.

- Watch the movie *The Secret of Roan Inish,* directed by John Sayles, and jot down any thoughts and feelings that are stimulated by the story.

- The next time you get an opportunity to do so, spend several minutes sitting by the ocean, meditating on what's happening around you and inside you.

Snake

Quality: Resurrection

Snake's Message for You

"I REPRESENT AND AM KIN to the ultimate substance of life, the very DNA that animates all of this. It's the twin serpents intertwined, expressing the basic duality of existence, that which resoundingly connects you to every other living being on this planet. I've been given a bad name in some circles, yet I'm highly revered and honored in so many others. *You have nothing to fear from me!* I can teach, I can heal, and I can show you the way to new life when the old one is finished and complete. I can help you clear and awaken all your chakras, bringing in new life force and vitality from the ground up. Close your eyes and track this healing energy as it rises up from the base of your spinal column along your entire backbone to the crown of your head. From there you can feel this energy as it cascades down the inside front of your body, bathing your internal organs in healing power.

"I'm the eternal and the now, the masculine and the feminine, the healer and the healed, the mother and the father, and the symbol and the spirit of all healing. Never underestimate or fear my power!"

If Snake Is Your Power Animal . . .

- You feel at home with esoteric and metaphysical subjects, and are fascinated by ancient and indigenous cultures and spiritual practices.

- You're a healer, whether the focus of your gifts is on the physical, emotional, mental, or spiritual dimension. This is true whether you apply your healing talents to plants, animals, or human beings.

- Your healing capacities have come about as a result of a series of initiations, whether metaphorical or actual near-death experiences. Each one has brought you greater understanding, wisdom, and healing power.

- You are extremely "sense-itive." Not only do you perceive others' auras or energies through the physical sensations in your body, but you also smell danger and register it in your gut. Pay attention to these sensations and smells and trust them, no matter how strange they may seem.

Ask for Snake's Help When . . .

- You're going through a major life or developmental transition, one that requires you to shed an old identity so that a new one can be formed.

- You need help releasing the destructive aspects of some current circumstance, situation, or relationship in order to make a clear choice about what to do once you've released them.

- You have any kind of physical, mental, emotional, or spiritual toxicity that could manifest as a physical illness, and you need to transmute these poisons to become healthy.

- You're moving into creative but unknown territory that involves a passage through darkness, one where you can't quite see where you're going and feel afraid of what's ahead.

- You want to increase your energy and vitality, particularly your sexual vitality.

How to Access Snake's Power

- Sit on a chair without armrests and close your eyes. Slowly and gently sway side to side in a wave-like pattern, being particularly aware of how your spine moves.

- While sitting comfortably erect, bring your awareness to the base of your spine and gradually move your attention and awareness upward until you reach the area where your spine connects with your head. Continue tracking this energy up to the top of your head, then allow it to cascade down the front of and inside your body so that it bathes your insides with healing power.

- Journal about two or three of your death and resurrection experiences ones, in which you were severely wounded physically or emotionally and not only survived, but came away with some powerful teachings and made very dramatic changes in your life.

- Many cultures have images of a snake eating its own tail (which the Greeks called *Ouroboros*) symbolizing completion, perfection, totality, and eternity. Meditate on this symbol:

Journal about your ideas and associations with it.

Squirrel

Quality: Preparedness

Squirrel's Message for You

"I NEVER WORRY. Not at all. I'm ready for any eventuality, and I don't just mean that I have all my nuts stored up for the winter. I have immense trust that as long as I do what I have to do, everything's taken care of. Can you say the same? You see me scurrying about, but I make no wasted movements nor needlessly expend my energy. Neither should you. All that 'busy-ness,' just so you can think that what you're doing is so important. You need to gather when it's time to gather, play when it's time to play, and relax when it's time to relax. You'll be amazed at how much more you can accomplish when your movements are motivated by clear intention.

Yes, action is the key, but action that has clear and conscious purpose, rather than random and chaotic hustle and bustle.

"Take the path through the forest, allowing your direction to be determined by your inner knowingness. And keep tracking your instincts so you can determine what course of action—or inaction—to take. The shifting sensations in your gut tell you when and what to gather, and when and what to release. Not just material possessions, but also judgments, fears, doubts, and anxieties. As long as you stay tuned in to your body and trust your physical sensations more than your egoistic mind, no harm will come to you. So take what you need—no more, no less—and give back what you will with gratitude. Trust that life is abundant, but don't just repeat mantras and affirmations—be willing to take the action that's required. Prepare by saving up whatever you need that will feed your body, fill your heart, and nurture your soul!"

If Squirrel Is Your Power Animal . . .

- You're excellent at organizing, strategizing, and implementing any plans you've made for yourself or others. You naturally gravitate toward the kind of work that incorporates these gifts.

- You're much better at learning by doing instead of observing, studying, or reading about things that interest you.

- You can be quite sociable, and you enjoy playing and doing physical activities with family and friends. However, you're wary and cautious with those you don't know, especially complete strangers.

- You're a good "boy scout," resourceful and prepared for just about anything that comes up. You usually have the supplies you need readily accessible.

Ask for Squirrel's Help When . . .

- Your life is so busy and full that you feel as if you're scurrying around without focus, and you want to feel more purposeful and directed.

- You've accumulated too much stuff and are ready and willing to give away and recycle those items that have served their purpose and are no longer needed.

- You find yourself worrying about the future a great deal, to the point that you're blocked or even frozen into inaction.

- You're going through a cycle in which you feel unsafe, and you want a spiritual guardian to help warn you of any potential danger or harmful situations you might inadvertently wander into.

How to Access Squirrel's Power

- For a few minutes, mimic the motion of Squirrel with short, staccato movements. As you do, keep your eyes wide open and closely observe your environment.

- Make a list of all the things you need that you don't presently possess, and devise a plan and strategy to go about obtaining them.

- Before you acquire those things you need or want, lighten your load by cleaning out your closets. Take all your old books, jewelry, and other material items, and give them to a thrift store or someone who's able to use them.

- Pay particular attention to the seasons, and coordinate your level of activity accordingly. For instance, "gather" during autumn, slow down and rest during winter, get outside during spring, and play during summer.

Swan

Quality: Grace

Swan's Message for You

"AH, SUCH SWEETNESS AND BEAUTY you possess—
whether you realize it or not. Look until you see, really *see*, the
beauty that's reflected in the mirror or in the still, calm waters of the
lake. Witness not only your inner and outer beauty, but also that which
surrounds you, from the tiniest flower to the grand panorama of the
stars at night. It's always there. All you need to do is slow down,
breathe, and open your eyes, ears, and heart. You're no ugly duckling.
Neither is your world, even with all its dark and shadowy elements.
It's always for you to choose to notice the magical dance of shadow
and light in all its mystery and allure, without fear or judgment.

"Let me help you walk through this world with grace and innocence, to move through life slowly dancing to your own private song, whether you're walking alone or in the company of others. Let me help you shift smoothly and effortlessly through the varied states of consciousness and emotional textures you experience, like moving from air to water, all the while letting intuition be the guiding force for your choices. Surrender and trust. It's really very simple."

If Swan Is Your Power Animal . . .

- You're quite adept at gliding through the waters of change easily and effortlessly, and you move smoothly through the daily rhythms of life.

- You're able to shift through various states of consciousness with ease, and you have great trust in your intuitive capacities, one of which is the ability to foresee the future.

- No matter what your physical appearance is like, you shine with inner beauty and walk in this world with humility and poise.

- You're very powerful physically and spiritually, yet your beauty and grace can deceive others into thinking that you're meek and passive.

- You possess an admirable ability to easily converse with anyone you encounter, and you have a distinctive style and dignity that's charming and irresistible to nearly everyone.

Ask for Swan's Help When . . .

- You need a strong dose of poise and confidence to help you handle a variety of social and business situations.

- You're feeling rather ugly, emotionally or physically, or you're just feeling the ugliness of life or some particular aspect of your life. You also realize you haven't been taking good care of yourself and need to give yourself some extra-special care.

- You feel as if you're stuck in rather mundane circumstances, having lost touch with the mystical and spiritual, and you'd like to retrieve your connection to these realms.

- You're ready for your soul mate, but you know that you must first find and meet your *inner* mate—that part of you that's complementary to your gender and your character—before manifesting your mate in third-dimensional reality.

How to Access Swan's Power

- Make a list of all the critical statements you habitually make about yourself, and when you're done, release these self-judgments by ceremonially burning or burying the list.

- Put on some soft, flowing music, and move to it slowly and gently, feeling the gracefulness and suppleness of such movements.

- Take a cleansing bath, with candles, music, and scented oil. While you're relaxing in the water, repeat: "I am beautiful, and I love myself just as I am."

- While outdoors, close your eyes, stand in a relaxed pose, and stretch your wings (arms) to their fullest, making slow, gentle horizontal movements with your arms while feeling the expansiveness in your heart area.

Turtle

Quality: Mother Earth

Turtle's Message for You

"SLOW DOWN! You've got all the time in the world! Going slower sometimes gets you there sooner. Remember the story about my land brother, Tortoise? That's a good one to keep in mind when you feel caught up in the 'hurry-up sickness' that so many humans are subject to. Listen closely, especially to the natural rhythms of your body. Pay closer attention to your need for rest, nourishment, exercise, and touch. By doing so, you not only honor yourself and your body, but also our Earth Mother. Since your body is birthed from Her, and to Her it will return, consider it to be a holy sacrament to honor Her in this way. In turn, our Earth Mother will return love, compassion, and abundance to you. She's a generous and abundant

resource who provides everything we need. Have faith and know that she'll always provide for you.

"It may be time for you to retreat into solitude and a period of silence. If that makes sense to you, do so consciously and with resolve. Put away your watch and just say no to any demands from the outer world. Just as I can move easily from water to land, so can I help you manifest your dreams and desires to bring them into material reality. First you must swim in the deep subconscious of your imagination, cruising unhurriedly and without destination. Then bring yourself to the shores of physical creation, to give birth to those inspirations that came to you because you slowed down enough to receive them! Just remember that all these material blessings were fathered by Spirit and given physical life by our Earth Mother."

If Turtle Is Your Power Animal . . .

- You're an ancient soul, and anyone who looks into your eyes can see that immediately. You have a great depth of understanding and compassion that you readily express, especially with those to whom you're closest.

- You must be true to your own pace. Even though it may be a little slower than others', you move with grace and fluidity, and you get the job done. Trying to keep up with others only generates greater frustration and anxiety for yourself.

- You're quite willing to listen to others' troubles and sorrows, and you have the uncanny ability to do so without taking on their burdens or being drained by their neediness.

- Your faith in life's generosity and abundance is an inspiration to others. You never lack for anything that you truly need, and you know it.

Ask for Turtle's Help When . . .

- You're feeling overwhelmed with your own challenges, or when your life is frenetic and fast-paced and you want to get your troubles off your back.

- You have an important creative project to complete, and worry about having the time to do so.

- You need to get away from the world for a while, to be in the silence and solitude of nature.

- You're feeling anxious and fearful about money, worrying that you won't have enough. You need reassurance about the abundance of life, to *know* that you're always cared for and will have everything you truly need.

How to Access Turtle's Power

- Take a day or two just for yourself, doing only what *you* want, without a schedule. Perhaps engage in an activity you've always wanted to try. Spend some of this time writing in your journal, particularly if you're receiving any messages.

- Every day for the next week, spend a few minutes moving at a slower pace than usual. Don't just walk slower, but also slow down even the simplest of hand movements, like picking up your pen and so forth. Make sure you're breathing slowly and steadily when you do so.

- When there's an opportunity to go swimming, periodically swim underwater with slow and easy movements, and note how this feels.

- Place a shell of energy around you by imagining a ball of translucent green light surrounding you. Do this especially when you perceive any threats, whether physical or psychological.

Whale

Quality: Inner Depths

Whale's Message for You

"ALTHOUGH I BREATHE AIR, I live in the ocean, as my ancestors have done for a long, long time. We've lived through many cycles of the earth's evolution and have witnessed many human civilizations that have come and gone. Your most ancient self came from the ocean, and in the deepest memory you have, you know that to be fact. Like you, I depend on both the water and the air to survive, although my home is in the depths of the sea. It's your challenge and your salvation to immerse yourself in this fluidity, into the flow and natural movements of life. It's also necessary to come up for air when you've been meditating or immersed in any altered state of consciousness or creative endeavor. When you do, take a good look at the world around you, breathing in the air that is so plentifully available. Not only can you appreciate the depth and beauty of your internal psychic realm, but your physical surroundings as well. As you do so, listen to the sounds of the natural world, both inside and out, calling to your ancient soul. Know that each new moment is a rebirth into the wonders of being alive. Enjoy it!"

If Whale Is Your Power Animal . . .

- You're quite contained and self-reflective, letting just a few close friends know who you really are. Typically you disclose more of yourself in occasional and brief bursts of self-revelation that often surprise others.

- You're very psychic, with your strongest intuitive gifts being telepathy and clairaudience. Accept these gifts, develop them, and use them to benefit others.

- You work with sound in some way—through music, singing, chanting, or drumming—and you use it for healing yourself and others.

- You've always had an intense interest in the more primal origins of the human species and our ancient connection to all life. As you mature, you gain wisdom of universal truths and can more readily feel the heartbeat of the universe.

Ask for Whale's Help When . . .

- You've engaged in a lot of creative expression, but up until now it's been mostly a private pursuit. Now you want to break into the material world through some form of artistic or creative expression that allows you to express your passion fully.

- You've been stuck in a deep pool of emotions and you're ready to pull yourself out, yet it feels overwhelming to do so.

- You want to get over your shyness about expressing yourself vocally and musically. It's important to do so from the depths of your soul rather than just your personality or ego.

- You want greater abundance in your life and wish to establish some consistency with the flow of money and supplies.

How to Access Whale's Power

- Play a drum, rattle, native flute, or didgeridoo, or simply listen to the sounds of nature for a few minutes, whether by yourself, with a friend, or in a group. You may find some interesting sounds, chants, or songs emerging from this experience.

- Spend some time next to a large body of water, such as a lake or ocean, away from your usual routines. Notice how being near the water affects you.

- Try *Whale breathing:* Lie on your back, let all the air out of your lungs, take a deep breath, and exhale with a "Ha!" sound. Repeat this a few times at a leisurely pace.

- Express yourself by toning, chanting, or singing. As you're experimenting and playing with various sounds, find one that feels comfortable for you. Let this be your sound or call. You may even find that a simple song comes forth.

Wolf

Quality: Guardian

Wolf's Message for You

"ONE LOOK IN MY EYES and you can see the truth of who I am. Like some of my brother and sister four-leggeds, we've gotten a bad rap. We mean no harm to anyone. We have soul arrangements with all who give their lives so that we can continue ours. I love my family. With no false modesty, I am a supreme guardian and teacher. I take this role seriously—not as a burden, but as a welcome assignment and commitment. And the best teachings come through example and story, rather than through lecture and fundamentalist rules. It's also one of your natural responsibilities to teach others, not about matters of the mind, but about matters of the heart and soul. Teach what it takes to live with others in harmony—not through instruction, but by your actions and through personal and mythic stories. Find that balance between true freedom and the interdependency that's an inherent characteristic of living with other beings. You have no need to prove who you are to anyone, nor do you ever have to fight to prove that you're right. Have confidence in who you are and your place in the community. Don't be afraid to take the lead or to stand out, and never be reluctant to surrender that lead when necessary in the spirit of cooperation and harmony."

If Wolf Is Your Power Animal . . .

- You have a strong sense of family and community and an intuitive sense of social order, and you're very willing to give and receive affection when it comes to your friends and family.

- You tend to be uncomfortable around people who talk only from their intellect, yet you thrive and relax with people who speak from their heart or gut. Your senses are very keen and you have a well-developed "b.s. detector."

- You're very expressive, both verbally and nonverbally, and can tell a story with a great deal of passion, sincerity, and animation.

- You avoid confrontations, but if cornered, you'll fight. Usually there's no need for any of this, since your presence naturally and easily commands respect from others.

Ask for Wolf's Help When . . .

- You feel lost—whether it be in a relationship, a project, or your career choice—or you've strayed from your life path.

- You're having trouble discerning the truth of what others are saying. Not the factual truth, but whether they're speaking sincerely from their heart and soul.

- You're feeling the need for extra protection, whether it be for your physical safety or protection from psychic attacks.

- You want to improve your communication by adding more body language and voice inflection, either in preparation for a presentation to a group or for everyday communication.

- You notice that you're socially polarized, either by isolating yourself or being overly enmeshed with others, and you need to make changes in the appropriate direction to regain balance.

How to Access Wolf's Power

- Tell a story drawn from your personal experiences, and do so by exaggerating your body language (gestures, facial expressions, postures, and vocal inflections). You can do this with one other person or in a small group.

- Show your family and friends you love them by letting them know both through words and simple, loving actions.

- For one entire day, see if you can discern what the teaching or lesson is for every significant experience you have.

- When you feel that your life has become stagnant, seek out a new adventure or go on a journey with or without a particular destination.

Afterword

<u>A Prayer for the Wild Things</u>

*Oh, Great Spirit, we come to you with love and gratitude for all
living things. We now pray especially for our relatives of the wilderness—the four-legged, the winged, those that live in the water,
and those that crawl upon the land. Bless them that they might
continue to live in freedom and enjoy their right to be wild.
Fill our hearts with tolerance, appreciation, and respect for all living
things so that we all might live together in harmony and peace.*

WE CANNOT LIVE WITHOUT our friends the animals.
They give us so much, and without them our species would not
have survived as long as it has. Through their very existence, they
touch the wild, instinctual nature in each one of us; and our

domesticated animals provide companionship and love that's unparalleled.

I produced this book and CD so that you may remember our complex and interwoven relationship with all of God's creatures. By connecting with your spirit animal guides, you'll open a treasure chest that can never be closed again. Through your willingness to work with these spiritual beings, you'll discover a deeper and more intimate connection with the animals that exist here on this earth. You'll also enjoy a greater appreciation of and respect for your own instinctual nature, and learn to increasingly trust it to help guide you through the joys and challenges of living in the world as it is today.

No matter whether you have relationships with other spirit guides, your power animals will be valuable assets to you in so many ways. May you be blessed with many adventures with your power animals, and know that you're always safe and protected—both in this world and in the world of Spirit.

Mitakuye Oyasin ("All my relations"),
Steven Farmer, Laguna Beach, California

APPENDIX

Power Animal Key Characteristics

Animal Spirit	Characteristic
BEAR	Introspection
BEAVER	Productiveness
BUFFALO	Provisions
BUTTERFLY	Transformation
COUGAR (MOUNTAIN LION/PUMA)	Leadership
COYOTE	Paradox
DEER	Gentleness
DOLPHIN	Communication
DOVE	Serenity
DRAGONFLY	Light
EAGLE	Spirit
ELEPHANT	Resolve
FOX	Shape-Shifting
FROG	Purification
GIRAFFE	Foresight
HAWK	Perspective
HORSE	Freedom
HUMMINGBIRD	Joy
KANGAROO	Abundance
LION	Nobility
LIZARD	Dreamtime
LYNX (BOBCAT)	Secrets and confidentiality

Animal Spirit	Characteristic
OPOSSUM	Strategy
OTTER	Inner Feminine
OWL	Wisdom
PANTHER (LEOPARD/JAGUAR)	Passion
RABBIT	Fertility
RACCOON	Resourcefulness
RAVEN (CROW)	Magic
SEAL (SEA LION)	Imagination
SNAKE	Resurrection
SQUIRREL	Preparedness
SWAN	Grace
TURTLE	Mother Earth
WHALE	Inner Depths
WOLF	Guardian

How to Use the CD

THERE ARE FIVE TRACKS on the enclosed CD. The first three feature drumming with a particular rhythm, the fourth has a similar rhythm using a rattle, and the fifth offers a unique type of rhythm and sound using the didgeridoo and click sticks.

The rhythms used on all five tracks will put you in an altered state of consciousness, or trance, which will facilitate your shamanic journey. The drumming and rattling is at the rate of 4 to 7 beats per second, a type of rhythm used by shamans cross-culturally to induce a state of consciousness necessary for their work. Scientific research has demonstrated that the brain's electrical activity actually slows from its normal waking state of 14 to 20 cycles per second (the *beta rhythm*) to the much slower rate of 4 to 7 cycles per second *(theta rhythm)* after listening to this type of rhythm for a few minutes. In other words, a steady, monotonous rhythm of 4 to 7 beats per second can induce a moderately deep trance state, similar to the deeper states achieved during meditation and that are used by shamans to do their work.

Here's an outline of the tracks and how to use them:

Track 1: Journey to Retrieve Your Power Animal. This should be the first guided meditation journey you do. I'll lead you through the process that's described step-by-step in Chapter 8, so be sure to carefully review that chapter before you proceed. I've invoked guardian spirits during the creation of this track, so you'll be well protected during the journey. After you've retrieved your power animal, take her with you on any subsequent journeys. If you should encounter anything frightening, use the power you've funded through your power animal companion to pass by or neutralize the intimidating force. Note your starting point into the lower world so that you'll know how to return, and also so you'll remember how to get there during your next journey.

Track 2: Guided Meditation Journey for Divination. If you've been able to successfully retrieve your power animal, this should be your second journey (if not, repeat Track 1 until you succeed in finding and bringing her back). I'll also guide you throughout this journey, where you'll go to the lower world accompanied by your power animal. There you'll consult with her on a question you have or regarding some guidance you're seeking. When you do seek counsel from your power animal, she may directly answer your question or may take you to another animal spirit guide who will then proceed to show you the answer. No matter who ultimately gives you the response, you'll receive it through any of the following four pathways: a vision, an auditory communication, a feeling, or a thought—or any combination thereof.

Track 3: Self-Directed Shamanic Journey with Drum.
This track provides shamanic drumming with no voice-over. Once you've discovered your power animal and gained some experience with her, you can embark on your own journey. Take your power animal with you, and be clear on your intention prior to traveling to the lower world. The purpose can be for divination, to further explore the lower world, to seek a ceremony for healing, or simply to "hang out" and play with your power animal and other spirit beings in the lower world. Also, it's important to take your power animal with you whenever you explore non-ordinary reality, as she'll serve to empower and protect you and can help you confront anything that's frightening or intimidating.

Track 4: Self-Directed Shamanic Journey with Rattle.
Similar to Track 3, only this is rattling with a rhythm of 4 to 7 shakes per second. It tends to be softer, and at times you may prefer it to the drumming track. It's a good one to experiment with.

Track 5: Self-Directed Shamanic Journey with Didgeri-doo (with Ash Dargan). This track, with the Australian Aboriginal didgeridoo and click sticks, will provide a foundation for a different sort of journey. You can choose to go to the lower world, or if you wish, you can simply let the sound and the rhythm of the didgeridoo take you to the realms of non-ordinary reality in its own way. Again, first make sure your power animal is with you, and be prepared to experience the ancient and unusual.

Recommended Readings and Organizations

Readings

Animal Dreaming, Scott Alexander King. Victoria, Australia: Project Art and Photo, 2003.

Animal Magick: The Art of Recognizing & Working with Familiars, D.J. Conway. Llewellyn Publications: St. Paul, Minnesota, 2002.

Animal-Speak: The Spiritual & Magical Powers of Creatures Great & Small, Ted Andrews. Llewellyn Publications: St. Paul, Minnesota, 2001.

Animal Wisdom: The Definitive Guide to the Myth, Folklore and Medicine Power of Animals, Jessica Dawn Palmer. Element: Great Britain, 2002.

Kinship with All Life, J. Allen Boone. HarperSanFrancisco, 1954.

Medicine Cards, Jamie Sams and David Carson. New York: St. Martin's Press, 1988.

Totems: The Transformative Power of Your Personal Animal Totem, Brad Steiger. HarperSanFrancisco: 1997.

The Vision, Tom Brown, Jr. New York: The Berkley Publishing Group, 1988.

The Way of the Shaman, Michael Harner. HarperSanFrancisco, 1990.

Organizations

The following are some organizations that directly or indirectly support the animal kingdom:

Defenders of Wildlife: 1130 17th St., NW, Washington, DC 20030 • (202) 682-9400 • **www.defenders.org**

The Fund for Animals: 200 West 57th St., New York, NY 10019 • (212) 246-2096 • **www.fund.org**

National Wildlife Federation: 11100 Wildlife Center Dr.,
Reston, VA 20190-5362 • (800) 822-9919
www.nwf.org

Natural Resources Defense Council (NRDC): 40 West 20th St.,
New York, NY 10011 • (212) 727-2700
www.nrdc.org

The Nature Conservancy: 4245 North Fairfax Dr., Ste. 100,
Arlington, VA 22203-1606 • (703) 841-5300
www.nature.org

Oceana: 2501 M St., NW, Ste. 300, Washington, DC
20037-1311 • (202) 833-3900 • **www.oceana.org**

People for the Ethical Treatment of Animals (PETA):
501 Front St., Norfolk, VA 23510 • (757) 622-7382
www.peta.org

Sierra Club: 85 Second St., 2nd Floor, San Francisco, CA
94105 • (415) 977-5500 • **www.sierraclub.org**

Surfrider Foundation USA: P.O. Box 6010, San Clemente, CA
92674-6010 • (949) 492-8170 • **www.surfrider.org**

World Wildlife Fund: 1250 24th St. NW, Washington, DC
20037 • (800) 225-5993 • **www.wwf.org**

Acknowledgments

FIRST AND FOREMOST, thanks to my muse, companion, wife, lover, friend, and first-look editor, Doreen Virtue. *Mi destino eres tú; eras y siempre serás tú.*

To all who supported, inspired, and prayed for this project, thanks to:

Kevin Buck, Lynnette Brown, Chris Prelitz, Becky Prelitz, Alan Garner, Carol Michaels, Gary Miller, Martha Granados, Shannon Kennedy, Liz Dawn, Ariel Wolfe, Holmes Bryant, and Dan Clark. My friends and my clan!

Michelle Pilley, Megan Slyfield, and Jo Lal for pointing me in the right direction for this project.

Leon, Kristen, Rachelle, and the rest of the gang from Hay House Australia; and all the great people of Oz, in particular Sethlans and cousin Leela.

Ted Andrews, Jamie Sams, Brad Steiger, D. J. Conway, Michael Harner, and Jade Wah'oo-Grigori for their clear and down-to-earth teachings and writings that were so stimulating and helpful.

Eric "Animal Chin" Nesmith for his very cool animal portraits.

Ash Dargan for his awesome didgeridoo playing on the CD.

Scott Alexander King for his breakthrough book on Australian animals.

Christina Redfern, for taking care of Pismo while we traveled.

The people at Hay House: Louise Hay for her inspirational leadership, Reid Tracy for his encouragement and faith in this project, Jill Kramer and Shannon Littrell for their their peerless editing, Christy Salinas and Amy Rose Szalkiewicz for their beautiful design and artwork, Richelle Zizian for her enthusiasm, and Rocky George for impeccable engineering of the CD.

Last but not least, for all the spirit guides—especially the animal spirit guides—who urged me on, guided me, reminded me of the purpose of this project, and blessed me with their inspiration and communications: This one's for you.

About the Author

STEVEN D. FARMER, PH.D., is a spiritual psychotherapist, shamanic practitioner, ordained minister, and author of *Sacred Ceremony: How to Create Ceremonies for Healing, Transitions, and Celebrations* as well as several other books. Dr. Farmer offers workshops and lectures on a variety of spiritual and shamanic topics. He makes his home in Laguna Beach, California, with his wife, Doreen. They have four grown children (two sons and two daughters). For further information, see **www.poweranimals.com**.

If you have an experience with a power animal that you would like to share, please submit your story to: **poweranimalstory @poweranimals.com**

NOTES

NOTES

NOTES

NOTES

Hay House Titles of Related Interest

<u>Books</u>

American Indian Cultural Heroes and Teaching Tales,
by Kurt Kaltreider, Ph.D.
The Dolphin, by Sergio Bambaren
Healing with the Fairies, by Doreen Virtue, Ph.D.
It's Not about the Horse, by Wyatt Webb
The Journey to the Sacred Garden (book-with-CD),
by Hank Wesselman, Ph.D.
Silent Power (book-with-CD), by Stuart Wilde (available March 2005)
Sixth Sense, by Stuart Wilde
Spirit Medicine (book-with-CD),
by Hank Wesselman, Ph.D., and Jill Kuykendall, RPT
Visionseeker, by Hank Wesselman, Ph.D.

<u>Card Decks and Kits</u>

Connecting with Your Angels Kit, by Doreen Virtue, Ph.D.
The Four Agreements Cards, by DON Miguel Ruiz
Sacred Contracts (an interactive experience for guidance),
by Caroline Myss and Peter Occhiogrosso
Magical Mermaids and Dolphins Oracle Cards, by Doreen Virtue, Ph.D.

All of the above are available at your local bookstore,
or may be ordered by visiting:
Hay House USA: **www.hayhouse.com**
Hay House Australia: **www.hayhouse.com.au**
Hay House UK: **www.hayhouse.co.uk**
Hay House South Africa: **orders@psdprom.co.za**

We hope you enjoyed this Hay House book. If you would like to receive a free catalog featuring additional Hay House books and products, or if you would like information about the Hay Foundation, please contact:

Hay House, Inc., P.O. Box 5100
Carlsbad, CA 92018-5100
(760) 431-7695 or **(800) 654-5126**
(760) 431-6948 (fax) or **(800) 650-5115 (fax)**
www.hayhouse.com

Published and distributed in Australia by: Hay House Australia Pty. Ltd.
18/36 Ralph St. • Alexandria NSW 2015 • *Phone:* 612-9669-4299
Fax: 612-9669-4144 • www.hayhouse.com.au

Published and distributed in the United Kingdom by: Hay House UK, Ltd.
Unit 62, Canalot Studios • 222 Kensal Rd., London W10 5BN
Phone: 44-20-8962-1230 • *Fax:* 44-20-8962-1239
www.hayhouse.co.uk

Published and distributed in the Republic of South Africa by:
Hay House SA (Pty), Ltd., P.O. Box 990, Witkoppen 2068
Phone/Fax: 27-11-706-6612 • orders@psdprom.co.za

Distributed in Canada by: Raincoast • 9050 Shaughnessy St., Vancouver, B.C. V6P
6E5 • *Phone:* (604) 323-7100 • *Fax:* (604) 323-2600

Tune in to **www.hayhouseradio.com**™ for the best in inspirational talk radio featuring top Hay House authors! And, sign up via the Hay House USA Website to receive the Hay House online newsletter and stay informed about what's going on with your favorite authors. You'll receive bimonthly announcements about: Discounts and Offers, Special Events, Product Highlights, Free Excerpts, Giveaways, and more!
www.hayhouse.com

A
THEOLOGICAL
MISCELLANY

A
THEOLOGICAL
MISCELLANY

T. J. M^cTAVISH

W PUBLISHING GROUP
A Division of Thomas Nelson Publishers
Since 1798

www.wpublishinggroup.com

Published by W Publishing Group, a Division of Thomas Nelson, Inc., P.O. Box 141000, Nashville, Tennessee 37214.

W Publishing Group books may be purchased in bulk for educational, business, fundraising, or sales promotional use. For information, please e-mail SpecialMarkets@ThomasNelson.com.

Produced with the assistance of The Livingstone Corporation (www.LivingstoneCorporation.com).

Unless otherwise indicated, Scripture quotations are from the Revised Standard Version of the Bible (RSV), copyright 1946, 1952, 1971 by the Division of Christian Education of the National Council of the Churches of Christ in the USA. Used by permission. Other Scripture references are from the following sources:
The Holy Bible, New International Version (NIV). Copyright ©1973, 1978, 1984, International Bible Society. Used by permission of Zondervan Bible Publishers.
The New Revised Standard Version Bible (NRSV), ©1989 by the Division of Christian Education of the National Council of the Churches of Christ in the USA.
The King James Version of the Bible (KJV).
The New King James Version (NKJV®) copyright © 1979, 1980, 1982, Thomas Nelson, Inc., Publishers.
The New American Standard Bible (NASB), © 1960, 1977, 1995 by the Lockman Foundation.
The *Holy Bible,* New Living Translation (NLT), copyright © 1996. Used by permission of Tyndale House Publishers, Inc., Wheaton, IL 60189. All rights reserved.

Library of Congress Cataloging-in-Publication Data

McTavish, T. J.
    A theological miscellany / by T.J. McTavish.
      p. cm.
    ISBN 0-8499-1839-1
    1. Christianity--Miscellanea. 2. Church history--Miscellanea. 3. Bible--Miscellanea. I. Title.
    BR96.M38 2005
    230--dc22

                                 2004027066

Printed in the United States of America

05 06 07 08 09   QW 9 8 7 6 5 4 3 2 1

PREFACE

What you're holding is more than just a book. It's a labor of love. It's blood, sweat, and tears. It's the sum total of the knowledge I've been endowed with by the One who's seen fit to . . . uh, endow me. It's gold among the dross of other books. It's a shining testament to . . .

Okay, maybe it *is* just a book. But it's an extraordinarily unique one. In fact, it may very well save you a great deal of embarrassment. How many times have you been at a swanky dinner party when the conversation has turned to the popes who have served the shortest terms, or the five points of Calvinism, or famous bald men in the Bible, only to slink down into your chair in horror, realizing that you had nothing intelligent to add to the conversation? You didn't even know there were *three* points of Calvinism, much less *five*.

Well, be embarrassed no longer! Dive deeply into these pages . . . or skim the surface if you're afraid to commit. You'll come away amazed at your new-found sense of assurance in future theological conversations, your grasp of deep philosophical and biblical truths, and your annoyance at having wasted precious hours here while you could have been watching *Gilligan's Island* reruns.

Best wishes,
T. J. McTavish
November 2004

Thou art beside thyself;

much learning doth make thee mad.

—*Acts 26:24* (KJV)

The term *Fathers of the Church* refers to the writings from the early Christian centuries by theologians, preachers, popes, and others. To be regarded as a Father, one must have orthodox doctrine; but this does not exclude all doctrinal error. An occasional material heresy can be found even in the greater lights among the Fathers.

❋ THE "FATHERS OF THE CHURCH" ❋

The term *Fathers of the Church* refers to the writings from the early Christian centuries by theologians, preachers, popes, and others. To be regarded as a Father, one must have orthodox doctrine; but this does not exclude all doctrinal error. An occasional material heresy can be found even in the greater lights among the Fathers.

Greek Fathers
Justin Martyr (100–165)
Athenagoras of Athens (late second century)
Irenaeus of Gaul (140–202)
Clement of Alexandria (150–215)
Hippolytus of Rome (170–236)
Origen of Alexandria (185–254)
Eusebius of Caesarea (263–340)
Cyril of Jerusalem (315–386)
Basil the Great (330–379)
Gregory of Nazianzus (329–389)
Gregory of Nyssa (330–395)
Theodore of Mopsuestia (350–428)
John Chrysostom (344–407)
Cyril of Alexandria (died 444)
John of Damascus (675–749)

Latin Fathers
Tertullian (160–220)
Cyprian of Carthage (died 258)
Lactantius (250–317)
Athanasius (297–373)
Hilary of Poitiers (315–367)
Ambrose of Milan (339–397)
Jerome (342–420)
Augustine of Hippo (354–430)
Prosper of Aquitaine (390–463)
Pope Gregory I "the Great" (540–604)

❋ THE PSALMS OF PENITENCE ❋

"Enter not into judgment with thy servant; for no man living is righteous before thee" (Ps. 143:2). This is the mood of seven of the Psalms, traditionally called the *Penitential Psalms*. In liturgical churches these psalms are often used on Ash Wednesday or during Lent. They are Psalms 6, 32, 38, 51, 102, 130, and 143.

❦ THE NATIONAL ASSOCIATION OF EVANGELICALS' ❦ STATEMENT OF FAITH

The National Association of Evangelicals exists "to extend the kingdom of God through a fellowship of member denominations, churches, organizations, and individuals, demonstrating the unity of the body of Christ by standing for biblical truth, speaking with a representative voice, and serving the evangelical community through united action, cooperative ministry, and strategic planning."

To that end, the organization embraces this statement of faith:

We believe the Bible to be the inspired, the only infallible, authoritative Word of God.

We believe that there is one God, eternally existent in three persons: Father, Son and Holy Spirit.

We believe in the deity of our Lord Jesus Christ, in His virgin birth, in His sinless life, in His miracles, in His vicarious and atoning death through His shed blood, in His bodily resurrection, in His ascension to the right hand of the Father, and in His personal return in power and glory.

We believe that for the salvation of lost and sinful people, regeneration by the Holy Spirit is absolutely essential.

We believe in the present ministry of the Holy Spirit by whose indwelling the Christian is enabled to live a godly life.

We believe in the resurrection of both the saved and the lost; they that are saved unto the resurrection of life and they that are lost unto the resurrection of damnation.

We believe in the spiritual unity of believers in our Lord Jesus Christ.

❦ THREE POPES ARE TWO TOO MANY ❦

Occasionally in the history of the Roman Catholic Church, rivals have claimed the title of bishop of Rome or Supreme Pontiff. Some twenty-five *antipopes*, as they are styled, have been officially counted, and even in the twentieth century tiny splinter groups formed around someone claiming the title of pope. From 1309–1377, the popes were exiled in Avignon, France. From 1378–1417, a period known as the Great Schism,* there were both a pope in Rome and an antipope in Avignon, and later a third pope in Pisa. John XXIII, of the Pisa line, convened the Council of Constance (1414–1418), hoping to be declared the sole pope, eliminating the other two, Gregory XII and Benedict XIII. The council, however, deposed him and Benedict, and Gregory resigned. In 1417, Oddo Colonna was elected pope as Martin V, ending the period of "two popes too many."

*The term *Great Schism* is also applied to the split between the Eastern and Western Churches in 1054.

❀ THE BIRTH OF JESUS AND THE MILLENNIUM ❀

According to Matthew, Jesus was born during the reign of Herod, who ruled Judea under the Romans. Herod died around April 1 in what we know as 4 BC. The Magi spoke with Herod before finding the child Jesus (Matt. 2:1–8). However, Herod was seriously ill during his last years, and he was in no condition to receive unfamiliar visitors; he stayed in Jericho part of the time and died there. The visit of the Magi, then, would have occurred earlier. Since their trip, from wherever they started, would have taken them some time before they reached the place where they found Jesus, a date of 4 BC for his birth is probably too late. Sometime in 6 BC might be more likely.

The third millennium would have started with the beginning of the 2001st year after the birth of Jesus. Starting with 6 BC, the 2001st year would have begun in 1995 (there is no year zero). When the year 2000 began, we would already have been in the third millennium for five years.

❀ THE CONSTRUCTION OF JEHOVAH ❀

As one philosopher quipped, "God made himself out of nothing." But we're talking about the *name* Jehovah, familiar for centuries as God's personal name. It never existed in biblical times, however. It came about this way.

The Hebrew alphabet includes only twenty-two letters standing for consonants. Vowels in Hebrew manuscripts are indicated by signs, called *points* by scholars, placed with the letters. Pious Jews didn't want to pronounce the holy name of God, written YHWH (Yahweh), so they substituted the word *Adonai* (Lord). Eventually, scribes started putting the vowel points for Adonai with the letters for YHWH so readers would remember not to pronounce the divine name. In the late Middle Ages, scholars who didn't understand this practice came up with the hybrid form Jehovah (J is pronounced like Y, as in German and other languages).

❀ CALENDARS: EAST MEETS WEST ❀

Why do your Greek Orthodox friends usually celebrate Easter a week or two after you do? The Eastern churches follow the *Julian* calendar, devised by Julius Caesar in 46 BC. Its calculations were inaccurate, and the dates began to creep up on the vernal equinox (when the sun crosses the equator northward) that determines the date of Easter. In 1582, Pope Gregory XIII dropped ten days from the current year to even things out and changed the leap-year rules to keep the errors from recurring. The Western church adopted this *Gregorian* calendar, but the Orthodox churches never accepted it, and its liturgical year runs thirteen days behind that of the West.

❊ THE SIGNERS OF THE DECLARATION OF ❊ INDEPENDENCE AND THEIR RELIGIOUS AFFILIATIONS

Name	State	Denomination
John Adams	Massachusetts	Congregational (Unitarian)
Samuel Adams	Massachusetts	Congregational
Josiah Bartlett	New Hampshire	Congregational
Carter Braxton	Virginia	Church of England
Charles Carroll of Carrollton	Maryland	Roman Catholic
Samuel Chase	Maryland	Church of England
Abraham Clark	New Jersey	Presbyterian
George Clymer	Pennsylvania	Quaker/Church of England
William Ellery	Rhode Island	Congregational
William Floyd	New York	Presbyterian
Benjamin Franklin	Pennsylvania	Deist* (buried Episcopal)**
Elbridge Gerry	Massachusetts	Church of England
Button Gwinnett	Georgia	Church of England
Lyman Hall	Georgia	Congregational
John Hancock	Massachusetts	Congregational
Benjamin Harrison	Virginia	Unknown
John Hart	New Jersey	Presbyterian
Joseph Hewes	North Carolina	Church of England
Thomas Heyward Jr.	South Carolina	Unknown
William Hooper	North Carolina	Church of England
Stephen Hopkins	Rhode Island	Unknown
Francis Hopkinson	New Jersey	Church of England
Samuel Huntington	Connecticut	Congregational
Thomas Jefferson	Virginia	Deist
Francis Lightfoot Lee	Virginia	Unknown
Richard Henry Lee	Virginia	Unknown
Francis Lewis	New York	Unknown
Philip Livingston	New York	Presbyterian
Thomas Lynch Jr.	South Carolina	Unknown
Thomas McKean	Delaware	Presbyterian
Arthur Middleton	South Carolina	Unknown
Lewis Morris	New York	Unknown
Robert Morris	Pennsylvania	Church of England
John Morton	Pennsylvania	Unknown
Thomas Nelson Jr.	Virginia	Unknown
William Paca	Maryland	Church of England
Robert Treat Paine	Massachusetts	Congregational
John Penn	North Carolina	Unknown

❊ THE SIGNERS OF THE DECLARATION OF ❊ INDEPENDENCE AND THEIR RELIGIOUS AFFILIATIONS—CONT.

Name	State	Denomination
George Read	Delaware	Church of England
Caesar Rodney	Delaware	Church of England
George Ross	Pennsylvania	Unknown
Benjamin Rush	Pennsylvania	Presbyterian
Edward Rutledge	South Carolina	Church of England
Roger Sherman	Connecticut	Congregational
James Smith	Pennsylvania	Presbyterian
Richard Stockton	New Jersey	Presbyterian
Thomas Stone	Maryland	Church of England
George Taylor	Pennsylvania	Presbyterian
Matthew Thornton	New Hampshire	Presbyterian
George Walton	Georgia	Church of England
William Whipple	New Hampshire	Congregational
William Williams	Connecticut	Congregational
James Wilson	Pennsylvania	Church of England/Deist
John Witherspoon	New Jersey	Presbyterian
Oliver Wolcott	Connecticut	Congregational
George Wythe	Virginia	Church of England

*Deism is a belief that God, having created the universe, does not interfere in its regular operation or in historical events, nor does he reveal truth except through the natural order. During the eighteenth century, some thinkers held this view while still maintaining a nominal membership in a Christian church.

**The Episcopal Church was organized after the Revolutionary War as the successor to the Church of England in the United States.

❊ THE FOUR EVANGELISTS (GOSPEL WRITERS) ❊

Matthew
(Winged Man)

Mark
(Winged Lion)

Luke
(Winged Ox)

John
(Eagle)

❦ MUSLIM BELIEFS ABOUT JESUS ❦

The Qur'an mentions Jesus (usually called *Isa* in Islam) several times, giving him honored titles. These are some of its teachings, implied or expressed, about him.

Jesus was a prophet, but only one of a succession of prophets culminating in Muhammad. Jesus cannot be the Son of God because Allah is One and can have no son.

Jesus is called the *Word* and the *Messiah*. Angels told Mary, "God gives thee good tidings of a Word from him whose name is Messiah, Jesus, son of Mary."

Jesus is God's messenger and his Spirit. "The Messiah Jesus Christ Son of Mary was only the messenger of God and his word that he committed unto Mary, and a Spirit from him."

Jesus was raised up to God. The Qur'an quotes him saying, "Peace be upon me, the day I was born, and the day I die, and the day I am raised up alive!"

But Jesus did not die on the cross; "only a likeness was shown" to his enemies. Muslims take this to mean that God made someone else appear to be Jesus and allowed him to be crucified, while Jesus was taken up to heaven without having died. A true prophet cannot fail.

Jesus denied the Trinity. He refused to claim, "Take me and my mother as gods, apart from God." Muhammad knew only a distorted form of Christianity and misunderstood the Trinity as God, Jesus, and Mary.

❦ TEN PLAGUES OF EGYPT ❦

1. Water of the Nile turned to blood (Exod. 7:20)
2. Frogs covering the land (Exod. 8:6)
3. Gnats covering the land and its creatures (Exod. 8:17)
4. Flies ruining the land (Exod. 8:24)
5. A plague destroying cattle and other animals (Exod. 9:6)
6. Boils or sores on people and animals (Exod. 9:10)
7. Hailstorm (Exod. 9:23)
8. Locusts destroying all plants (Exod. 10:13–15)
9. Darkness for three days (Exod. 10:22)
10. Death of the firstborn of people and cattle (Exod. 12:29)

❋ TWELVE APOSTLES OR SIXTEEN? ❋

Jesus had twelve disciples, but we know a larger number of people, including some women (Mark 15:40–41; Luke 23:55), were associated with him in his work. Because Jesus was calling Israel back to its true faith in God, there had to be *twelve* designated apostles as a symbol of the fullness of the twelve tribes. But the membership in this group may have been a bit fluid, since we have at least fifteen names plus Matthias, who was enrolled after the Resurrection:

1. Simon (Bar-Jonah, Matt. 16:17, also called Peter)
2. Andrew, brother of Simon
3. James, son of Zebedee
4. John, son of Zebedee
5. Philip
6. Bartholomew
7. Thomas (called the Twin, John 20:24)
8. Matthew
9. James, son of Alphaeus
10. Thaddaeus
11. Simon the Cananaean (or Zealot, Luke 6:15)
12. Judas Iscariot
13. Levi (Luke 5:27, usually equated with Matthew)
14. Nathanael of Cana
15. Judas, son of James (Luke 6:16; "not Iscariot," John 14:22)
16. Matthias (replacing Judas Iscariot, Acts 1:26)

❋ WHAT'S SO SPECIAL ABOUT THE TRIBE OF ❋ BENJAMIN'S LEFT-HANDED SLINGSHOTS?

Judges 20:15–16 states, "And the Benjaminites mustered out of their cities on that day twenty-six thousand men that drew the sword, besides the inhabitants of Gibeah, who mustered seven hundred picked men. Among all these were seven hundred picked men who were left-handed; every one could sling a stone at a hair, and not miss."

Why was it important to sling a shot with your left hand? This is one theory: To conquer a walled city, you had to break through its gate. As you faced the gate from outside, the ramp to it sloped up from the right along the wall. If you could creep up the ramp close to the wall, it was harder for the defenders to hit you with arrows or spears, but that kept your right arm too close to the wall to use a weapon. Now, if you were *left-handed*—you get the picture.

❧ WHY TWELVE TRIBES? ❧

The number twelve is significant in the Bible as a symbol for the fullness of Israel. The twenty-four (twelve plus twelve) elders of the Revelation to John probably represent the fullness of all believers, both of the old covenant and the new (symbolized in Jesus' twelve apostles). But why were there twelve Israelite tribes in the first place? Yes, Jacob their ancestor had twelve sons. But Simeon's land was included in that of Judah, so Joseph's tribe was split into territories for his sons Ephraim and Manasseh to make up twelve. The number was important.

Ancient Mediterranean peoples sometimes formed groups around a sanctuary (scholars call such a group an *amphictyony*). Israelites had a sanctuary, the tabernacle, which they moved about until they permanently located it in Jerusalem. Worship in the sanctuary required animals for sacrifice and other supplies, to be provided by the tribes belonging to the confederation. Since the year has *twelve* months (based on the lunar cycle), perhaps each tribe was responsible for the sanctuary for one month of the year. Psalm 81:3–4 might refer to this twelve-month system: "Blow the trumpet at the new moon, / at the full moon, on our feast day. / For it is a statute for Israel, / an ordinance of the God of Jacob."

❧ THE SERENITY PRAYER ❧

"God grant us the serenity to accept the things we cannot change, courage to change the things we can, and wisdom to know the difference."

This is the Serenity Prayer, popularized through the work of Alcoholics Anonymous. Where it came from is still a mystery. Alcoholics Anonymous picked it up from a 1942 obituary in a New York newspaper. Protestant theologian Reinhold Niebuhr (1892–1971) later revealed he had written it as the ending of a sermon. After his death a similar prayer was found in the writings of Theodor Wilhelm, a German university professor who published using the name of the eighteenth-century Pietist Friedrich Oetinger (1702–1782). A similar prayer came to light appearing to be derived from a fourteenth-century source called the General's Prayer.

❧ HEAVEN: FACT OR FICTION? ❧

A recent U.S. poll found

81 percent believed in heaven	8 percent didn't believe in heaven
10 percent weren't sure	1 percent had no opinion

❧ THE SEVEN . . . NO, THREE . . . ❧ OR IS IT TWO? . . . SACRAMENTS

Since the early Christian centuries, believers have thought of certain actions as *mysteries*, special signs of the gospel of Christ at work in the life of his church. The Greek word *musterion* was translated into the Latin *sacramentum*, with the implication of an action sacred in itself. A sacrament came to be defined as "an outward and visible sign of an inward and spiritual grace." Protestants began to think differently about these special acts, and in many churches they are limited to actions expressly instituted by Jesus.

Roman Catholic and Orthodox churches recognize the first seven acts on this list as sacraments (or mysteries). Many Anglicans recognize the third through seventh as "minor sacraments." Most Protestants recognize only the first two, and evangelical Protestants usually call them *ordinances* of Christ. Since Jesus also commended foot washing (John 13:14), some communities, such as the Brethren, regard this act as an ordinance.

1. Eucharist (Holy Communion, Lord's Supper)
2. Baptism
3. Confirmation (Chrismation)
4. Confession (Penance, Reconciliation)
5. Marriage
6. Holy Orders (Ordination)
7. Holy Unction (Anointing of the Sick)
8. Foot Washing (Humility)

❧ HOW DID THE MASS BECOME THE MASS? ❧

In the oldest Roman liturgies, once the Communion was over, a deacon announced, *"Ite missa est,"* or "Go, it's the dismissal." The response was, *"Deo gratias,"* "Thanks be to God." Because the words *Ite missa est* came at the end, they signified that the Holy Communion was complete. Hence the term *missa* came to stand for the entire rite of the Eucharist. In popular Latin it became *messa* and passed into Middle English in the form *mæsse,* or Mass.

❧ CHRISTIANS WHO WON'T VOTE ❧

Some Christian, or Christian-derived, groups in North America encourage their members not to vote. They view voting as taking responsibility for an ungodly society. These groups include the Amish, Hutterites, and Jehovah's Witnesses.

❧ THE WEST HAS ROME; THE EAST HAS ... ❧

Catholics around the world look to the Holy Father in Rome for direction. Orthodox Christians have five patriarchs with a similar symbolic role.

Patriarchate	Present Patriarch Installed	Comments
Constantinople	Bartholomew, 1991	Nominal head of all Orthodoxy but directly rules a tiny minority in a Muslim environment. Constantinople is now Istanbul.
Alexandria	Peter VI, 1997	Jurisdiction over Africa
Jerusalem	Irenaeus, 2002	Jurisdiction over Palestine
Antioch	Ignatius IV, 1979	Located in Damascus; jurisdiction over Syria and nearby regions
Moscow	Alexius II, 1991	—

The Orthodox churches are organized by nationality, with self-governing or *autocephalous* bodies nominally loyal to one of the five patriarchs and headed by a bishop called a *metropolitan*, *archbishop*, or other title. Originally Rome was one of the five patriarchates, but it developed into the Roman Catholic Church.

❧ THE TRADITIONAL WAY TO PRAY ❧ THROUGH THE DAY

The early Christians followed Jewish practice in setting specified hours through the day for prayer. Christian monks—who were lay, not clergy—developed this schedule, and Benedict (480–550) refined it. These hours of prayer are usually called the *Daily Office*, and each hour includes psalms, Scripture readings, regular prayers, and other material.

Matins	Middle of the night, or before retiring
Lauds	After Matins, or early morning
Prime (first)	Around 6:00 AM
Terce (third)	Around 9:00 AM
Sext (sixth)	Around noon
None (ninth)	Around 3:00 AM
Vespers	Before dark
Compline	Before retiring

❀ BRANCHES OF JUDAISM ❀

What does it mean to be Jewish? An ancient Jew, the apostle Paul, grappled with this issue in his letter to the Romans, and today's Jews still struggle with it. Judaism in North America is not monolithic; several definable movements exist within the Jewish community.

Branch	Description	Representative Institution
Orthodox	Holds to observance of the Torah (books of Moses), the kosher food laws, male headship, and other traditional practices	Rabbinical Council of America
Reformed	The "liberal" branch, seeks to adapt Judaism to the modern world; synagogues are called *temples*	Central Conference of American Rabbis
Conservative	Pursues a middle way between Orthodox and Reformed Judaism	United Synagogue of America
Hasidic	An extreme form of Jewish orthodoxy focusing on cabala, a medieval mystical and meditative tradition	Many small groups centered around a teacher called a *rebbe*
Reconstructionist	Views Judaism as a religious culture arising from a humanistic outlook, not given by God	Jewish Reconstructionist Federation
Messianic	Accepts Jesus as Messiah but practices a form of Judaism; other Jews do not consider them Jewish	Many missionary organizations such as Jews for Jesus, plus local congregations

❀ THE MOST TRAVELED PREACHER EVER ❀ ... AND THE RUNNER-UP

John Wesley, founder of the Methodist movement, rode 250,000 miles in England on horseback and preached 42,000 sermons. Francis Asbury, whom Wesley appointed to organize Methodism in the United States, outrode him. He covered 300,000 miles, but in sparsely settled America he preached only 16,000 sermons.

❊ GREAT PREACHERS OF CHRISTIAN HISTORY ❊

Great preachers have always motivated the Christian community, and some of them have been remembered throughout history.

Preacher	Dates	Locations	Denomination
Ambrose of Milan	330–397	North Italy	Ancient church
John Chrysostom	344–407	Antioch and Constantinople	Ancient church
Peter the Hermit	1050–1115	Northeastern France	Catholic
Bernard of Clairvaux	1090–1153	Eastern France	Catholic
Dominic de Guzman	1170–1221	Spain, France	Catholic
Girolamo Savonarola	1452–1498	Florence	Catholic
John Wesley	1703–1791	England	Anglican (Methodist)
George Whitefield	1714–1770	England, American colonies	Anglican (Calvinistic Methodist)
Lyman Beecher	1775–1863	Litchfield, CT, and Cincinnati	Congregational
Theodore Parker	1810–1860	Boston	Unitarian
Charles Haddon Spurgeon	1834–1892	London	Baptist
Phillips Brooks	1835–1893	Boston	Episcopal
Harry Emerson Fosdick	1878–1969	New York City	Baptist, non-denominational
Helmut Thielicke	1908–1986	Germany	Evangelical church
Fulton J. Sheen	1895–1979	New York City	Catholic
Norman Vincent Peale	1898–1993	New York City	Reformed
D. Martyn Lloyd-Jones	1899–1981	London	Congregational
Billy Graham	1918–	—	Baptist

❊ THE FISH SYMBOL ❊

The Greek word for "fish," *ichthys*, has five letters (*ch* and *th* are each one letter in Greek). The five letters are the first letters of the expression "Jesus Christ, Son of God, Savior" in Greek.

Fish—Jesus Christ

ΙΧΘΥC

❧ CHURCHES THAT LOOK ORTHODOX ❧
BUT ARE CATHOLIC

The church has an onion-shaped dome, the liturgy is in some old language other than Latin, the "ambience" is that of an Orthodox church—yet the church is actually Catholic, in communion with the pope. Churches like this are called *Eastern Rite Catholic* or *Uniate* churches. They use one of the several ancient Eastern liturgies that their Orthodox counterparts also use, especially the Byzantine Liturgy of St. John Chrysostom. Often their priests are married, which Roman priests aren't.

Rite	Rite Type	Main Countries of Origin	Typical Language
Armenian	Armenian	Armenia, Turkey	Classical Armenian
Chaldean	Chaldean	Iraq	Syriac, Arabic
Coptic	Alexandrian	Egypt	Coptic, Arabic
Ge'ez	Alexandrian	Ethiopia	Ge'ez
Greek	Byzantine	Greece, Turkey	Greek
Malankar	Antiochene	India	Syriac, Malayalam
Maronite	Antiochene	Lebanon	Syriac, Arabic
Melkite	Byzantine	Syria, Lebanon	Arabic
Russian	Byzantine	Russia	Old Slavonic
Ruthenian (Carpatho-Russian)	Byzantine	Slovakia, Hungary	Old Slavonic
Ukrainian	Byzantine	Ukraine	Old Slavonic, Ukrainian
Syrian	Antiochene	Lebanon, Iraq	Syriac, Arabic
Syro-Malabar	Chaldean	India	Syriac, Malayalam

❧ THE FIVE FUNDAMENTALS OF FUNDAMENTALISM ❧

Fundamentalism arose from a statement conservative Christians issued at the Niagara Bible Conference of 1895. These leaders were concerned about trends in the major denominations of North America that they felt were departures from biblical Christianity. The five "fundamentals of the faith" that gave fundamentalism its name are these:

1. The inerrancy of Scripture
2. The deity and the virgin birth of Jesus Christ
3. The substitutionary atonement (i.e., Christ died for our sins)
4. The bodily resurrection of Jesus
5. The personal return of Christ

❈ DIFFERENT VERSIONS OF THE LORD'S PRAYER ❈

Many churches in North America regularly use the Lord's Prayer in worship, though most evangelical and Pentecostal churches do not. Catholics call it the "Our Father," as do Anglicans and others on occasion. When attending a church other than your own, it's a good idea to be alert to its favorite version of the prayer Jesus taught his disciples:

> Our Father who art in heaven,
> Hallowed be thy name,
> Thy kingdom come,
> Thy will be done,
> On earth as it is in heaven.
> Give us this day our daily bread;
> And forgive us our debts,
> As we also have forgiven our debtors;
> And lead us not into temptation,
> But deliver us from evil. (Matthew 6:9–13)

Catholic, Lutheran, Anglican/Episcopal, United Methodist, and some other denominations say, "Forgive us our trespasses as we forgive those who trespass against us." Baptist, Presbyterian, Christian, and evangelical churches are more likely to say, "Forgive us our debts, as we forgive our debtors."

Catholic worshipers end the prayer with "but deliver us from evil." (It is part of the Eucharistic Prayer before Communion.) Protestants continue with the doxology, "For thine is the kingdom and the power and the glory . . ."

Anglicans, Episcopalians, and Lutherans say, ". . . forever and ever. Amen." Everyone else usually says, ". . . forever. Amen."

A few churches use a version in more contemporary wording, though most stick with the "thy, thine" form.

If the prayer is sung, some of the wording may change. It's easier to sing, "Forgive us our sins, as we forgive those who sin against us."

❈ THE CITIES OF THE DECAPOLIS ❈

The Decapolis was a federation of ten Greek-speaking cities in the region east of the Sea of Galilee and the Jordan River. Jesus preached in the Decapolis (Mark 5:20; 7:31). The cities were

Abila • Canatha • Dion • Gadara • Gerasa • Hippos
Pella • Philadelphia • Raphana • Scythopolis

❋ CHURCHES THAT ARE NOT CATHOLIC, ❋ ORTHODOX, OR PROTESTANT

"Gallia est omnis divisa in partes tres," wrote Julius Caesar—"All Gaul is divided in three parts." Usually we think of Christianity the same way: you are either Protestant, Catholic, or Orthodox. Not so. Here are several ancient and still existing churches that were never part of the "big three."

Church	Origin	Head and Where Located	Comments
Abyssinian	Ethiopia	Abuna (Patriarch), Addis Ababa	The independent Coptic church of Ethiopia; follows many Jewish practices
Armenian	Armenia	Catholicos, Etchmiadzin	Armenia was the first nation to officially adopt Christianity, in 301.
Coptic	Egypt	Pope, Cairo	The ancient Christian church of Egypt; headed by its own pope
Jacobite	Syria, Iraq, India	Patriarch of Antioch, Damascus	Also called *Oriental Orthodox*
Nestorian	Iraq, Iran, India	Catholicos Patriarch, Chicago	Now a remnant; was the dominant Christian church of central Asia before Muslim expansion; sometimes called *Assyrian Church* or *Church of the East*

❋ THE ORIGIN OF THE TERM *DEVIL'S ADVOCATE* ❋

In the Roman Catholic Church, when a person is proposed for sainthood, the first big step is to have him or her declared "blessed," or *beatified.* Before this can happen, church officials conduct an investigation to see if any significant reasons exist for why that person should not be *canonized* as a saint. The official whose job it is to raise all possible objections is called the "promoter of the faith," but he is popularly styled the "devil's advocate." Catholic canon law requires that someone recognized as a saint should have led a holy life and that miracles should be associated with him or her, either while living or after death. If the "devil's advocate" isn't convincing enough in his objections, then the way is cleared for eventual canonization.

❋ POPES WITH THE SHORTEST REIGNS ❋

Pope	Year	Held Office
Urban VII	1590	13 days
Boniface VI	896	16 days
Celestine IV	1241	17 days
Sissinnius	708	21 days
Theodore II	897	21 days
Marcellus II	1555	22 days
Damasus II	1048	24 days
Pius III	1503	27 days
Leo XI	1605	27 days
Benedict V	964	33 days
John Paul I*	1978	34 days

*Karol Józef Wojtyla (John Paul II) took the name of his briefly reigning predecessor upon being elected pope.

❋ THE FIRST TWELVE TRANSLATIONS OF THE BIBLE ❋

1. Samaritan Pentateuch—Third or fourth century BC; not a translation, but a version of the Hebrew books of Moses in old Hebrew script

2. Septuagint (Greek)—Third to second centuries BC; there were multiple Greek versions of Old Testament books of which the Septuagint was most influential

3. Peshitta (Syriac)—Second-century translation of the Hebrew Scriptures with New Testament added later; still the authorized version of Syriac-speaking churches

4. Old Latin—Various translations made in the second to third centuries, surviving chiefly in quotations by the church fathers

5. Old Syriac (i.e., Aramaic)—Around 200; only Gospels survive

6. Sahidic (Coptic)—Around 200

7. Armenian—Third- to fourth-century translation of the New Testament, from Old Syriac

8. Gothic—Fourth century; only portions survive

9. Latin Vulgate—Completed 404 by Jerome; the authorized Roman Catholic version

10. Ethiopic (Ge'ez)—Fourth to fifth centuries

11. Philoxenian (Syriac)—508; only a few books survive

12. Georgian—Sixth century, translated from Armenian

❀ CHRISTIAN BESTSELLERS ❀

This list doesn't include the Bible, the all-time "bestseller." It is said that Bunyan's *Pilgrim's Progress* is second only to the Bible in the number of copies distributed, and that Sheldon's *In His Steps* has sold 28,500,000 copies.

Life of St. Antony, ascribed to Athansius, 360
The Imitation of Christ, Thomas à Kempis, 1425
Book of Martyrs (Acts and Monuments), John Foxe, 1563, later supplemented
Pilgrim's Progress, John Bunyan, 1678
The Christian's Secret of a Happy Life, Hannah Whitall Smith, 1875
Ben-Hur, Lew Wallace, 1880
In His Steps, Charles Monroe Sheldon, 1896
Quo Vadis? Henryk K. Sienkiewicz, 1896
The Robe, Lloyd Douglas, 1942
God's Smuggler, Brother Andrew (Andy van der Bijl), 1967
The Late Great Planet Earth, Hal Lindsey, 1970
The Purpose-Driven Life, Rick Warren, 2002
The Left Behind series, Tim LaHaye and Jerry B. Jenkins, 1995–2004

❀ THE CHALCEDONIAN CREED ❀

The Chalcedonian Creed, from the Council of Chalcedon (451), is not used in worship.

We, then, following the holy Fathers, all with one consent, teach men to confess one and the same Son, our Lord Jesus Christ, the same perfect in Godhead and also perfect in manhood; truly God and truly man, of a reasonable soul and body; consubstantial with the Father according to the Godhead, and consubstantial with us according to the Manhood; in all things like unto us, without sin; begotten before all ages of the Father according to the Godhead, and in these latter days, for us and for our salvation, born of the Virgin Mary, the Mother of God, according to the Manhood; one and the same Christ, Son, Lord, only begotten, to be acknowledged in two natures, inconfusedly, unchangeably, indivisibly, inseparably; the distinction of natures being by no means taken away by the union, but rather the property of each nature being preserved, and concurring in one Person and one Subsistence, not parted or divided into two persons, but one and the same Son, and only begotten, God the Word, the Lord Jesus Christ; as the prophets from the beginning [have declared] concerning Him, and the Lord Jesus Christ Himself has taught us, and the Creed of the holy Fathers has handed down to us. (Traditional English version)

❦ ONWARD CHRISTIAN SOLDIERS: ❦
THE CRUSADES OF CHRISTENDOM

Muslim Arabs captured Jerusalem in 637, but Christian pilgrimages to the Holy Land continued. In 1071, however, the more hostile Seljuk Turks took Jerusalem and went on to conquer most of Asia Minor, weakening the eastern Roman Empire. After an appeal from the emperor Alexius I Comnenus, Pope Urban II (ruled 1088–1099) urged an expedition to recover the Holy Land. These are the crusades that followed, as commonly reckoned.

First Crusade (1096–1099) . . . . Captured Antioch, established the Latin Kingdom of Jerusalem

Second Crusade (1147–1149) . . . . . No result; most crusaders never reached the Holy Land

Third Crusade (1188–1192) . . . . . Syrian ruler Saladin had recaptured Jerusalem in 1187; Richard I of England made a truce with him, allowing crusaders to visit Jerusalem

Fourth Crusade (1202–1204) . . . . . Never reached the Holy Land but placed a Latin ruler on the throne of the Eastern Empire in Constantinople

Children's Crusade (1212) . . . . Few children even reached the ports of France and Italy; perhaps the origin of the legend of the "Pied Piper."

Fifth Crusade (1217–1221) . . . . Took place mostly in Egypt, recovered the Holy Cross (supposed true cross)

Sixth Crusade (1228-1229) . . . . Frederick II (Holy Roman Emperor) governed Jerusalem for fifteen years, till its final re-capture by the Turks in 1244.

Seventh Crusade (1248–1254) . . . . Louis IX of France strengthened some Christian enclaves in Syria but could not retake Jerusalem.

Eighth Crusade (1270) . . . . Louis IX attacked Tunis but died there; soon the remaining Christian enclaves in Syria were lost to Islam.

The Holy Land finally passed again into Western hands during World War I, when British General Edmund Allenby captured it from the Ottoman Turks in 1917–1918.

❄ BIBLICAL WOMEN NAMED MARY ❄

In the Bible, the name *Mary* is *Miriam* in the Old Testament, *Mariam, Marias,* or *Maria* in the New Testament. These are the eight or nine women of the Bible bearing that name:

Miriam . . . . Sister of Moses and Aaron
Miriam . . . . Daughter of Mered and Bithiah, the
daughter of Pharaoh (1 Chron. 4:17)
Mary . . . . Mother of Jesus
Mary Magdalene . . . . . . Miriam of Magdala
The "other" Mary . . . . . Mother of James and Joses
(Matt. 27:61)
Mary . . . . Wife of Clopas (John 19:25, may
be same as above)
Mary . . . . Sister of Martha and Lazarus
Mary . . . . Mother of John Mark (Acts 12:12)
Mary . . . . Greeted by Paul in Romans 16:6

❄ THE SEVEN LAST WORDS OF CHRIST ❄

The traditional Seven Last Words of Christ on the cross are these, from the Revised Standard Version:

1. "Father, forgive them; for they know not what they do" (Luke 23:34).
2. "Woman, behold, your son!" (John 19:26).
3. "Truly, I say to you, today you will be with me in Paradise" (Luke 23:43).
4. "I thirst" (John 19:28).
5. "My God, my God, why hast thou forsaken me?" (Matt. 27:46; Mark 15:34).
6. "Father, into thy hands I commit my spirit!" (Luke 23:46).
7. "It is finished" (John 19:30).

These were not Jesus' *last* words, of course. His last words before his ascension into heaven were: "It is not for you to know times or seasons which the Father has fixed by his own authority. But you shall receive power when the Holy Spirit has come upon you; and you shall be my witnesses in Jerusalem and in all Judea and Samaria and to the end of the earth" (Acts 1:7–8).

His last recorded words to the apostle Paul were: "Take courage, for as you have testified about me at Jerusalem, so you must bear witness also at Rome" (Acts 23:11).

His last recorded words to the apostle John were: "Surely I am coming soon" (Rev. 22:20).

❈ THE UNFORTUNATE WIVES OF HENRY VIII ❈

England's King Henry VIII (ruled 1509–1547) broke with the Church of Rome in part over the issue of divorce. His first wife, Catherine of Aragon, bore him only one child who survived, a daughter. Catherine had been the widow of Henry's older brother Arthur, and Henry became convinced from a passage in Leviticus that their marriage was invalid. When the pope refused to grant an annulment, Henry made himself the head of the church in England and had Archbishop Thomas Cranmer annul the marriage. (In 1556, Cranmer was martyred by Catherine's daughter Mary, known as "Bloody Mary," in her effort to return England to the Catholic fold.)

Catherine of Aragon	Marriage annulled 1533	Mother of Mary I (ruled 1553–1558)
Anne Boleyn	Executed 1536	Mother of Elizabeth I (ruled 1558–1603)
Jane Seymour	Died 1537	Mother of Edward VI (ruled 1547–1553)
Anne of Cleves	Marriage annulled 1540	
Catherine Howard	Executed 1542	
Catherine Parr	Survived	

❈ THE SEVEN CHURCH COUNCILS ❈

Both the Catholic and Orthodox churches recognize seven ancient councils of the church, called the *Ecumenical Councils* (from the Greek *oikumene*, "inhabited world"). Some of the non-Orthodox Eastern churches recognize only the first three. The Anglican and Reformed traditions honor the councils but apply the test of Scripture to their deliberations. These are the Ecumenical Councils and the issues they dealt with. For a description of the issues, see the entries on *Heretics and Their Heresies* and *Obscure Christian -Isms*.

1. Nicaea, 325 . . . . Arianism
2. Constantinople I, 381 . . . . Apollinarianism
3. Ephesus, 431 . . . . Nestorianism
4. Chalcedon, 451 . . . . Eutychianism
5. Constantinople II, 553 . . . . Three Chapters Controversy (views of writers sympathetic to Nestorius)
6. Constantinople III, 680–681 . . . . . Monothelitism
7. Nicaea II, 787 . . . . Iconoclasm

❧ POPULAR BIBLICAL NAMES FOR CHILDREN ❧

There are twelve Bible names among the current top twenty for boys, whereas the top twenty for girls include only six. Some girls' names are feminine versions of boys' names (Danielle, Gabrielle), while a number of them represent biblical virtues or qualities (Grace; Faith; Zoe, the New Testament Greek word for *life*; Sophia, the word for *wisdom*). Madeline is from Mary Magdalene, and Jordan is the river. The Godhead does better on the feminine side; Trinity ranks fifty-seventh among girls, whereas Jesus is sixty-fifth among boys. If, however, you include ninth-ranked Christopher (which means "Christ-bearer") and twenty-third-ranked Christian, the boys do much better. Some names exist in multiple versions, partly due to ethnic variations.

Boys		Girls	
Jacob or James	Alexander	Sarah or Sara	Julia
Joseph or José	Zachary	Hannah	Jordan
Michael	Jonathan	Abigail	Faith
John or Juan	Samuel	Elizabeth	Trinity
Joshua	Christian	Grace	Zoe
Matthew	Benjamin	Maria or Mary	Madeline
Andrew	Nathan	Sophia	Rebecca
Ethan	Gabriel	Anna	Leah
Daniel	Noah	Chloe	Danielle
David	Caleb	Rachel	Gabrielle, Gabriella, or Gabriela

❧ CHURCH CANDLES ❧

The use of candles in Christian worship began with the custom of carrying candles in procession before the bishop of Rome (pope), then placing them around the altar. Beginning around the year 1200, worshipers actually placed candles on the altar, and the custom spread throughout the church. In Catholic and other churches, worshipers place smaller votive candles before statues of saints or on a special rack. This use of candles may go back to Israelite practice, in which a lamp stand (using oil lamps, not candles) was placed in the sanctuary.

Today candles have come to symbolize Christ, "the Light of the World," Christ's offering of himself (as the candle burns down), or a prayer request. Probably their original purpose was none of these. Ancient churches were built of stone, with thick walls and few windows until the Gothic churches of the Middle Ages. It was quite dark inside the church, even in daytime. Candles were needed for their light, if nothing else.

❋ CHRISTIAN ACRONYMS AND ABBREVIATIONS ❋

AD . . . . Anno Domini, The Year of Our Lord

CE . . . . Of the Common Era

B.V.M. . . . . Blessed Virgin Mary

COGIC . . . . Church of God in Christ

IFCA . . . . Independent Fundamental Churches of America

ECFA . . . . Evangelical Council on Fiscal Accountability

ECUSA . . . . Episcopal Church (USA)

EFCA . . . . Evangelical Free Church of America

KJV . . . . King James Version

NAE . . . . National Association of Evangelicals

NIV . . . . New International Version

NT . . . . New Testament

O.P. . . . . Order of Preachers (Dominicans)

O.S.B. . . . . Order of St. Benedict (Benedictines)

OT . . . . Old Testament

PCUSA . . . . Presbyterian Church (USA)

RV . . . . Revised Version (English, 1881)

RSV . . . . Revised Standard Version

SBC . . . . Southern Baptist Convention

S.J. . . . . Society of Jesus (Jesuits)

UCC . . . . United Church of Christ

❋ EARMARKS OF A "CHRISTIAN" CULT ❋

What makes a religious movement a cult? Analysts offer several criteria for labeling a movement a cult:

- Teachings that modify, or go beyond, clear statements of Scripture.

- Sacred or special writings or traditions that reinterpret or supersede the Bible.

- Manipulation of members or potential members (condemnation for anyone who leaves the movement or questions its teaching).

- A controlling authority structure, often with one idolized leader.

- An attitude of exclusiveness: "We are the only true church with the only truth."

❦ OF CATHEDRALS AND BASILICAS ❦

Basilica, Dyersville, Iowa

In North America a large, imposing church is sometimes called a *cathedral*—such as the Washington National Cathedral or Robert Schuller's Crystal Cathedral in Garden Grove, California. The name *cathedral*, however, comes from the Latin word *cathedra*, meaning "throne." A church is correctly called a cathedral only if a bishop is "seated" there, as in the Catholic, Orthodox, or Anglican traditions. Even a small building can be a cathedral if it is the bishop's church.

The term *basilica* is derived from the Greek word for "king." In the Roman world, basilicas were large, oblong halls in major cities where the emperor held court when visiting. The church took over the basilica as its favored building style. Today, however, the Roman Catholic Church designates a church or cathedral as a basilica if it has a unique ceremonial role or special historical or architectural merit. Examples are the Basilica of St. Thérèse in Lisieux, France, devoted to the veneration of this saint, or the Basilica of the Agony in the Garden of Gethsemane at Jerusalem. There are at least thirty-seven basilicas in the United States, such as the Basilica of the National Shrine of the Assumption of the Blessed Virgin Mary in Baltimore, and the Basilica of Saint Francis Xavier in the small town of Dyersville, Iowa. Canada has at least nine, including the Basilica-Cathedral of Notre Dame in the old city of Quebec.

❦ THE APOSTLES' CREED ❦

The Apostles' Creed, or "Roman Symbol," is a fourth-century baptismal creed.

> *I believe in God the Father Almighty, Maker of heaven and earth; and in Jesus Christ his only Son our Lord, who was conceived by the Holy Ghost, born of the Virgin Mary, suffered under Pontius Pilate, was crucified, dead, and buried. He descended into hell; the third day he rose again from the dead. He ascended into heaven, and sitteth on the right hand of God the Father Almighty; from thence he shall come to judge the quick and the dead.*
>
> *I believe in the Holy Ghost, the holy catholic Church, the communion of saints, the forgiveness of sins, the resurrection of the body and the life everlasting. Amen.*
> (Book of Common Prayer, 1928)

❀ RIVERS OF THE BIBLE ❀

The Bible often mentions rivers and streams, vital in a region of sporadic rainfall. These are some of the most important.

Tigris . . . . One of the four rivers of Eden, along with the following

Euphrates . . . . The "great river" (Gen. 15:18) or simply "the River" (Gen. 31:21 NIV), considered the boundary between Mesopotamia* and areas to the west "Beyond the River" (Ezra 6:8)

River of Egypt . . . . . Probably a *wadi* or torrential stream that divided Egypt from the land of Israel (Gen. 15:18)

Jabbok . . . . Where Jacob wrestled and his name was changed to Israel (Gen. 32)

Nile . . . . Where Pharaoh's daughter found the baby Moses (Exod. 2); he turned its waters into blood (Exod. 7)

Jordan . . . . Divides the Promised Land into areas known historically as "Trans-Jordan" and "Cis-Jordan" (West Bank). Joshua led the Israelites across it, and Jesus was baptized in it.

Abana and Pharpar . . The rivers of Damascus that Naaman thought were more impressive than the Jordan (2 Kings 5)

Kishon . . . . The brook where Elijah slew the prophets of Baal (1 Kings 18)

Chebar . . . . In Mesopotamia, where Ezekiel had his visions

River in the "city of God" . . . . The "river whose streams make glad the city of God" (Ps. 46:4 NIV). The Kidron in Jerusalem is a small brook, so this river is a visionary one, perhaps the same as the following.

River of Life . . . . The visionary river flowing from the sanctuary (Ezek. 47); the river in the new Jerusalem (Rev. 22), Jesus spoke of the "rivers of living water" flowing from the life of the believer (John 7:38).

Rivers in the desert . . Isaiah 43, perhaps the same as above

Mesopotamia means "between the rivers," a Greek name for the area known as Babylon or Chaldea (modern Iraq).

A Theological Miscellany

❋ YOUR RELIGIOUS NEIGHBORS ❋

Religious groups are not evenly distributed across the United States. The denominational preferences of your neighbors are likely to change depending on what part of the country you live in.

- If you live in New England, New York, New Jersey, most of Pennsylvania, or anywhere near the Great Lakes, your neighbors will probably be Catholic.

- If you live in Delaware, Maryland, central Pennsylvania, the northern part of West Virginia, southern Ohio, Indiana, central Illinois, southern Iowa, Nebraska, or Kansas, there is a good chance your neighbors are Methodists.

- If you live in Virginia, southern West Virginia, Kentucky, southern Illinois, Missouri, the Carolinas, Georgia, Tennessee, Arkansas, Oklahoma, Georgia, Alabama, Mississippi, northern Louisiana, most of Texas, or northern or central Florida, you will definitely have Baptist neighbors.

- If you live in south Florida, southern Louisiana, or near the Rio Grande Valley in Texas, your neighbors could well be Catholic.

- If you live in western Wisconsin, Minnesota, northern Iowa, the Dakotas, or eastern Montana, you will probably have Lutheran neighbors.

- If you live in western Montana, Wyoming, Colorado, New Mexico, Arizona, California, western Nevada, or Alaska, it is likely that your neighbors are Catholic.

- If you live in Utah, Idaho, or eastern Nevada, you will have Mormon neighbors.

- If you live in Washington State, Oregon, or Hawaii, your neighbors may not attend church at all.

❋ ORIGINS OF CHRISTMAS ❋

The New Testament contains no command to celebrate the birth of Jesus, and Scripture doesn't indicate the time of year when he was born. The traditional December 25 date came from a Roman winter festival, the *Natalis Solis Invicti*, a festival of the sun after the winter solstice when the days in the Northern Hemisphere begin to lengthen. Despite objections from early Christian theologians concerned about confusing Christ with the sun god, Christians had begun to celebrate the birth of Jesus on this day by the fourth century. Perhaps they felt this would keep weaker believers from falling back into the popular Roman custom.

❈ JOHN WESLEY'S "GENERAL RULES" ❈

For a preacher of God's free grace who irked his Calvinist critics, John Wesley was no slacker about living a methodical Christian life, and he expected the same commitment from his Methodist followers. In 1739 he formulated the General Rules of the "United Society," at the request of several who asked for help in "working out their own salvation" (see Phil. 2:12).

There is only one condition required of those who desire admission into these societies, a "desire to flee from the wrath to come, and to be saved from their sins." But wherever this is really fixed in the soul, it will be shown by its fruits. It is therefore expected of all who continue therein, that they shall continue to evidence their desire of salvation.

First, by doing no harm, by avoiding evil of every kind, especially that which is most generally practiced. . . .

Secondly, by doing good, by being in every kind merciful after their power as they have opportunity, doing good of every possible sort, and, as far as possible, to all men:

To their bodies, of the ability which God giveth; by giving food to the hungry; by clothing the naked, by visiting or helping them that are sick or in prison.

To their souls, by instructing, reproving, or exhorting all that we have any intercourse with; trampling under foot that enthusiastic doctrine that "We are not to do good unless our hearts be free to do it."

. . . By all possible diligence and frugality, that the gospel be not blamed. By running with patience the race set before them, denying themselves and taking up their cross daily; submitting to bear the reproach of Christ; to bear the filth and offscouring of the world; and looking that men should say all manner of evil of them for the Lord's sake.

Thirdly, by attending upon all these ordinances of God; which are,

The Public Worship of God;

The Ministry of the Word, either read or expounded;

The Supper of the Lord;

Family and private prayer;

Searching the Scriptures;

Fasting, or abstinence.

These are the General Rules of our Societies; all of which we are taught of God to observe, even in His written Word, which is the only rule, and the sufficient rule, both of our faith and practice. And all these we know his Spirit writes on truly awakened hearts. If there be any among us who observe them not, who habitually break any of them, let it be known unto them who watch over that soul, as they who must give an account. We all admonish him of the error of his ways: we will bear with him for a season; but then if he repent not, he hath no more place among us; we have delivered our own souls.

❊ SOME CHRISTIAN "OLOGIES" ❊

The suffix -*ology* comes from the Greek word *logos* ("word"), meaning the expression, science, or body of knowledge of a subject. These are some "ologies" and their subjects.

Angelology . . . . Angels	Hagiology . . . . The saints
Bibliology . . . . The Bible	Hamartiology . . . . . . The nature and extent of sin
Christology . . . . The nature of Jesus Christ	Mariology . . . . The Virgin Mary
Cosmology . . . . The universe	Martyrology . . . . Martyrs (a catalog or history)
Ecclesiology . . . . The church	Pneumatology . . . . . . The Holy Spirit
Epistemology . . . . How people know	Soteriology . . . . Salvation, or how Christ saves
Eschatology . . . . The "last things" or end times	Theology . . . . God

❊ CHRISTIAN FEASTS THAT CHANGE ❊ DAYS FROM YEAR TO YEAR

Christmas is always December 25 (in the Western church); why does the date of Easter change every year? Christians in the early centuries disagreed about the day for celebrating Christ's resurrection. Some wanted to observe it on the fourteenth of the Jewish month of Nisan, the day of Passover, while others argued for a schedule independent of the Jewish calendar. The bitter controversy quieted down after 325, when the Council of Nicaea determined that Easter should be celebrated on the first Sunday after the first full moon following the vernal equinox. The moon circles the earth in a twenty-eight-day cycle, so the date changes each year.

Some days of the church year depend on the date of Christmas. The Advent season begins the fourth Sunday before, while Epiphany Day is the twelfth day after Christmas. Other days, however, depend on the date of Easter. Ash Wednesday comes forty days before, not counting Sundays, and Pentecost is the fiftieth day (as its name means in Greek) afterward. This means that the Epiphany season expands or contracts with the changing dates of Ash Wednesday, and the Pentecost season varies in length at the other end of the "sliding" part of the liturgical year.

❧ CHRISTMAS TRADITIONS AROUND THE WORLD ❧

Aleuts (Alaska, U.S.) . . . . Celebrators eat *piruk* (fish pie) or smoked salmon; caroling children carry a colored star on a long pole.

Austria . . . . "St. Nicholas" gives sweets, toys, and nuts to children with a list of good deeds. Baked carp is the traditional Christmas dinner.

Bangladesh . . . . Worshipers light the way to church using arches made from banana trees, with oil lamps.

China . . . . Santa Claus is called "Christmas Old Man" (Dun Che Lao Ren).

Egypt . . . . Christians fast during Advent; on Christmas Eve (January 6) they attend church wearing new clothes, and on Christmas Day they visit friends and share *kaik*, a type of shortbread.

England . . . . Christmas dessert is a rich, fruity pudding with brandy sauce.

Ethiopia . . . . Christmas Eve worshipers circle the church three times with lighted candles; Christmas food includes *injera*, a sourdough bread.

France . . . . Children leave their shoes by the fireplace to be filled with gifts by Père Noël; players or puppeteers reenact the story of Christ's birth in church squares.

Germany . . . . Children leave letters on their window sills for Christkind, a winged figure in white robes bringing gifts; families bake gingerbread houses; in some homes, the Christmas tree and gifts are kept in a locked room, opened only on Christmas Day.

Greenland . . . . Celebrators eat *mattak*, whale skin containing a strip of blubber.

Iraq . . . . Families light a fire of dried thorns in their courtyard on Christmas Eve; if it burns to ashes, they will have a good year. Another bonfire is lit in church on Christmas Day, and there is a procession with an image of the child Jesus.

Ireland . . . . On the day after Christmas, St. Stephen's Day, there are football matches and other events; boys go from door to door with a fake wren on a stick, singing and playing instruments and asking for money "for the starving wren," actually for themselves.

❀ CHRISTMAS TRADITIONS AROUND THE WORLD—CONT. ❀

Labrador (Canada) . . . . Children are given turnips with a lighted candle.

Mexico . . . . La Posada is a procession reenacting Joseph and Mary's search for shelter before the birth of Jesus; celebrators go from house to house carrying their images. (Many Hispanic countries have the same custom.)

Netherlands . . . . Sinterklaas Eve, when St. Nicholas distributes gifts, is December 5.

Portugal . . . . Hoping to receive gifts and treats on January 6, children place their shoes, filled with carrots and straw, on window sills to lure the horses of the Magi.

Russia . . . . Babushka, or "Grandmother," is a legendary figure who distributes presents to children; she failed to go with the Magi but changed her mind and is still trying to find Jesus.

Sweden . . . . Christmas trees are set up only a day or two before Christmas; the Christmas goat (*julbok*) distributes the gifts; Christmas dinner includes *lutfisk* (boiled codfish).

❀ THE CHRISTIAN FLAG ❀

The Christian flag is one of the world's oldest unchanged flags. Charles C. Overton, a Sunday school superintendent on Staten Island, New York, designed it in 1897. When a guest speaker failed to appear, Overton noticed an American flag in the room and gave an impromptu talk on the meaning of flags. It suddenly occurred to him that there should be a Christian flag, and he designed the one still in use. The flag is white (for purity and peace), with a blue field (faithfulness, truth, and sincerity) and a red cross (the sacrifice of Christ). These colors are the same as the American flag but were also used in the Israelite tabernacle.

❧ A CHURCH BULLETIN FROM AD 150 ❧

What was early Christian worship like? The New Testament doesn't go into detail about it, but two sources from the following century begin to connect the dots. They are the anonymous *Didache* (dee-duh-KAY), or *Teaching of the Twelve Apostles*, and the *First Apology* of Justin Martyr. Justin was a lawyer who converted to Christianity and wrote a defense of the faith (traditionally called an *apology*) addressed to the Roman emperor. For his trouble he was put to death sometime around 165. Hence he's called Justin *Martyr*—that was not his last name.

Here's what the bulletin or "worship folder" might look like, combining what we know from our two sources.

First Church, Illyricum
Lord's Day XXII, Annum XII Caesar Antoninus Pius

Presider: Presbyter M. Diotrephes Demetrios
Deacons: F. Urbanus Cimber, Stephanos Philippos
Prophetess: Priscilla Lydia

Welcome to First Church. We're glad you came to worship with us on this Lord's Day. Please remember that only Christians baptized in the name of the Lord are invited to share in the Lord's Table. If you haven't received the "washing" for rebirth, please leave after the teaching time. We hope you'll understand and soon decide to become a Christian and take our membership training course.

Please remain standing for the entire service—men to the right, women to the left.

Our guest prophet today is Flavius Eumenes of Amphipolis. Please be generous in providing for his needs as he moves on toward Brundisium this week.

We thank the family of G. Archippus Pudens for opening their spacious home to our gathering this Lord's Day. We urge you to take care not to allow young people to sit on the window ledges—remember Eutychus!

The Thanksgiving Meal will be taken to members who are absent today due to illness or work; please remind the deacons of friends or family members who need to be visited.

The Writings
Read by Presbyter Demetrios
From the book of the prophet Isaiah
From the memoirs of the apostle Paul
From the memoirs of the apostle Matthew

Teaching from the Writings
Presbyter Demetrios

Hymn "My Soul Magnifies the Lord"
Led by the Prophets

❦ A CHURCH BULLETIN FROM AD 150—CONT. ❦

Prayers
Led by Deacon Philippos
You may join in offering prayers for your needs and those of others, especially for those baptized this week.

Kiss of Peace
Greet one another with a holy kiss. Please confine your greeting to your own (men's or women's) side of the room.

The Gifts
The deacons will present the bread, wine, and water.

Thanksgiving before the Meal
Presbyter Demetrios
Presider: Praise and glory to the Father of all, through the name of the Son and the Holy Spirit. We thank you that we have been deemed worthy to receive these things at your hand.
Response: Amen.
Presider: We give thanks, our Father, for the holy vine of David, your servant, which you have made known to us through Jesus, your servant.
Response: To you be the glory forever.
Presider: We give you thanks, our Father, for the life and knowledge that you have made known to us through Jesus, your servant.
Response: To you be the glory forever.
Presider: Just as this broken bread was scattered upon the mountains and then was gathered together and became one, so may your church be gathered together from the ends of the earth into your kingdom.
Response: For yours is the glory and the power through Jesus Christ forever.
The deacons will serve the Thanksgiving Meal.

Thanksgiving after the Meal
The presider will give thanks for the faith made known to us, ending with "through Jesus, your servant."
Response: To you be the glory forever.
The presider will give thanks for spiritual food and drink, ending with "we give thanks because you are mighty."
Response: To you be the glory forever.
The presider will pray for the gathering of the church, ending with "into your kingdom, which you have prepared for it."
Response: For yours is the power and the glory forever.
Presider: May grace come, and may this world pass away.
Response: Hosanna to the God of David.
Presider: If anyone is holy, let him come; if anyone is not, let him repent.

❀ A CHURCH BULLETIN FROM AD 150—CONT. ❀

Response: Maranatha! Amen.

Thanksgiving by the Prophets and Spiritual Songs
You may bring your gifts for the poor to Presbyter Demetrios during the singing. And don't forget to pray the Lord's Prayer three times every day, as is our custom.

❀ CHRISTIAN COMPOSERS PAST AND PRESENT ❀

Many composers through history have written music for the church, or churches have employed them as organists or music directors. Not all of them, perhaps, have been known to be devout. This is a short list of some who apparently were practicing Christians of one variety or another.

Composer	Lived	Country	Faith
Giovanni Pierluigi da Palestrina	1525–1594	Italy	Catholic
Tomás Luis de Victoria	1548–1611	Spain, Italy	Catholic (priest)
Heinrich Schütz	1585–1672	Germany	Lutheran
Dietrich Buxtehude	1637–1707	Germany	Lutheran
Johann Sebastian Bach	1685–1750	Germany	Lutheran
Antonio Soler	1729–1783	Spain	Catholic (priest)*
Franz Josef Haydn	1732–1809	Austria	Catholic
William Billings	1746–1800	U.S. (MA)	Congregational
Johann Friedrich Peter	1746–1813	U.S. (PA)	Moravian**
Felix Mendelssohn	1809–1847	Germany	Lutheran (had Jewish roots)
Anton Bruckner	1824–1896	Austria	Catholic
Igor Stravinsky	1882–1971	Russia, France, and U.S.	Orthodox, Catholic
Edmund Rubbra	1901–1986	England	Catholic
Lennox Berkeley	1903–1990	England	Catholic
Olivier Messiaen	1908–1992	France	Catholic
Arvo Pärt	1935–	Estonia	Orthodox
John Tavener	1944–	England	Orthodox

*Soler was a member of a religious order. Antonio Vivaldi (1678–1741) was also a priest, but he does not appear to have been especially devout.

**Peter was educated for the ministry.

❄ A TRADITIONAL EASTER VIGIL ❄

The Great Vigil of Easter is a traditional service held the night preceding Easter morning. Here is an outline of the usual order of worship. The word *Alleluia* should not occur anywhere until the time indicated below.

1. The service begins in dim light. The large paschal (Easter) candle is lit at the rear of the church, with traditional or appropriate prayer, then carried toward the front of the church. The person carrying the candle (usually a deacon) calls out, "The Light of Christ!" and the people respond, "Thanks be to God!" This occurs three times.
2. After the candle is set in place, the candle-bearer or another singer sings the traditional *Exsultet*, beginning, "Rejoice now, heavenly hosts and choirs of angels . . ."
3. A series of Scripture readings follows, setting forth the story of redemption. If not all of them are read, the passage from Exodus should not be omitted. Each reading may be followed by a selection from the Psalms (the usual choices given here) or appropriate music, followed by a suitable prayer or collect.

    a. *The Creation*—Genesis 1:1–2:2, with Psalm 33:1–11 or 36:5–10
    b. *The Flood*—Genesis 7:1–5, 11–18; 8:8–18; 9:8–13, with Psalm 46
    c. *Abraham's Sacrifice of Isaac*—Genesis 22:1–18, with Psalm 33:12–22 or Psalm 1
    d. *Israel's Deliverance at the Red Sea*—Exodus 14:10–15:1a, with Exodus 15:1b–18
    e. *God's Presence in a Renewed Israel*—Isaiah 4:2–6, with Psalm 122
    f. *Salvation Offered Freely to All*—Isaiah 55:1–11, with Isaiah 12:2–6 or Psalm 42:1–7
    g. *A New Heart and a New Spirit*—Ezekiel 36:24–28, with Psalm 42:1–7
    h. *The Valley of Dry Bones*—Ezekiel 37:1–14, with Psalm 30 or 143
    i. *The Gathering of God's People*—Zephaniah 3:12–20, with Psalm 98 or 126

4. Candidates for baptism are baptized at this time, and/or the congregation renews its baptismal vows using the words of the Apostles' Creed.
5. The leader and people then exchange the traditional Easter greeting. Before the greeting, appropriate preparatory music may be sung, and after the greeting, worshipers may ring bells.
    "Alleluia! Christ is risen!"
    "The Lord is risen indeed! Alleluia!"
6. The *Gloria in excelsis*, *Te Deum* or other triumphant hymn may be sung.
7. After prayer, the epistle is read: Romans 6:3–11, followed by Psalm 114.
8. The gospel is read: Matthew 28:1–10; Mark 16:1–8; or Luke 24:1–12.
9. A homily (short sermon) may be preached here.
10. General prayers may be offered here.
11. The service of Holy Communion (Eucharist) follows.
12. The service concludes with appropriate joyful music and the dismissal.

❋ DENOMINATIONAL AFFILIATIONS ❋
OF U.S. PRESIDENTS

George Washington . . . . Church of England (Episcopal)*
John Adams . . . . Congregational (Unitarian)**
Thomas Jefferson . . . . Episcopalian (Deist)***
James Madison . . . . Episcopalian
James Monroe . . . . Episcopalian
John Quincy Adams . . . . Congregational (Unitarian)**
Andrew Jackson . . . . Presbyterian
Martin Van Buren . . . . Dutch Reformed
William Henry Harrison . . . . Episcopalian
John Tyler . . . . Episcopalian
James Knox Polk . . . . Presbyterian
Zachary Taylor . . . . Episcopalian
Millard Fillmore . . . . Unitarian
Franklin Pierce . . . . Episcopalian
James Buchanan . . . . Presbyterian
Abraham Lincoln . . . . Raised Baptist, nondenominational
Andrew Johnson . . . . Raised Baptist, nondenominational
Ulysses S. Grant . . . . Presbyterian
Rutherford B. Hayes . . . . Methodist
James A. Garfield . . . . Disciples of Christ
Chester A. Arthur . . . . Episcopalian
Grover Cleveland . . . . Presbyterian
Benjamin Harrison . . . . Presbyterian
Grover Cleveland . . . . Presbyterian
William McKinley . . . . Methodist
Theodore Roosevelt . . . . Dutch Reformed
William Howard Taft . . . . Unitarian
Woodrow Wilson . . . . Presbyterian
Warren G. Harding . . . . Baptist
Calvin Coolidge . . . . Congregationalist
Herbert Hoover . . . . Quaker
Franklin Delano Roosevelt . . . . Episcopalian
Harry S. Truman . . . . Baptist
Dwight D. Eisenhower . . . . Presbyterian
John F. Kennedy . . . . Roman Catholic
Lyndon Baines Johnson . . . . Disciples of Christ
Richard M. Nixon . . . . Quaker
Gerald Ford . . . . Episcopalian
Jimmy Carter . . . . Southern Baptist

❧ DENOMINATIONAL AFFILIATIONS ❧ OF U.S. PRESIDENTS—CONT.

Ronald Reagan . . . . Presbyterian
George H. W. Bush. . . . . Episcopalian
William Jefferson Clinton . . . . Southern Baptist
George W. Bush . . . . Methodist

*Washington was a member of the established church in Virginia, which had been part of the Church of England before the American Revolution. The Protestant Episcopal Church was not formed until 1789, shortly after Washington was inaugurated.

**The American Unitarian Association was formed in 1825. Before that, the Orthodox and Unitarian Congregational churches of Massachusetts were not differentiated.

***Jefferson was nominally a member of the established church in Virginia, which became part of the Protestant Episcopal Church, but by belief he was a nonsupernaturalist Deist who created his own version of the Bible.

❧ WHERE THE FOUR *H*'S CAME FROM ❧

The 4-H clubs are well-known organizations for rural youth in the United States and Canada. What the *H*'s stand for is stated in the 4-H Pledge:

I pledge:
My Head to clearer thinking,
My Heart to greater loyalty,
My Hands to larger service, and
My Health to better living,
For my club, my community, my country, and my world.

The four *H*'s go back to the description of four ways in which the young Jesus grew (Luke 2:52):
"And Jesus increased in wisdom and in stature, and in favor with God and man." The parallels can be seen as follows:

Head . . . . Wisdom
Heart . . . . Favor with God
Hands . . . Favor with man
Health . . . Stature

❀ WELL-KNOWN LATIN HYMNS ❀

"All Glory, Laud, and Honor"—*Gloria, laus et honor*, Theodulph of Orleans, ninth century

"Christ Is Made the Sure Foundation"—*Angularis fundamentum*, seventh century

"All Creatures of Our God and King"—*Cantico di fratre sole*, Francis of Assisi, 1225

"Good Christian Men, Rejoice"—Attributed to Heinrich Suso (1295–1366)

"Humbly I Adore Thee"—*Adoro te devote*, Thomas Aquinas, thirteenth century

"A Hymn of Glory Let Us Sing"—*Hymnum canamus Domino*, Venerable Bede, eighth century

"Jesus, the Very Thought of Thee"—*Jesu dulcis memoria*, Bernard of Clairvaux, twelfth century

"Jesus, Thou Joy of Loving Hearts"—*Jesu dulcis memoria*, Bernard of Clairvaux, twelfth century (another translation)

"O Come, All Ye Faithful"—*Adeste fidelis*, eighteenth century

"O Come, O Come, Emmanuel"—*Veni Emanuel*, twelfth century

"O Sacred Head, Now Wounded"—*Salve caput cruentatum*, Bernard of Clairvaux, twelfth century

"O Sons and Daughters, Let Us Sing"—*O filii et filiae*, Jean Tisserand, fifteenth century

"O What Their Joy and Their Glory Must Be"—*O quanta qualia sunt illa Sabbata*, Peter Abelard, twelfth century

"The Strife Is O'er, the Battle Done"—*Finita jam sunt praelia*, twelfth century

"To Thee before the Close of Day"—*Te lucis ante terminum*, seventh century

"Unto Us a Boy Is Born"—*Puer nobis nascitur*, fifteenth century

❀ AVERAGE SIZE OF A CHURCH ❀ IN CANADA AND THE UNITED STATES

There are an estimated 350,000 churches in the United States, and an estimated 9,000 Protestant churches in Canada (not counting Catholic and other bodies).

The average attendance of churches in the United States is around 90. In Canada, evangelical churches report an average attendance of 135 and growing, while for traditional Protestant denominations the figure is 113 and declining.

Evangelical churches typically have a higher average attendance than membership, while the reverse is true of older mainline denominations. In the United States, about 45 percent of the population claims to regularly attend a church. For Canada, the figure is said to be around 20 percent.

❋ SANTA CLAUS AND OTHERS LIKE HIM ❋

Jolly old Saint Nick, a.k.a. St. Nicholas or Santa Claus, is pretty much a denizen of North America, but he has his counterparts in the Christmas visitors, gift-givers, or pranksters of many countries:

Austria	Christkind
Belgium and the Netherlands	Noël, Sinterklaas, Christkind, and Black Pete
Brazil	Papa Noel
Chile	Viejo Pascuerro
China	The Christmas Old Man (Dun Che Lao Ren)
Denmark	Julinisse
England	Father Christmas, Kriss Kringle
Finland	Old Man Christmas
France	Père Noël or le Petit
Germany	Kriss Kringle, Christkind, or St. Nicholas
Hawaii	Kanakaloka
Italy	Befana
Japan	Santa Kurohsu
Mexico	The Three Kings
Poland	The Star Man or Wise Men
Russia	Babushka, a grandmother figure
Spain	The Three Kings
Sweden	Jultomten or the Christmas Brownie, and the Christmas goat (*julbok*)

❋ THE SEVEN SORROWS OF THE VIRGIN MARY ❋

A traditional Catholic list of events that brought sorrow to Jesus' mother:

1. The prophecy of Simeon, that "a sword will pierce through your own soul also" (Luke 2:35)
2. The flight into Egypt to escape from Herod (Matt. 2:13–14)
3. Losing Jesus while returning from the feast in Jerusalem (Luke 2:42–45)
4. Meeting Jesus on the way to Calvary (perhaps based on Luke 23:27–28)
5. Standing at the foot of the cross (John 19:26)
6. When Jesus was taken down from the cross (Luke 23:53)
7. Jesus' entombment (John 19:41–42)

❊ WORLD RELIGIONS AT THEIR CORE ❊

There are many ways of stating the principles at the core of Christian faith. Here is one attempt to do so, in order to compare Christianity with other major world religions. Notice that only in Christianity is the core of faith bound up with a relationship to a particular person, instead of following certain practices.

Christianity

1. God created all things to glorify him.
2. Sin, or disregard for God's purpose, separates people from God and destroys life.
3. God works through history, especially through a people he calls, to restore his purpose.
4. God has realized his renewal of creation in the life, death, and resurrection of Jesus.
5. God brings people into the life of his renewed creation through their membership in Christ.

Judaism

Judaism would accept the first three points of Christianity, described above, perhaps stated differently.

Islam (the "Five Pillars")

1. God (Allah) is One, and Muhammad is his authoritative spokesman.
2. A cycle of daily prayers is the duty of every worshiper.
3. Believers are obligated to help the needy.
4. Worshipers of Allah are to purify themselves through fasting.
5. All who are able must make a pilgrimage to Mecca.

Buddhism (the "Noble Truths")

1. Life is full of grief and suffering.
2. Suffering arises from attachment to desires.
3. Ridding yourself of desire brings an end to suffering.
4. The "Eightfold Path" brings freedom from suffering: right outlook, thought, speech, action, livelihood, effort, mindfulness, and contemplation.

Hinduism

1. God is manifested in many gods such as Brahma (creator), Vishnu (sustainer), Shiva (destroyer), Krishna, Ganesha, and others.
2. *Avatars* are incarnations of the gods, becoming gods themselves—hence Hinduism's many gods.
3. The *Vedas, Upanishads*, and other sacred writings are reverenced.
4. Certain principles govern life, including:

❊ WORLD RELIGIONS AT THEIR CORE—CONT. ❊

a. *karma*—a soul's particular quality, good or bad
b. *reincarnation*—The soul is reborn in another form based on its *karma*; hence all life is sacred.
c. *dharma*—various moral and religious laws
d. *maya*—Final truth is illusory. Hinduism, therefore, has wide diversity of belief and practice and absorbs ideas from other religions.

❊ THE OLDEST MANUSCRIPTS ❊ OF THE NEW TESTAMENT

The oldest fragments of the New Testament were written on *papyrus*, an early paper made from reeds. Later manuscripts, called *codices* (singular *codex*), were in book form and used *vellum*, sheets made from the skin of lambs, kids, or calves. The New Testament was not written on scrolls, as were the separate books of the Hebrew Scriptures. In scholarly practice, papyri were numbered and preceded with *P*. The oldest codices, called *uncials* because they were written in capital letters only, were symbolized by letters (there is an alternate numbering scheme).

Manuscript	Symbol	Contents	Date
John Rylands Papyrus	P 52	Part of John 18	Around AD 150
Chester Beatty Papyri	P	Fragments of Gospels, Acts, and Epistles	Around 200
Bodmer Papyri	P	Parts of Luke and John, the Epistles of Peter and Jude	Third century AD
Codex Vaticanus	B	Complete Greek Bible	Fourth century AD
Codex Sinaiticus	?	Complete Greek Bible	Fourth century AD
Codex Alexandrinus	A	Most of the Greek Bible	Around AD 500
Codex Ephraemi rescriptus	C	Most of the Greek Bible	Fifth century AD
Codex Bezae	D	Gospels and Acts, both Greek and Latin	Fifth or sixth centuries AD
Codex Claromontanus	D_2	Epistles of Paul	Sixth century AD

❋ BIBLICAL WEIGHTS AND MEASURES ❋

OLD TESTAMENT

Weight

gerah (1/20 shekel)	0.6 gram
beka (1/2 shekel)	1/5 ounce
pim (2/3 shekel)	1/4 ounce
shekel	2/5 ounce
mina, 50 shekels	1¼ pounds
talent, 3,000 shekels	75½ pounds

Length, Distance, and Area

finger	7/10 inch
handbreadth (4 fingers)	3 inches
span (2 handbreadths)	8¾ inches
cubit (6 handbreadths)	17½ inches
pace	length of a step
semed (yoke)	5/8 acre

Capacity, Dry

kab	1⅛ quarts
omer (1/10 ephah)	2 quarts
seah (1/3 ephah)	2/3 peck
ephah	½ bushel
lethech (½ homer)	2½ bushels
homer, cor	5⅛ bushels

Capacity, Liquid

log	2/3 pint
hin	1 gallon
bath	5½ gallons
cor, homer	55 gallons

NEW TESTAMENT

Weight

talent	a large weight
pound	12 ounces

Length, Distance, and Area

fathom	6 feet
stadion (furlong)	⅛ mile
milion (mile)	9/10 mile

Capacity, Dry

modios (bushel)	¼ bushel

Capacity, Liquid

metretes (firkin)	10 gallons
litra (pound)	12 ounces

❋ THE FOUR CHIEF ARCHANGELS ❋

Archangel	Name Means	Reference	Feast Day (West)
Michael	"Who is like God?"	Daniel 10, 12; Jude; Revelation 12	September 29
Gabriel	"Man of God"	Daniel 8, 9; Luke 1	March 24
Raphael	"God has healed"	Books of Tobit and Enoch (Apocryphal)	October 24
Uriel	"God is my light"	Book of Enoch (Apocryphal)	July 28

❊ POPULAR SAINTS ❊

Which saints have been the most popular among Roman Catholics in North America? One good indication is how many churches have been named after them. A survey of twenty major cities in Canada and the United States yielded the following, in order of frequency. More than one saint held some of these names, but we have described the most likely possibility. This list does not include the twelve disciples or the apostle Paul, also often called *Saint* by Protestants.

Patrick . . . . Missionary to Ireland, fifth century
Michael . . . . Archangel, mentioned in Daniel, Jude, and Revelation
Anthony . . . . Founder of monastic movement, fourth century
Ann . . . . Traditionally the mother of the Virgin Mary
but not mentioned in the Bible
Bernadette . . . . Her visions of the Virgin Mary gave
rise to healing pilgrimages to Lourdes, France
Theresa . . . . Spanish mystic, sixteenth century
George . . . . Legendary early Christian martyr, patron saint of England
Augustine . . . . Theologian, fifth century
Nicholas . . . . Pope, ninth century
Cecelia . . . . Legendary early Christian martyr, patron saint of music
Helena . . . . Mother of the Roman emperor Constantine,
third to fourth century
Catherine . . . . Visionary, fourteenth century

❊ DANTE'S LEVELS OF HELL ❊

Dante Alighieri (1265–1321), in his *Inferno* (part of the *Divine Comedy* trilogy), developed a picture of nine layers, or rings, of hell:

1. Limbo, the place of virtuous non-Christians and unbaptized children
2. The Lustful, those who sinned in the flesh
3. The Gluttonous, who lived with excess
4. The Avaricious and Prodigal, who lived greedily and wastefully
5. The Wrathful and Gloomy, who lived lives of crudity and vindictiveness
6. Heretics, who refused to believe in God or the afterlife
7. The Suicides, who committed violence against God and nature
8. Malebolge, abode of various types of the fraudulent and malicious
9. Cocytus, the lowest level where Satan, the Arch Traitor, eternally chews the bodies of Judas and other betrayers

❋ FAMOUS MISSIONARIES ❋

Some well-known Christian missionaries since the 1500s.

Missionary	Lived	Nationality	Missionary to
Francis Xavier	1506–1552	Navarre (Spain)	Japan, China
Jacques Marquette	1636–1675	France	American Indians, Great Lakes region
David Brainerd	1718–1747	Connecticut (Colonial America)	American Indians in Middle Colonies
Junipero Serra	1713–1784	Spain, Mexico	American Indians in California
William Carey	1761–1834	England	India
Samuel Marsden	1764–1838	England	Australia, New Zealand
Adoniram Judson	1788–1850	United States	Burma
John Geddie	1815–1872	Canada	Eastern Melanesia, South Pacific
David Livingstone	1813–1873	Scotland	Southern Africa
Robert Moffatt	1795–1883	Scotland	South Africa
Alexander Mackay	1849–1890	Scotland	Uganda
James Chalmers	1841–1901	Scotland	Cook Islands, New Guinea
Hudson Taylor	1832–1905	England	China
George Grenfell	1849–1906	England	Congo
Mary Slessor	1848–1915	Scotland	Nigeria, Benin
Solomon Ginsburg	1867–1927	Poland/ England	Brazil
Charles T. Studd	1860–1931	England	China, India, Africa
Jonathan Goforth	1859–1936	Canada	China
Jim Elliot	1927–1956	United States	Ecuador
Albert Schweitzer	1875–1965	Alsace (Germany/ France)	French Equatorial Africa
Gladys Aylward	1900–1970	England	China

❋ FIVE PHILISTINE CITIES ❋

The Philistines, who gave the Israelites so much grief after their settlement in Canaan, also gave their name to the land we now call *Palestine*. Their five main cities, located in what is now called the *Gaza Strip*, were Ashkelon, Ashdod, Ekron, Gath, and Gaza.

❀ THE ORIGIN OF CHAPTERS AND VERSES ❀

The Bible originally had no chapter or verse references. When people referred to portions of Scripture, they used subject matter or first words as a title.

Stephen Langton, archbishop of Canterbury, divided the Latin Bible into chapters in 1205 to make it easier to cite biblical texts. Scholars working with Cardinal Hugo de Santo Care made a chapter division around 1248. The practice spread to other languages, with the chapters divided into lettered sections, usually seven. Rabbi Nathan printed a Hebrew Bible with verse divisions in Venice in 1524. Robert Estienne (Stephanus, or Stevens) of Paris, a Protestant, introduced numbered verses in his printed editions of the Greek New Testament in 1551 and the Hebrew Bible in 1571. The Geneva Bible of 1560 was the first English Bible with both chapter and verse numbers.

In the English Bible, there are 594 chapters before Psalm 118 and 594 chapters after Psalm 118; 594 plus 594 equals 1,188. Psalm 118:8 says, "It is better to take refuge in the LORD / than to put confidence in man."

❀ MUSICAL INSTRUMENTS OF THE BIBLE ❀

Instrument	Selected References	Comments
Cymbal	1 Chronicles 15:16 (NASB); Psalm 150:5 (KJV)	Several types; evidently there was a difference between "loud cymbals" and "high sounding cymbals"
Gong	1 Corinthians 13:1 (NASB)	Mentioned by Paul; used in pagan temples
Harp	Psalm 150:3 (NASB); Revelation 5:8 (NASB)	Usually an instrument of ten strings
Horn	Joshua 6:5 (NLT); Psalm 81:3	Ram's horn (shofar, qeren, yobel) used for signaling
Lyre	Psalm 43:4 (NASB); Isaiah 5:12 (NASB)	Several types, some of them mentioned among Nebuchadnezzar's instruments (Dan. 3)
Pipe	Psalm 150:4 (NASB); Luke 7:32 (KJV)	A reed flute, associated with both rejoicing and mourning
Sistrum	2 Samuel 6:5 (NKJV)	A rattle-like instrument
Tambourine	Exodus 15:20 (NLT); Psalm 68:25 (NASB)	Typically played by women, associated with dance
Trumpet	Numbers 10:8–10 (NASB)	Of silver, used similarly to the ram's horn

❊ THE FAMOUS LAMBETH QUADRILATERAL ❊

The Lambeth Conferences are periodic gatherings of the bishops of all the churches in the worldwide Anglican Communion. They are held at Lambeth Palace, the London residence of the archbishop of Canterbury. The 1888 conference put forth the Anglican view of the essentials for the reunification of the Christian church in four articles known as the *Lambeth Quadrilateral*. They are also called the *Chicago Lambeth Articles*, having originated in the 1886 General Convention of the Protestant Episcopal Church in Chicago.

1. The Holy Scriptures of the Old and New Testaments, "containing all things necessary to salvation," are the ultimate standard of faith.
2. The Apostles' Creed is the baptismal symbol, and the Nicene Creed is the sufficient statement of Christian faith.
3. Baptism and the Lord's Supper, which Christ ordained, are the two sacraments.
4. The office of bishop, adapted to local conditions (the *historic episcopate*), is the focal point for the unity of the church.

❊ THE NICENE CREED ❊

The Nicene Creed, or Niceno-Constantinopolitan Creed, is thought to have been enlarged from the statement of the Council of Nicaea (325) after the Council of Constantinople (381).

> *We believe in one God, the Father, the Almighty, maker of heaven and earth, of all that is, seen and unseen.*
>
> *We believe in one Lord, Jesus Christ, the only Son of God, eternally begotten of the Father, God from God, Light from Light, true God from true God, begotten, not made, of one Being with the Father. Through him all things were made. For us and for our salvation he came down from heaven: by the power of the Holy Spirit he became incarnate from the Virgin Mary, and was made man. For our sake he was crucified under Pontius Pilate; he suffered death and was buried. On the third day he rose again in accordance with the Scriptures; he ascended into heaven and is seated at the right hand of the Father. He will come again in glory to judge the living and the dead, and his kingdom will have no end.*
>
> *We believe in the Holy Spirit, the Lord, the giver of life, who proceeds from the Father and the Son. With the Father and the Son he is worshiped and glorified. He has spoken through the Prophets. We believe in one holy catholic and apostolic Church. We acknowledge one baptism for the forgiveness of sins. We look for the resurrection of the dead, and the life of the world to come. Amen. (*Book of Common Prayer, 1979*)*

❦ WHO REFORMED THE REFORMATION? ❦

Martin Luther's break with Rome may seem a radical enough step, but others in the sixteenth century wanted to go even farther than Luther, Calvin, Zwingli, or the other "standard" Reformers. Today the term *Anabaptist* is generally applied to members of this "radical Reformation." It refers to people who rebaptize because they do not recognize the validity of baptism in the established churches—whether Catholic or Reformed—which they considered corrupt. But the radical reformers were concerned with more than baptism. They had several major beliefs:

1. The church must be restored to its primitive form, with no links to the state.
2. The Scriptures are the supreme authority in matters of faith. Other Reformers believed this, but the radicals applied the principle more consistently.
3. Infant baptism has no basis in Scripture, hence the practice of rebaptizing converts.
4. The Lutheran doctrine of justification by faith alone does not have enough foundation in Scripture; a holy life separated from the corruptions of society is also necessary for salvation.
5. Both church and civil society must be rebuilt according to the principles of the kingdom of God; for some of these reformers, this meant forming communities of shared life and resources similar to the communist ideal.
6. Some communities held a heightened expectation of the imminent return of Christ.

Both the Catholic Church and the major Reformers denounced and persecuted leaders of various groups in this radical reform movement, and as a result many of their followers eventually found their way to North America. Their spiritual descendants today are the Mennonites, Amish, Hutterites, and similar groups, and many of their beliefs have had a lasting influence on the thinking and practice of Baptists, Quakers, and the evangelical churches in general.

❦ JESUS GOES TO HOLLYWOOD: ❦ MOVIES ABOUT THE LIFE OF CHRIST

A few of these films would not be thought consistent with a Christian viewpoint.

The Robe (1953) • *King of Kings* (1927, 1961) • *The Greatest Story Ever Told* (1965)
Jesus Christ Superstar (1973) • *Jesus of Nazareth* (1977) • *Jesus* (1979)
The Last Temptation of Christ (1988) • *The Gospel of John* (2003)
The Passion of the Christ (2004)

❊ WOMEN WHO LED THE ISRAELITES ❊

Miriam—Prophetess, sister of Moses and Aaron. She led a celebration after the Exodus (Exod. 15:20) and later a protest against Moses' authority (Num. 12:1).

Deborah—She was a prophetess who judged Israel (Judg. 4:4).

Jael—She killed the Canaanite general Sisera (Judg. 4:21).

Bathsheba—Wife of David and mother of Solomon. She convinced the aged David to name her son his successor in place of the expected Adonijah (1 Kings 1:15–18).

Athaliah—Queen of Judah. She ruled as a usurper between the death of her son Ahaziah and the coronation of the boy Joash (2 Kings 11:1–3).

Huldah—Prophetess. She encouraged King Josiah to reform worship according to the rediscovered Book of the Law (2 Kings 22:14–20).

Esther—Queen of Persia. She convinced King Ahasuerus to let the Jews protect themselves and established the customs of Purim (Esther 9:25–32).

Judith—Widow of Bethulia. She killed the invading general Holofernes and encouraged the Jews to throw off his army.

The Queen Mother—Bathsheba and Athaliah. She seems to have played an important role in the life of Judah. The Bible often gives the names of the mothers of the kings, and the king mentions the Queen Mother (in the phrase "son of thy handmaid" in Pss. 86 and 116). Catholic theologians sometimes justify the veneration of the Virgin Mary, mother of Jesus Christ, on the basis of the Queen Mother's role.

❊ BALD AND FAT MEN OF THE BIBLE ❊

Eglon, king of Moab, was "a very fat man" (Judg. 3:17). Eli, the priest, was "an old man, and heavy" (1 Sam. 4:18).

Elisha was called "baldhead" by some boys (2 Kings 2:23). Perhaps, as a prophet, he was tonsured like a monk and the boys were actually belittling him as a man of God. (After they finished taunting Elisha, the boys were mauled by two bears.)

Paul

Paul, the apostle, may have been bald. The apocryphal Acts of Paul describes him as "a man little of stature, thin-haired upon the head, crooked in the legs, of good state of body, with eyebrows joining, and nose somewhat hooked."

❧ BIBLE MONEY IN TODAY'S DOLLARS ❧

In the Old Testament, the *shekel* is a unit of weight in silver. Thus people could use it for money. At recent rates for silver, it would be worth about $2.50 today. Abraham paid Ephron the Hittite 400 shekels of silver for land to bury his wife, Sarah, or $1,000 in current North American value. A *talent* was 3,000 shekels, or about $7,500. A gold talent would be worth $476,400 U.S.

In the New Testament world, both Greek and Roman coins were in use. One mentioned often in the New Testament is the Roman *denarius*. It was one twelve-hour-day's wage for a day laborer (Matt. 20:9–10). Based on current U.S. and Canadian minimum-wage laws, that would be about $72, not counting overtime. But a better comparison would be Palestinians working in Israel, for whom a day's wage is about $19 U.S. The Greek *drachma* was worth about the same as a denarius.

Other New Testament coins can be valued in relation to the denarius, using the Palestinian rate, as follows:

Lepton (mite, Jewish coin) . . . . . Worth about the same as the following but required for a contribution to the temple, which would not accept Greek or Roman coinage because a Gentile ruler's head was stamped on it.

Quadrans (farthing, Roman) . . . ¼₄ denarius, 29 cents. The widow's contribution to the temple treasury (Mark 12:42) was about 58 cents.

Assarius (farthing, Roman) . . . . . ¹⁄₁₆ denarius, $1.19, the price of two sparrows (Matt. 10:29).

Stater (Greek) . . . . 4 denarii, $76, the tax Peter was to pay for Jesus and himself (Matt. 17:27).

❧ THE ORIGINS OF EASTER ❧

Easter is the oldest festival of the Christian church, perhaps going back to the second century. Its origin as a feast is found in the Jewish Passover, since Jesus' resurrection took place in connection with the Passover celebration.

The early medieval church was marked by the *Paschal controversies*, bitter disputes over how to determine the date of the Easter celebration. In the Western church Easter can fall anywhere from March 21 through April 25, depending on the date of the Paschal full moon.

The link between Easter and Passover has been important in Christian theology and worship. As Passover celebrates the exodus of the Israelites from Egyptian slavery, Easter celebrates the new "exodus" of Christ and his own from sin and death to new life.

❦ ENGLISH BIBLE TRANSLATIONS, POPULAR, ❦ HISTORIC, AND OBSCURE

These are some of the historic or widely used translations of the complete Bible, out of the approximately five hundred translations of the Old and New Testaments that have been produced. Several important Jewish translations that include only the Hebrew Scriptures are not included, nor are New Testament–only versions.

1380s . . . . John Wycliffe—Completed by John Purvey

1525 . . . . William Tyndale—First printed English Bible

1560 . . . . Geneva Bible—First English Bible with numbered verses

1610 . . . . Douay-Rheims Bible—Catholic, from Latin

1611 . . . . Authorized Version (King James)

1881 . . . . Revised Version—England

1901 . . . . American Standard Version

1926 . . . . The Bible: A New Translation by James Moffatt, England

1952 . . . . Revised Standard Version

1955 . . . . The Holy Bible: A Translation from the Latin Vulgate—
Catholic, by Ronald Knox

1960 . . . . Confraternity Edition—Catholic, from Latin

1961 . . . . New English Bible

1965 . . . . The Amplified Bible

1966 . . . . Jerusalem Bible—Catholic

1970 . . New American Bible—first Catholic English Bible from the original languages

1971 . . . . New American Standard Bible

1971 . . . . The Living Bible—paraphrase by Kenneth Taylor

1976 . . . . Today's English Version (Good News)—by Robert Bratcher

1978 . . . . New International Version

1982 . . . . New King James Version

1985 . . . . New Jerusalem Bible—Catholic

1986 . . . . International Children's Bible

1987 . . . . New Century Version

1990 . . . . New Revised Standard Version

1992 . . . . Revised English Bible—revision of New English Bible

1996 . . . . . . Contemporary English Version—revision of Today's English Version

1996 . . . . New Living Translation

2002 . . . . English Standard Version—revision of Revised Standard Version

❧ ENGLISH BIBLE TRANSLATIONS, POPULAR, ❧ HISTORIC, AND OBSCURE—CONT.

Some Unusual Translations

1808 .... The Holy Bible, Containing the Old and
New Covenant—first English translation of the
Septuagint (Greek Old Testament), by Charles Thomson,
secretary of the Continental Congress

1867 .... The Holy Scriptures, Translated and Corrected by
the Spirit of Revelation—adaptation of King James
Version by Joseph Smith, with Mormon emendations;
published after his death

1903 .... The Holy Bible in Modern English—
by Ferrar Fenton, a businessman and amateur translator

1957 .... The Holy Bible from Ancient Eastern
Manuscripts—by George M. Lamsa, based on Syriac Peshitta version

1960 .... New World Translation—Jehovah's Witnesses

❧ THE LITURGICAL COLOR SCHEME ❧

Many churches change the color of altar and pulpit hangings (sometimes called *ante-pendia*) or clergy garb (stoles and other vestments) depending on the seasons and days of the liturgical calendar. The following is a typical scheme for Western churches.

Advent	Violet or Blue (sometimes Rose for the third Sunday, called *Gaudete*)
Christmas	White
Epiphany Day	White
Epiphany Season	Green
Palm Sunday and Holy Week	Red
Good Friday, Holy Saturday	Black, or altar is bare
Easter and Ascension	White
Pentecost	Red
Pentecost Season	Green*
Trinity Sunday	White
All Saints' Day	White
Christ the King	White

*Green, the "neutral color," is typically used during "ordinary time," the period between Pentecost and Advent.

✳ BAPTIST GROUPS IN NORTH AMERICA ✳

Fifty-one Baptist fellowships or associations are organized in the United States and Canada.

Alliance of Baptists

American Baptist Association

American Baptist Churches in the USA

Association of Reformed Baptist Churches of America

Association of Regular Baptist Churches (Canada)

Baptist Bible Fellowship International

Baptist General Conference

Baptist General Conference of Canada

Canadian Baptist Ministries

Canadian Convention of Southern Baptists

Central Baptist Association

Conservative Baptist Association of America

Continental Baptist Churches

Convention of Atlantic Baptist Churches

Cooperative Baptist Fellowship

Evangelical Free Baptist Church

Fellowship of Evangelical Baptist Churches in Canada

Full Gospel Baptist Church Fellowship

Fundamental Baptist Fellowship Association

Fundamental Baptist Fellowship of America

General Association of Baptists (Duck River Baptists)

General Association of General Baptists

Global Independent Baptist Fellowship

Independent Baptist Fellowship of North America

Independent Baptist Network

Institutional Missionary Baptist Conference of America

L'Association des Églises Missionnaire Baptiste Landmark du Québec

Liberty Baptist Fellowship

National Association of Free Will Baptist Churches

National Baptist Convention of America, Inc.

National Missionary Baptist Convention of America

New England Evangelical Baptist Fellowship

New Testament Association of Independent Baptist Churches

North American Baptist Conference

Original Free Will Baptist Convention

Primitive Baptist Church

Progressive National Baptist Church

Separate Baptists in Christ

Southern Baptist Convention

Seventh Day Baptist General Conference

Sovereign Grace Landmark Independent Baptist Churches

Two-Seed-in-the-Spirit Predestinarian Baptists

Ukranian Evangelical Baptist Convention of Canada

United American Free Will Baptist Church

United American Free Will Baptist Conference

World Baptist Fellowship

❊ HEBREW-ARAMAIC WORDS WE STILL USE TODAY ❊

Some words used in English are derived from Hebrew, the language of most of the Old Testament, and its sister language, Aramaic, which the Jews spoke during the New Testament period. A few proper names also seem to be derived from Hebrew. This list includes some terms in addition to the more obviously theological words, such as *amen, hallelujah, messiah, Pharisee, rabbi,* and *Satan.*

abbey, abbot .... An abbey is a monastic community governed by an abbot, from *abba*, "father."

alphabet .... From *aleph* and *beth*, the first two letters of the Hebrew alphabet

behemoth .... A large creature (Job 40:15), perhaps the origin of the name of the Bahamas

cabal .... An intrigue, from *qabbalah*, "secret lore"

cherub .... A small angel, and by extension a pleasant little child, from paintings by Michelangelo; but originally the cherubim were the much more fearsome guardian figures with the ark of the covenant

Europe .... From *erev*, "evening." Europe was the land of the setting sun for the ancient Hebrews and Phoenicians.

gauze .... From the city of Gaza

hosanna .... An exclamation of joy, from the cry "Save us, we beseech thee" (Ps. 118:25).

jubilee .... A celebration, especially a fifty-year anniversary, from *yobel*, the ram's horn blown to signal the Year of Jubilee (Lev. 25:9)

leviathan .... A large creature or sea monster (Ps. 104:26, et al.)

sabbath, sabbatical ..... The seventh day or a period of rest from normal activity, as in a faculty member's sabbatical year, from the Hebrew *shabbat*, based on the word for the number seven

scallion .... A type of onion, from the city of Ashkelon

seraph .... A member of a traditional order of angels, from the Hebrew plural *seraphim*, "burning ones" (see Isa. 6:2)

shibboleth .... A belief or motto that defines who belongs to one's party or group. The Hebrew word has no relevant meaning but was used in an intra-Israelite feud to filter out men from the other side who could not pronounce it correctly (Judg. 12:5–6).

sodomy .... The practice of homosexual behavior, from the city of Sodom (Gen. 19:4–5)

❧ SUPERSCRIPTIONS IN THE PSALMS ❧

About half of the psalms have introductory notes, or *superscriptions*. These notes may indicate the type of psalm, the collection to which it belongs, instructions for performance (the instruments used and perhaps the name of a tune), an event in the life of David to which the psalm relates, or the name of another who composed the psalm. Here are some of the superscriptions, as given in the Revised Standard Version.

Psalm	Superscription
3	A Psalm of David, when he fled from Absalom his son.
5	To the choirmaster: for the flutes. A Psalm of David.
7	A Shiggaion of David, which he sang to the LORD concerning Cush a Benjaminite.
16	A Miktam of David.
17	A Prayer of David.
18	To the choirmaster. A Psalm of David the servant of the LORD, who addressed the words of this song to the LORD on the day when the LORD delivered him from the hand of all his enemies, and from the hand of Saul. He said:
34	A Psalm of David, when he feigned madness before Abimelech, so that he drove him out, and he went away.
45	To the choirmaster: according to Lilies. A Maskil of the Sons of Korah; a love song.
50	A Psalm of Asaph.
51	To the choirmaster. A Psalm of David, when Nathan the prophet came to him, after he had gone in to Bathsheba.
56	To the choirmaster: according to The Dove on Far-off Terebinths. A Miktam of David, when the Philistines seized him in Gath.
60	To the choirmaster: according to Shushan Eduth. A Miktam of David; for instruction; when he strove with Aram-naharaim and with Aram-zobah, and when Joab on his return killed twelve thousand of Edom in the Valley of Salt.
67	To the choirmaster: with stringed instruments. A Psalm. A Song.
72	A Psalm of Solomon.
75	To the choirmaster: according to Do Not Destroy. A Psalm of Asaph. A Song.
90	A Prayer of Moses, the man of God.
100	A Psalm for the thank offering.
145	A Song of Praise.* Of David.

*The title of the book of Psalms in Hebrew is *tehillim*, "Praises," but only Psalm 145 is called a "praise" in its superscription. The English title "Psalm" is a translation of Hebrew *mizmor*, a piece sung to the accompaniment of a stringed instrument.

❊ CHRISTIANS WHO LIVE IN COMMUNES ❊

The early Christians in Jerusalem "were together and had all things in common" (Acts 2:44). Since apostolic times, groups of Christians have tried communal living. There have been, and still are, communes with a distinctly Christian orientation as well. The following is a partial list.

The Munster commune of the 1530s comprised an entire Dutch city taken over by a radical Anabaptist movement; a Catholic army destroyed it.

The Hutterites of Canada and the northwestern United States form one of the oldest and largest communal systems. They originated as a German-speaking Anabaptist group in central Europe, and after moving to Russia, emigrated to America in the late 1800s.

Herrnhut was the Moravian-Pietist commune Count Nikolaus Zinzendorf established and led in Saxony in 1927. The Moravians were influential in the life of John Wesley.

The Shakers, or United Society of Believers in Christ's Second Coming, were founded in England by Mother Ann Lee in 1758. Their nickname came from their enthusiastic movements, or dancing, during worship. They spread to the American colonies and became famous for their handcrafts. They were celibate, and only a handful remain in a Maine community.

The Harmony Society, or Rappites, was a German pietist group of the 1800s in Pennsylvania and Indiana. The community was known for the quality of its textile and other manufacturing. Partly due to the practice of celibacy, it declined and disbanded in 1905.

Bethany Fellowship, an evangelical community in the Minneapolis area, was founded in 1945. It trains and supports missionaries and recently sold its Christian publishing house.

Jesus People USA is a communal group in Chicago famous for its association with the former Rez Band (the Resurrection Band, which was formed by Glen Kaiser in 1971). The community has become a member congregation of the Evangelical Covenant Church.

Reba Place Fellowship is a community in Evanston, Illinois, associated with Reba Place Church, a member of the Illinois Mennonite Conference.

❊ ARAMAIC PASSAGES OF THE BIBLE ❊

Many Christians know the Old Testament was written in Hebrew and the New Testament in Greek. What is not so well known is that a few parts of the canonical Old Testament are written in Aramaic, a language the Jews spoke after the Babylonian exile. It is also called *Chaldee*, after Chaldea, an old name for Babylonia. The Bible passages in Aramaic are Ezra 4:8–6:18; Ezra 7:12–26; and Daniel 2:4–7:28.

❋ STATIONS OF THE CROSS ❋

One aspect of Christian worship is to reenact and take part in events of the life of Christ. Outstanding examples of this are the Lord's Supper, "following the Lord in baptism," and processions on Palm Sunday. Worshipers in many Catholic and Anglican churches also pray around the Stations of the Cross during Lent or Holy Week, passing by a series of carvings or icons (pictures) depicting Jesus' journey toward the tomb. A few of the events, such as the appearance of Veronica, are legendary. The "stations" are often arranged around the outer walls of the church's worship space.

Pilate condemns Jesus to death	Jesus tells the women of Jerusalem not to weep for him.
Jesus receives his cross	Jesus falls a third time.
Jesus falls under the cross	Jesus is stripped of his clothing.
Jesus meets his mother	Jesus is nailed to the cross.
Simon of Cyrene takes up the cross	Jesus dies on the cross.
Veronica wipes the face of Jesus	Jesus' body is taken down from the cross.
Jesus falls a second time	Jesus' body is placed in the tomb.

❋ SOME CHRISTIAN "OLATRIES" ❋

The suffix -olatry is derived from the Greek verb latreuo, meaning "I worship." Any kind of false worship might be labeled an "olatry."

Angelolatry	Veneration of angels
Bibliolatry	Bible worship; making a particular interpretation of the Bible more important than Jesus Christ as a criterion of faith
Ecclesiolatry	Obsession with church traditions in the place of devotion to Christ
Hagiolatry	Worship of saints
Hierolatry	Worship of saints or sacred things
Idolatry	Worship of idols; any excessive preoccupation with values other than God
Mariolatry	Veneration of the Virgin Mary to the point of worship, or substituting her for Jesus

❀ BIRDS HAVE NESTS, ❀ FOXES HAVE DENS, CLERGY HAVE . . .

Many Protestant churches do not maintain homes for their clergy, preferring to include a housing allowance as part of their compensation. Others, however, still provide such housing. Catholic priests, having taken a vow of poverty, own little property and must live in what the church provides. Some of the terms used for clergy housing:

Parsonage—Many Protestant churches
Rectory—Catholic, Episcopal, Church of England
Manse—Presbyterian, Lutheran
Vicarage—Church of England
Episcopal Residence—Methodist bishops
Palace—Old term for the residence of an Anglican or Catholic bishop, one still used for Lambeth Palace, the London residence of the archbishop of Canterbury

❀ COUNTRIES WITH THE MOST ANGLICANS ❀

The Church of England is the established church in England, claiming between 27 and 33 million adherents. However, only around 9 million have been confirmed, and the number of those regularly receiving Holy Communion on Easter Sunday is estimated at between 1,700,000 and 2,800,000. Out of 70 million nominal Anglicans in the world, more than half (53 percent) live in the developing world, 35 million of them in Africa alone. The most Anglican country in the world is Nigeria, whose 17.5 million adherents make up 14 percent of the total population. There are 8 million Anglicans in Uganda. The Episcopal Church in the USA, the largest Anglican body in North America, is about 14 percent of the size of the Church of Nigeria and less than 1 percent of the total population of the United States.

❀ MOST POPULAR NAMES FOR THE POPE ❀

John	24*	Pius	12
Gregory	16	Stephen	10
Benedict	15	Boniface	9
Clement	14	Alexander	8
Innocent	13	Urban	8
Leo	13		

*There were two popes John XXIII. The first is considered an "antipope" and is normally not counted. Other splinter group antipopes have taken some of these names.

❋ TYPES OF CHRISTIAN CHORAL MUSIC ❋

Anthem . . . . In the broad sense, a choral piece with religious lyrics usually sung only by a choir

Antiphon . . . . A piece sung responsively by two different groups, or the response in such a piece (see *Verse*)

Cantata . . . . A composition of choral or solo "numbers" usually based on one seasonal theme or the lessons appointed for a certain day of the church year

Chant . . . . A nonmeasured* setting of a biblical or liturgical text, usually sung in unison and unaccompanied

Chorale . . . . A hymn usually sung in a slower, statelier manner

Gospel Song . . . . A measured* song with stanzas, sung by a congregation; it differs from the hymn in focusing on the singer's faith rather than God, the object of faith

Hymn . . . . The term commonly applied to any measured song, with stanzas, sung by a congregation

Mass . . . . A setting of the Catholic Mass (those portions not said by the priest nor varying with the calendar)

Motet . . . . Similar to an anthem but usually with many interweaving parts and unaccompanied

Oratorio . . . . A composition of both choral and solo "numbers," more extended than a cantata and usually based on a biblical theme, character, or story

Psalm . . . . There are several forms of psalm singing; see separate entry.

Refrain . . . . A portion of a song repeated after each stanza; also called *chorus*

Requiem . . . . A composition commemorating the dead, usually a setting of the Requiem Mass

Stanza . . . . That part of a song repeated with the same music but different words; often erroneously called *verse*

Verse . . . . The part of a responsive song that varies each time, while the antiphon remains the same; also applied to stanza

Worship Chorus . . . . A song sung by the congregation in a more "contemporary" style than the traditional hymn or gospel song; also called *praise chorus*

Measured means having a regular beat and bar lines.

❦ THE ATHANASIAN CREED ❦

The Athanasian Creed, or *Quicunque Vult*, from its opening words in Latin, is traditionally ascribed to Athanasius (296–373) but is of a later time. It is seldom used in worship today.

Whosoever will be saved, before all things it is necessary that he hold the catholic faith; which faith except every one do keep whole and undefiled, without doubt he shall perish everlastingly. And the catholic faith is this: That we worship one God in Trinity, and Trinity in Unity; neither confounding the persons nor dividing the substance. For there is one person of the Father, another of the Son, and another of the Holy Spirit. But the Godhead of the Father, of the Son, and of the Holy Spirit is all one, the glory equal, the majesty coeternal. Such as the Father is, such is the Son, and such is the Holy Spirit. The Father uncreated, the Son uncreated, and the Holy Spirit uncreated. The Father incomprehensible, the Son incomprehensible, and the Holy Spirit incomprehensible. The Father eternal, the Son eternal, and the Holy Spirit eternal. And yet they are not three eternals but one eternal. As also there are not three uncreated nor three incomprehensible, but one uncreated and one incomprehensible.

So likewise the Father is almighty, the Son almighty, and the Holy Spirit almighty. And yet they are not three almighties, but one almighty. So the Father is God, the Son is God, and the Holy Spirit is God; and yet they are not three Gods, but one God. So likewise the Father is Lord, the Son Lord, and the Holy Spirit Lord; and yet they are not three Lords but one Lord. For like as we are compelled by the Christian verity to acknowledge every Person by himself to be God and Lord; so are we forbidden by the catholic religion to say; There are three Gods or three Lords.

The Father is made of none, neither created nor begotten. The Son is of the Father alone; not made nor created, but begotten. The Holy Spirit is of the Father and of the Son; neither made, nor created, nor begotten, but proceeding. So there is one Father, not three Fathers; one Son, not three Sons; one Holy Spirit, not three Holy Spirits. And in this Trinity none is afore or after another; none is greater or less than another. But the whole three persons are coeternal, and coequal. So that in all things, as aforesaid, the Unity in Trinity and the Trinity in Unity is to be worshipped. He therefore that will be saved must thus think of the Trinity.

Furthermore it is necessary to everlasting salvation that he also believe rightly the incarnation of our Lord Jesus Christ. For the right faith is that we believe and confess that our Lord Jesus Christ, the Son of God, is God and man. God of the substance of the Father, begotten before the worlds; and man of substance of His mother, born in the world. Perfect God and perfect man, of a reasonable soul and human flesh subsisting. Equal to the Father as touching His Godhead, and inferior to the Father as touching His manhood. Who, although He is God and man, yet

❆ THE ATHANASIAN CREED—CONT. ❆

He is not two, but one Christ. One, not by conversion of the Godhead into flesh, but by taking of that manhood into God. One altogether, not by confusion of substance, but by unity of person.

For as the reasonable soul and flesh is one man, so God and man is one Christ; who suffered for our salvation, descended into hell, rose again the third day from the dead; He ascended into heaven, He sits on the right hand of the Father, God, Almighty; from thence He shall come to judge the quick and the dead. At whose coming all men shall rise again with their bodies; and shall give account of their own works. And they that have done good shall go into life everlasting and they that have done evil into everlasting fire. This is the catholic faith, which except a man believe faithfully he cannot be saved.

❆ CLIMBING THE CHURCH LADDER: ❆ LEVELS OF HOLY ORDERS

In addition to the roles of apostle, evangelist, prophet, and pastor-teacher, the New Testament mentions deacons ("servers"), presbyters ("elders"), and bishops ("overseers") as functionaries in the church. Various Christian groups handle these distinctions in different ways. This is a sketch.

In many evangelical churches, those designated as deacons and elders are laypeople. Pastors are elders, too, but are not usually so called.

In some churches, elders can be either lay or clergy. Presbyterians have both "ruling elders" (lay) and "teaching elders" (clergy, now often called *ministers of word and sacrament*). The "Christian" churches and some others have "preaching elder" as their ministerial title.

In Methodist churches, people are ordained deacons as a steppingstone toward full ordination as an elder. A bishop is an elder who has been *consecrated* (not *ordained*) to preside over an area or conference.

In Anglican, Catholic, or Orthodox churches, the deaconate (deacons) and priesthood are levels of Holy Orders for the ministry. (The term *priest* is derived from *presbyter*.) Bishops are a third order of ordination; Catholic and Orthodox theology holds that the fullness of the church resides in the office of the bishop. In these churches are also permanent deacons who perform certain roles in the church and are not on a path toward the priesthood.

In virtually all Christian groups, ordination to the offices of deacon, elder (priest), or bishop is done through the laying on of hands and prayer according to the model of Acts 13:3. The Catholic church formerly recognized several "minor orders" of subdeacon, acolyte, exorcist, reader, and doorkeeper, but they are now suppressed as orders and laypersons usually perform their remaining functions.

❦ AFRICANS IN THE BIBLE ❦

Moses' wife, a Cushite . . . Num. 12:1 . . . . . . Cush was the region south of Egypt (modern Sudan and Ethiopia), but there was a Cush in Asia as well. Moses' wife, Zipporah, was a Midianite, so either the Cushite wife was a second wife or Cush was another name for Midian, not in Africa.

The Queen of Sheba . . . . 1 Kings 10:1–5 . . . Sheba, who was highly impressed with Solomon, was traditionally equated with Ethiopia, but modern authorities locate it in the southern part of the Arabian Peninsula near modern Yemen.

The Ethiopians . . . . Amos 9:7 . . . . In this passage, Amos quoted God: "'Are you not like the Ethiopians to me, / O people of Israel?' says the LORD. / 'Did I not bring up Israel from the land of Egypt, / and the Philistines from Caphtor / and the Syrians from Kir?'" His point was that the Lord is involved in the affairs of other peoples, including those from Africa.

Simon of Cyrene . . . . Mark 15:21 . . . . . Simon carried Jesus' cross. Cyrene was modern Libya; people from Cyrene were also present on the Day of Pentecost (Acts 2:10).

The Ethiopian eunuch . . Acts 8:27 . . . . According to this verse, the eunuch was "a minister of Candace, queen of the Ethiopians." Unless he was a proselyte like Nicolaus of Antioch, one of the first deacons (Acts 6:5), this official is the first non-Jewish convert to Christianity mentioned after the Resurrection.

Simeon called Niger . . . . Acts 13:1 . . . . Simeon was a prophet in Antioch. *Niger* means "black" (from Latin, but in the Greek text), but whether this Simeon was a black African or simply a dark-skinned Mediterranean is impossible to tell.

❧ TITLES OF CHURCH WORKERS ❧
WHO AREN'T PASTORS OR PRIESTS

Everyone is familiar with clergy titles, such as *minister*, *pastor*, or *priest*, or a number of others. The titles of *elder* and *deacon* are used for both clergy and laypeople. Here are some titles for *nonclergy* functionaries in the church.

Acolyte . . . . Person, often young, who lights the altar candles and serves at the altar in other ways

Altar boy (girl) . . . . A young person who assists the presiding clergy with the vessels of Holy Communion or performs other altar duties

Beadle . . . . Official appointed to care for the place of worship; in some early New England churches, the beadle carried a pole with which to awaken dozing worshipers

Cantor . . . . Singer who leads a responsorial psalm or other music

Chorister . . . . Member of a choir

Clerk . . . . Person assigned to record actions by a church board (vestry, session) or to record baptisms and marriages. The word *clerk* is derived from *cleric*, as is the word *clergy*.

Crucifer . . . . Person who carries the cross in a procession

Lector . . . . A person who reads a Scripture lesson; also simply called Reader

Minister . . . . When used of laypeople, it often refers to liturgical assistants such as Communion ministers, prayer ministers, or ministers of music.

Precentor . . . . Person appointed to lead singing

Sexton . . . . Originally, the official responsible for maintaining church property, including vestments, books, and sacramental vessels, or placed in charge of the church cemetery or ringing the church bell; now sometimes another term for the janitor. The word comes from the Latin *sacrista*.

Steward . . . . A term formerly applied to members of the board of a Methodist church

Superintendent . . . . Term often applied to the head of a Sunday school and, of course, used for many other types of church officials

Torchbearer . . . . Person, often young, who carries candles in a procession

Trustee . . . . Member of the board responsible for making decisions about church property. In some cases, the trustees are the legal owners of the property.

❦ TITLES OF CHURCH WORKERS ❦
WHO AREN'T PASTORS OR PRIESTS—CONT.

Usher . . . . Person responsible for seating worshipers, distributing materials, or collecting the offering

Verger . . . . Official assigned to keep order in a service, or to lead a procession or reader to the proper place; carries a baton called a *verge* (you saw them in the National Cathedral during President Reagan's funeral)

❦ COMPARATIVE HEIGHT OF BIBLICAL MOUNTAINS ❦

Mount Ararat . . . . 16,900 (in modern Turkey)		Mount Zion 2,533	
Mount Lebanon 10,000		Mount Nebo* 2,500	
Mount Hermon 9,230		Mount Moriah 2,430	
Mount Sinai (*Jabal Musa*) 7,500		Mount Tabor 1,930	
Mount Ebal 3,080		Mount Carmel 1,700	
Mount Gerizim 2,850		Mount Gilboa 1,700	
Mount of Olives 2,690		Mount of Jesus' Temptation . . . 1,148	

Elevations are approximate feet above sea level.

*Mount Nebo rises 3,850 feet above the surface of the Dead Sea, which is 1,350 feet below sea level.

❦ RELIGION AND VOTING ❦

A survey following the 2000 presidential election in the United States revealed a link between politics and participation in religious organizations. Almost two-thirds of voters who attended religious services at least once a week voted for the Republican candidate, while two-thirds of those who seldom attend church services voted for the Democratic ticket. The survey did not identify the religious groups, but it would seem that voters in conservative or evangelical groups would be more likely to be frequent church attendees, while those in more mainline or "liberal" groups might be, on the average, less active.

❋ SOME PRESIDENTS OF THE ❋ NATIONAL ASSOCIATION OF EVANGELICALS

1942–44 . . . . Harold J. Ockenga (Presbyterian)

1946–48 . . . . Rutherford L. Decker (Southern Baptist)

1948–50 . . . . Stephen W. Paine (Wesleyan Methodist)

1958–60 . . . . Herbert S. Mekeel (Presbyterian USA)

1962–64 . . . . Robert A. Cook (Evangelical Free)

1968–70 . . . . Arnold Oldon (Evangelical Free)

1978–80 . . . . Carl H. Lundquist (Baptist General Conference)

1982–84 . . . . Arthur E. Gay Jr. (Conservative Congregational)

1984–86 . . . . Robert W. McIntyre (Wesleyan)

1988–90 . . . . John H. White (Reformed Presbyterian)

1990–92 . . . . B. Edgar Johnson (Nazarene)

1992–95 . . . . David Rambo (Christian and Missionary Alliance)

1995–98 . . . . Don Argue (Assemblies of God)

1999–2001 . . . . Kevin Mannoia (Free Methodist)

2002–03 . . . . Leith Anderson, Interim (Baptist General Conference)

Current . . . . Ted Haggard (Southern Baptist/Nondenominational)

❋ TYPES OF CHURCH GOVERNMENT ❋

Who decides the major (and minor) issues affecting the life of a church? Christians have struggled over this question as much as over any theological issue. Advocates for four historic forms of church government have all claimed the New Testament church's practice as the basis for their views:

1. Episcopal—Responsibility for the church rests with a bishop (Greek *episkopos*, "overseer") within a particular region. Examples: Roman Catholic, Greek Orthodox, Anglican/Episcopal.

2. Presbyterial—The local church receives direction from a body of presbyters (from Greek for "elders") from its sister churches. Examples: Presbyterian, United Methodist, Lutheran.

3. Congregational—The local church governs itself, ultimately through a congregational meeting. Examples: Baptist, Congregational, Churches of Christ ("Christian").

4. Monarchical—Decisions are made by the local pastor. Examples: many Pentecostal churches.

❀ CHRISTIAN SYMBOLS ❀

Hand of God
God the Father

Triumphant Lamb
Victorious Christ

Descending Dove
Holy Spirit

Trefoil
The Holy Trinity

Celtic Cross

Ship
The Church

Purse and Coins
Jesus' Betrayal by Judas

Chalice and Wafer
The Eucharist

Alpha-Omega
Monogram
Jesus, the Beginning
and the End

Chi Rho
First Two Letters of
"Christ" in Greek

Cross and Globe
(Orb)
Christ's Worldwide
Dominion

Latin Cross

Greek Cross

Jerusalem Cross

Russian or
Eastern Cross

Maltese Cross

❧ THE ROSARY ❧

The rosary is a series of prayers developed during the Middle Ages that Catholics use to venerate the Virgin Mary and seek her help.

The rosary beads form a circle with an extension ending in a crucifix. The circle is divided into five decades (groups of ten), each marked off by a larger or more separated bead, and the extension has five beads—two large or separated, with three others between them. The entire rosary, when recited, consists of twenty decades, or four circles, of the beads. Each circle of recitation contemplates five "mysteries" of Christ and the Virgin Mary. Traditionally there were three groups of mysteries: the Joyful, the Sorrowful, and the Glorious. Pope John Paul II added the Luminous Mysteries in 2002. As an example, the five Glorious Mysteries are the resurrection of Jesus, his ascension, the descent of the Holy Spirit, Mary's assumption into heaven, and her coronation as Queen of Heaven and Earth.

A standard procedure for praying the rosary:

1. Holding the crucifix, make the sign of the cross, and recite the Apostles' Creed.
2. Pray the "Our Father" (Lord's Prayer) on the first large bead.
3. Say a "Hail Mary" for an increase of faith, hope, and charity on each of the next three beads: "Hail Mary, full of grace; the Lord is with thee: blessed art thou among women, and blessed is the fruit of thy womb, Jesus. Holy Mary, Mother of God, pray for us sinners, now and at the hour of our death. Amen."
4. Recite the Gloria Patri on the next large bead: "Glory be to the Father, and to the Son, and to the Holy Ghost. As it was in the beginning, is now, and ever shall be, world without end. Amen."
5. Say the "Fatima Prayer": "My Jesus, forgive us our sins, save us from the fires of hell, and lead all souls to heaven, especially those in most need of thy mercy."
6. Contemplate the first Mystery (a mystery about Christ or the Virgin Mary, e.g., the resurrection of Jesus) in the first group, and pray the Our Father on the large bead.
7. On each of the next ten small beads ("decade"), recite a Hail Mary while reflecting on the Mystery.
8. On the next large bead, recite the Gloria Patri and the Fatima Prayer.
9. Continue in the same manner with the other four Mysteries on the following decades, until the circuit is complete.

❋ COMPARING THE THREE JEWISH ❋ TEMPLES OF THE BIBLE

The Israelite-Jewish sanctuary on Mount Zion in Jerusalem is commonly called the *temple*, but the Old Testament usually calls it the "house of the Lord" (Hebrew *bet-Yahweh*) or "house of God" (*bet-'Elohim*). It was built three times.

Solomon's Temple

The temple of Solomon was completed around 960 BC. The architect, Hiram, was a Phoenician, and the temple in many ways resembled sanctuaries outside Israel. First Kings 5–8 describe its construction and dedication. During David's reign the sanctuary (the tabernacle or tent) had been in Gibeon. Nebuchadnezzar, king of Babylon, destroyed Jerusalem and its temple in 587 BC.

The "Second Temple"

The book of Ezra records events surrounding the rebuilding of the temple. The community of returned exiles from Babylon, apparently led by the prince Zerubbabel, completed it around 515 BC. Little is known about this temple, but it stood for almost five hundred years, longer than either of the other two.

Herod's Temple

Herod (called "the Great") was an Idumean, whose people had been forcibly converted to Judaism. In 37 BC he managed to get himself appointed ruler of Judea by the Romans, who controlled the area. He was unpopular with his subjects and began the rebuilding of the temple in part to win their favor. It was a far more magnificent structure than the first two temples, and it took more than eighty years to complete. Construction began around 20 BC and was going on during the ministry of Jesus, who foretold its end (Mark 13:1–2). Shortly after its completion in AD 63, Herod's temple was destroyed in the Jewish revolt of AD 66–70.

Reconstruction of Herod's Temple

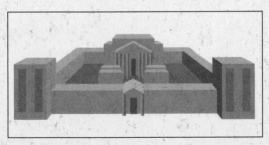

❊ BISHOPS AND THEIR JURISDICTIONS ❊

The word *bishop* comes from the Greek *episkopos*, which means "overseer" or "superintendent." In the New Testament it seems to refer to the man who had chief oversight for the church in a certain location. Today various Christian or historically related groups use the term *bishop* in different ways. This list indicates some of the typical jurisdictions, or areas of responsibility, bishops hold in several major groups in North America.

Group	Jurisdiction	Comments
African Methodist Episcopal	Episcopal District	
African Methodist, Episcopal Zion	Episcopal District	
Anglican (various groups including "continuing"* and missionary churches)	Diocese	Missionary bishops may work where a diocese has not yet been organized, as in the Anglican Mission in America.
Charismatic Episcopal Church	Diocese	Never part of Episcopal Church; new group formed in 1992
Christian Methodist Episcopal Church	Episcopal District	Predominantly African-American group
Church of Jesus Christ of Latter Day Saints (Mormon)	Ward	A ward is a local Mormon congregation.
Episcopal Church in the United States of America	Diocese	
Evangelical Lutheran Church in America	Synod (regional)	
Missionary Baptist	Local Church	An African-American group
Pentecostal/ Charismatic churches (various)	Local Church	African-American congregations are more likely to call their pastors "Bishop," but the practice exists among other groups also.
Reformed Episcopal Church	Diocese	Established in 1873
Roman Catholic Church	Diocese	In the U.S. the diocese is incorporated as the bishop. The man holding the office legally owns all

✵ BISHOPS AND THEIR JURISDICTIONS—CONT. ✵

Group	Jurisdiction	Comments
		church properties within his diocese except those belonging to religious orders or other nondiocesan Catholic organizations.
United Methodist Church	Area	An area consists of one or more regional Annual Conferences.

*A "continuing" Anglican church is a body that has formed to continue established worship practices and doctrinal standards modified by the Episcopal Church in the United States or the Anglican Church of Canada.

✵ WHY THE HUGUENOT DID FRANCE ✵ NEVER BECOME PROTESTANT?

John Calvin (Jean Cauvin), the Protestant Reformer, was French, so why did France never become Protestant? Actually the Reformation spread rapidly through France despite persecution, and many of the nobility became Protestants. They came to be called *Huguenots*, a name of uncertain origin though it may be a corruption of the German term *Eidgenossen*, "confederates." Civil war and assassinations broke out between militant Catholics, Protestants, and a third group that simply wanted political order. The St. Bartholomew's Day massacre of 1572 took the life of the Huguenot leader Admiral Gaspard de Coligny, among others.

After Henry of Navarre, originally a Protestant, became king of France, he issued the Edict of Nantes in 1598, which gave the Huguenots the right to live securely in their fortified towns. Louis XIV (reigned 1643–1715), however, revoked the edict in 1685 and the persecution of Protestants resumed. About three hundred thousand Huguenots made their way to the Netherlands, Switzerland, Germany, England, Ireland, America, and eventually South Africa. In the American colonies they founded French-speaking churches, most of which eventually merged into the Presbyterians after French ceased to be spoken.

After the Enlightenment and the Revolution, religious persecution diminished in France and the spiritual descendants of the Huguenots remain a small, but often influential, community. Maurice Couve de Murville, French foreign minister (1958–1968) was a member of the Reformed Church. The Oratory of the Louvre, across the street from the famed art museum of Paris, is a Reformed "temple" or church; a statue of Admiral Coligny stands in the courtyard. The only French Calvinist congregation in the United States is the Huguenot Church of Charleston, South Carolina; founded in 1687, it has not had an unbroken history but was reestablished in 1983.

❀ LIFESTYLES OF MONKS, ❀ HISTORIC AND CONTEMPORARY

Cenobites . . . . This term refers in general to monks who live in a monastic community, but there are many variations of such life. Some cenobites live similarly to hermits, having solitary cells but within a common building or enclosure. They may observe a rule of silence, such as the famous Trappists, except during the community worship. Other monastic communities follow a less-strict rule.

Cloistered . . . . A cloister is an enclosed area, originally an arcade linking the building of a cathedral complex. Today the term *cloister* refers to the house of a religious order, but the term *cloistered* refers in particular to monastics who never leave their building or compound.

Discalceds . . . . Monastic orders whose members do not wear shoes are called *discalced*, from a Latin word meaning "shoeless." Originally these monks went barefoot (Francis of Assisi is an example), but today they wear sandals.

Hermits . . . . A hermit withdraws to a solitary life, often in a cave and sometimes in a loose community with other hermits. This "eremitic" life was popular among devoted Christians from the third century till the Middle Ages.

Anchorites . . . . These persons withdrew to a solitary life of silence, prayer, and deprivation. Eventually they came to be enclosed in walled-up cells, sometimes attached to churches. Julian of Norwich (1342–1413) was a female anchorite.

Stylites . . . . Simeon Stylites (390–459) lived in solitude on top of a pillar (Greek *stylos*) near Antioch, gradually increasing its height to sixty feet until his death. Other stylites followed his example during the fifth through tenth centuries and afterward.

❀ U.S. CITIES WITH THE MOST ❀ CHRISTIAN ORGANIZATIONS

By telephone directory listings, there are 108 Christian ministries, organizations, and publishers in greater Orlando, Florida; 54 in Colorado Springs, Colorado; and 28 in and around Wheaton or Carol Stream, Illinois. This does not count local churches or Christian educational institutions.

❧ THE CHIEF END OF MAN, ACCORDING ❧ TO THE WESTMINSTER CONFESSION

Question: What is the chief and highest end of man?
Answer: Man's chief and highest end is to glorify God, and fully to enjoy him forever.

A certain Catholic catechism contains a similar statement:

> The desire for God is written in the human heart, because man is created by God and for God; and God never ceases to draw man to himself. Only in God will he find the truth and happiness he never stops searching for.

❧ RAILROAD CHAPEL CARS ❧

Several churches and missionary organizations operated railroad chapel cars in the western United States from 1890 through the 1940s. The cars were pulled by regular passenger or freight trains and set out on sidings along railway lines. By means of these cars, missionaries and priests were able to preach and administer the sacraments in remote or newly settled areas, and they reportedly founded churches in more than three thousand locations.

The Episcopal Church operated three cars. The first was the Cathedral Car of North Dakota Church of the Advent, which the Pullman Company of Chicago built in 1890. The Episcopal Diocese of Northern Michigan operated two additional cars converted from existing railway rolling stock.

Baptist chapel cars traveled throughout the West beginning in 1891. Evangel was the first car the American Baptist Publication Society operated, followed by Emmanuel, Glad Tidings, Good Will, Messenger of Peace, and Herald of Hope. The last Baptist car, Grace, was dedicated in 1915 and is displayed today at Green Lake, Wisconsin. Smith and Barney of Dayton, Ohio, built most of the Baptist cars.

The Catholic Extension Society had three chapel cars: St. Anthony, St. Peter, and St. Paul. The first was dedicated in 1907, a wooden Wagner Palace car reconditioned by the Pullman Company; the other two were steel. The St. Paul apparently served until 1954.

❧ SATAN: REAL OR IMAGINED? ❧

In 1990, 55 percent of the American public believed the devil to be real. Five years later:
70 percent believed in the devil   10 percent weren't sure
19 percent did not believe in the devil   1 percent had no opinion

❋ MOST-REPEATED WORDS IN THE BIBLE ❋

Some words appear quite often in the English Bible. The frequency of their occurrence could suggest some of the Bible's major concerns.

Say, says, said, saying . . . . 6,915 times in 6,446 verses
Come, comes, came, coming . . . . 3,633 times in 3,496 verses
Go, goes, went, gone, going . . . . 3,367 times in 3,120 verses
Give, gives, gave, given, giving . . . . 2,202 times in 2,093 verses
Life, live, lives, lived, living . . . . 1,406 times in 1,254 verses
Word, words . . . . .1,216 times in 1,170 verses
Hear, hears, heard, hearing . . . . 1,199 times in 1,145 verses
Speak, speaks, spoke, spoken, speaking . . . . 994 times in 966 verses
Death, die, dies, died, dying . . . . 975 times in 870 verses
Right, righteous, righteousness . . . . 921 times in 872 verses
Call, calls, called, calling . . . . 840 times in 805 verses
Heart, hearts . . . . 837 times in 783 verses
Sin, sins, sinned, sinning, sinner, sinners . . . . 813 times in 743 verses
Love, loves, loved, loving . . . . 706 times in 642 verses
Kill, kills, killed, killing, slay, slays, slain, slew, slaying . . . . 695 times in 665 verses
Child, children . . . . 621 times in 553 verses
Work, works, worked, working . . . . 585 times in 545 verses
Bless, blesses, blessed, blessing . . . . 500 times in 470 verses
Wife, wives . . . . 493 times in 452 verses
Faith, faithful, faithfulness . . . . 417 times in 397 verses
Glory, glories, glorify, glorified, glorifies . . . . 415 times in 387 verses
Salvation, save, saves, saved, saving . . . . 407 times in 398 verses
Peace, peaceful . . . . 367 times in 338 verses
Pray, prays, prayer, prayed, praying . . . . 303 times in 389 verses
Praise, praises, praised, praising . . . . 284 times in 253 verses
Believe, believes, believed, believing, believer, believers . . . 281 times in 265 verses
Soul, souls . . . . 243 times in 230 verses
Judge, judged, judging . . . . 195 times in 178 verses
Grace, gracious . . . . 181 times in 171 verses
Witness, witnesses . . . . 181 times in 169 verses
Steadfast love or loving-kindness . . . . 177 times in 175 verses
   (Hebrew *hesed*, "covenant love")
Mercy, mercies, merciful . . . . 160 times in 153 verses
Obey, obeys, obeyed, obeying . . . . 141 times in 137 verses
Trust, trusts, trusted, trusting . . . . 112 times in 111 verses

❋ CZAR NICHOLAS II—SAINT AND MARTYR ❋

Russian revolutionaries executed Czar Nicholas II and his family, the Romanovs, in 1918 at Ekaterinburg in Siberia. Following the demise of the Soviet Union, their remains were discovered and were reburied in 1998 in the Tomb of the Czars in St. Petersburg. In 2000, the Russian Orthodox Church declared the czar and his family official saints and martyrs. The declaration called them "people who sincerely sought to live by the commandments of the Gospel" and stated that in their humble endurance of suffering, "the evil-defeating light of the faith of Christ was revealed."

❋ DAYS OF THE WEEK ❋

The days of the week in the English language owe their names to ancient Greek and Roman practice, as carried through the Germanic peoples. The Greeks named the days of the week after the sun, the moon, and the five known planets, which were in turn named after the gods Ares, Hermes, Zeus, Aphrodite, and Cronus. The Romans substituted their equivalent gods for those of the Greeks: Mars, Mercury, Jupiter, Venus, and Saturn. The second through seventh days in Latin-derived languages such as French retain the Roman names: *lundi* (Luna, the moon), *mardi, mercredi, jeudi, vendredi, samedi*. The Germanic peoples substituted similar gods for the Roman ones for these days (except Saturday), resulting in the names of our days:

> Sunday (the sun)
> Monday (the moon)
> Tuesday (Tiu, equivalent to Ares and Mars)
> Wednesday (Woden, equivalent to Hermes and Mercury)
> Thursday (Thor, equivalent to Zeus and Jupiter)
> Friday (Freya, equivalent to Aphrodite and Venus)
> Saturday (Cronus, Saturn)

In the Latin-derived languages, however, Sunday is not named after the sun, but after the Lord (Latin *dominus*), as in Spanish *domingo*, French *dimanche*.

In modern Hebrew the days of the week are simply numbered, as in *yom rishon*, "first day," and so on through *shabbat* (seventh).

❆ FAMOUS PHYSICALLY DISABLED ❆ OR HANDICAPPED CHRISTIANS

This short list does not include people who became disabled as a result of a final illness.

The apostle Paul was harassed by a "thorn in the flesh" (2 Cor. 12:7 KJV). Some interpreters have suggested he had a vision problem, based on Galatians 4:15 and 6:11.

Origen of Alexandria, early Christian theologian, castrated himself.

Teresa of Avila had a severe illness that left her legs paralyzed for three years (she eventually improved).

Fanny Crosby, the hymn writer, was blind from infancy.

Helen Keller (died 1968) became both blind and deaf due to illness at the age of nineteen months.

Harold Wilke (died 2003), a United Church of Christ minister and founder of the National Organization on Disability, was born without arms.

The Ethiopian official whom Philip converted was rendered a eunuch (Acts 8:27).

Peter Abelard, medieval theologian, was castrated by thugs sent by the uncle of his lover, Héloïse.

John Milton, the Puritan writer, was blind for the last twenty-three years of his life.

William Seymour, pioneer of the Pentecostal revival of the early 1900s, was blinded in one eye by smallpox while in his twenties.

Ken Medema, Christian concert artist and music therapist, has been blind from birth.

Joni Eareckson Tada, Christian writer and speaker, became a quadriplegic in a diving accident as a young woman.

❆ THE WESLEY GRACE ❆

John Wesley composed a "grace" to be prayed before meals. It is usually sung to the tune "Old Hundredth," familiar to many Protestants as the doxology.

> Be present at our table, Lord;
> Be here, and everywhere, adored.
> These mercies* bless, and grant that we
> May feast in fellowship* with thee.

*Wesley's original words were "creatures" and "paradise."

❊ FIRST BIBLES OFF THE PRINTING PRESS ❊

Johann Gutenberg (1398–1468) is regarded as the inventor of printing in Europe. Johann Fust and Peter Schoeffer took over Gutenberg's printing operation in Mainz, Germany, in 1455; the following year, they published the Gutenberg Bible as their first printed book.

The next three Bibles published were the 1462 Bible printed in Mainz by Fust and Schoeffer, on vellum with illustrations (forty-nine copies are known); the 36-Line Bible, so called because it has thirty-six lines per page, printed in Bamberg in or before 1460 (only fourteen copies remain); and the Mentelin Bible, printed in Strasbourg in 1460 (twenty-seven copies survive). All of these first Bibles were printed in Latin.

The first Bible printed in English was William Tyndale's translation of the New Testament, printed in Germany in 1525. Possessing it was punishable by death in England, and only two copies of its first printing are known to have survived. Building on Tyndale's work, Miles Coverdale printed the first complete Bible in English in 1535, partly based on Luther's German Bible.

John Rogers printed Matthew's Bible, probably in the Netherlands, in 1537. It was an edition of the work of Tyndale and Coverdale and was the first English Bible authorized in England, though not for use in churches. Henry VIII and archbishop Thomas Cranmer authorized the Great Bible for church use; first published in 1539, it was essentially a revision of Matthew's Bible and was reprinted seven times.

The first complete English Bible translated entirely from the original languages was the Geneva Bible of 1560, which set a standard for scholarship and was reprinted as late as 1644. Though used in Scotland, it was not acceptable to English authorities because of its notes and comments, and the Bishop's Bible of 1568 was printed as a substitute. Finally the Authorized Version of 1611, known as the King James, superseded all previous English Bibles in Protestant usage.

The first Bible printed in the American colonies was in the Algonquin language; translated by the missionary John Eliot, it was printed in 1663. The first English Bible printed in America was a 1782 edition of the Authorized Version printed in Philadelphia by Robert Aitken.

❊ TEN WORDS OR PHRASES ❊
NOT FOUND IN THE BIBLE

This may surprise some folks, but these words and phrases just can't be found in the Bible.

Accepting Christ • Glossolalia (a term for speaking in
tongues) • Personal Savior • Going to heaven • Inerrancy • Infallibility •
Second Coming • Eternal security • Theology • Trinity

❀ SAINTS NAMED CATHERINE ❀

Name	Lived	Original Name	Nationality	Canonized
Catherine of Alexandria	d. 305		Alexandria (Egypt)	Legendary
Catherine of Siena	1347–1380	Catherine di Benincasa	Italy	1461
Catherine of Sweden (Catherine Vastanensis)	1331–1381	Catherine Gudmarsson	Sweden	1484
Catherine of Bologna	1413–1463	Catherine de' Vigri	Italy	1712
Catherine of Genoa	1447–1510	Caterina Fieschi Adorno	Italy	1737
Catherine del Ricci	1522–1590	Alessandra Lucrezia Romola	Italy	1746
Catherine of Palma	1533–1574	Catalina Tomas	Spain	1930
Catherine Labouré	1806–1876	Catherine Labouré	France	1947
Catherine Vincentia Gerosa	1784–1847	Catherine Gerosa	Italy	1950
Katherine Drexel	1858–1955	Katherine Drexel	United States	2000

Future Saints Catherine?

Name	Lived	Original Name	Nationality	Canonized
Catherine Cosie (Osanna of Cattaro)	1493–1565	Catherine Kosic	Montenegro	Beatified 1934
Catherine Tekakwitha	1656–1680	Catherine Tekakwitha	Native American (Algonquin/Mohawk)	Beatified 1980
	d. 1794	Catherine Cottenceau	France	Beatified 1984
	d. 1794	Catherine du Verdier de la Sorinière	France	Beatified 1984
	1754–1836	Catherine Jarrige	France	Beatified 1996
	1801–1857	Caterina Cittadini	Italy	Beatified 2001
	1839–1894	Caterina Volpicelli	Italy	Beatified 2001
Catalina de Maria	1823–1896	Saturnina Rodriguez	Argentina	Beatification Pending

❀ THE SEVEN CONTRARY VIRTUES ❀

These are derived from the poem "Psychomachia" ("Battle for the Soul") by Prudentius, around 410. The virtues are the antidotes for the corresponding Seven Deadly Sins.

1. Humility   3. Abstinence   5. Patience   7. Diligence
2. Kindness   4. Chastity   6. Liberality

❀ POPULAR HYMNS OF FANNY CROSBY ❀

Frances Jane Van Alstyne (1823–1915), known by her maiden name as Fanny J. Crosby, lost her sight at six weeks of age. She began writing poetry as a child. She became a pupil, then teacher, at the New York City Institution for the Blind. In 1858 she married the blind musician Alexander Van Alstyne. Beginning in 1864, she published more than two thousand hymns, many of them under almost one hundred other names because publishers were embarrassed by the quantity of her output. She is said to have written more than eight thousand hymns or, more correctly, "devotional lyrics." Purists do not consider her work to be of high poetic quality, but the simplicity and earnestness of her verse have endeared her songs to Christian worshipers in North America. These are some of her most-used hymns.

"All the Way My Savior Leads Me" (1875)
"Blessed Assurance, Jesus Is Mine" (1873)
"I Am Thine, O Lord" ("Draw Me Nearer," 1875)
"Jesus Is Tenderly Calling" (1883)
"Jesus, Keep Me Near the Cross" (1869)
"Pass Me Not, O Gentle Savior" (1868)
"Praise Him, Praise Him" (1869)
"Redeemed, How I Love to Proclaim It!" (1882)
"Rescue the Perishing" (1869)
"Safe in the Arms of Jesus"
"Saved by Grace" (1891)
"Savior, More Than Life to Me" (1875)
"Take the World, but Give Me Jesus" (1879)
"Tell Me the Story of Jesus" (1880)
"Thou My Everlasting Portion" ("Close to Thee," 1874)
"Though Your Sins Be as Scarlet" (1887)
"To God Be the Glory" (1875)
"Trusting Jesus" (1877)
"Watch and Pray" (1885)

❊ U.S. REVIVALS ❊

Revival	Approximate Dates	Focal Location	Major Figures
Dutch Reformed Revival	1720s	Raritan Valley, New Jersey	Theodorus J. Frelinghuysen
Log College Revival	1730–1760	Middle Colonies	Gilbert Tennent
Great Awakening	1734–1760	Western Massachusetts, spreading through eastern seaboard	Jonathan Edwards, George Whitefield
Yale Revival	1801	New Haven, Connecticut	Timothy Dwight
Frontier Revival	1801 and following	Cane Ridge, Kentucky, and throughout frontier	Barton W. Stone
Second Great Awakening	1820–1835	Western New York, spreading through northern states	Charles Grandison Finney, Lyman Beecher
Holiness Movement	1835–1910	New York City, spreading through North America	Phoebe Palmer, Charles Cullis
Pentecostal Revival	1901	Topeka, Kansas, and Los Angeles, spreading through North America	Charles F. Parham, William J. Seymour
Latter Rain Revival	1948	North Battleford, Saskatchewan; Detroit; spreading through North America	George Hawtin, Myrtle D. Beall
Wheaton College Revival	1950	Wheaton, Illinois	V. Raymond Edman
Jesus Movement	1967	West Coast, spreading throughout North America	Ted Wise, Arthur Blessit, Tony and Susan Alamo

❧ BIBLE MEN NAMED JOSHUA ❧

At least seventeen men in the Bible had a variation of the name Joshua. The full Hebrew name of Joshua is *Yehoshua'*. The name is derived from the Hebrew word meaning "salvation" or "deliverance." A variant of the name is *Yeshua'*. The Greek form of this name is *Iesous*, or Jesus. A shorter form is *Hoshea'* (same as Hosea).

1. Joshua (Hoshea), son of Nun, successor to Moses
2. Joshua of Beth-shemesh, on whose land the ark halted (1 Sam. 6:14)
3. Hoshea, son of Azaziah, an Ephraimite chief under David (1 Chron. 27:20)
4. Joshua, governor of Jerusalem under King Josiah (2 Kings 23:8)
5. Hosea, son of Beeri, the prophet
6. Hoshea, son of Elah, king of Israel
7. Hoshaiah, father of the commander Azariah (Jer. 42:1)
8. Jeshua, a Levite in the time of King Hezekiah (2 Chron. 31:15)
9. Jeshua, a Levite (Ezra 2:40)
10. Jeshua, father of Ezer (Neh. 3:19)
11. Jeshua, son of Kadmiel, a Levite (Neh. 12:24)
12. Hoshea, one of the "chiefs of the people" (Neh. 10:23)
13. Hoshaiah, a prince of Judah (Neh. 12:32)
14. Joshua, high priest in the time of the prophet Zechariah (Zech. 3:1)
15. Jesus of Nazareth
16. Jesus Barabbas*
17. Jesus called Justus, a Jewish worker with Paul (Col. 4:11)

*Several ancient manuscripts of the New Testament support the possibility that Barabbas's name was Jesus Barabbas.

❧ OTHER FAMILY TRAGEDIES ❧
EXPERIENCED BY MARTIN LUTHER KING SR.

The assassination of Dr. Martin Luther King Jr. on April 4, 1968, was a blow to all Americans, but especially to his father, the Reverend Martin Luther King Sr., pastor of Ebenezer Baptist Church in Atlanta, Georgia. But in July 1969, his other son and copastor, the Reverend A. D. Williams King, drowned in a pool accident. Then on June 30, 1974, the senior King's wife, Alberta Williams King, was shot while playing the organ in Ebenezer Baptist Church. "How much can a man take?" he asked, but at her funeral he said, "I cannot hate any man." Martin Luther King Sr. died November 11, 1984, at age eighty-four.

Incidentally, Martin Luther King Jr. was originally named Michael Luther King, but later his father changed both of their names to Martin.

❧ LEAST POPULAR BIBLICAL NAMES ❧

Girls' Names

Hoglah (Josh. 17:3)—Not very complimentary unless you think swine are beautiful

Jezebel (1 Kings 19:2)—Sort of like naming your son Hitler

Lo-Ruhamah (Hos. 1:6 NIV)—Means "not pitied"

Zillah (Gen. 4:23)—Not a bad name, but what if she marries . . . see *Gog*

Zipporah (Exod. 2:21)—Moses' wife. People might think your daughter is a fast (zippy) woman.

Boys' Names

Ahitub (1 Sam. 22:9)—Means "my brother is goodness" but sounds like taking an elevated bath

Bukki (1 Chron. 6:51)—Your family had better live in Ohio.

Dodo (2 Sam. 23:24)—Father of Elhanan. Even if your child is smart, no one would believe it.

Gog (Ezek. 38:2)—Imagine the headline if he marries Zillah.

Josheb-basshebeth (2 Sam. 23:8)—Gesundheit

Maher-shalal-hash-baz (Isa. 8:3)—Means "speeding is the spoil, hastening is the prey"

Romamti-ezer (1 Chron. 25:4)—Sounds romam-tic except for the "ezer" part

Zaphenath-paneah (Gen. 41:45)—The name Pharaoh gave to Joseph when he married the daughter of a priest. "I, Zaphenath-paneah, take thee, Asenath . . ."

❧ ST. PATRICK'S CATHEDRAL(S) ❧

St. Patrick's Cathedral in New York City is well known, but there are at least twelve St. Patrick's Cathedrals around the world. Three are in Ireland, and ironically only one is Catholic. A church is a cathedral if it is the seat of a bishop; often an existing church has become a cathedral with the founding of a new diocese (area headed by a bishop). Here's a list.

Catholic:

Melbourne, Australia
Parramatta, Australia
Bridgetown, Barbados
Bangalore, India
Pune (Poona), India

Armagh, Northern Ireland
New York, New York
Rochester, New York
Thunder Bay, Ontario
Karachi, Pakistan

Church of Ireland (Anglican):

Armagh, Northern Ireland
Dublin, Ireland

❀ FOUR THEORIES OF ATONEMENT ❀

Jesus saves—but *how?* At the heart of Christian faith is the conviction that the death of Christ made atonement for our sin and reconciled us to God. *Atonement* is another English word for *reconciliation*. Theologians have had different ideas about how this atonement happens.

Theory	Summary of View	Scripture Examples	Major Figures and Venues
Classic or "dramatic"	Atonement is a *work of God;* Christ's death is *God's victory* over the powers of evil, through which people are delivered from them.	2 Corinthians 5:19; Colossians 2:13–15	Church fathers, Eastern Orthodoxy, Martin Luther
Latin or "judicial"	Atonement is the *work of Christ* as representative of mankind; his sacrificial death *pays the price* demanded by God for sin.	Romans 3:24; Old Testament concept of atonement through sacrifice	Anselm of Canterbury, Catholic thought since the Middle Ages, Protestant Orthodoxy after Luther, modern evangelicalism
Moral or "subjective"	Christ's *example* of self-sacrifice creates a *response of love* in people and lifts them to God.	Luke 7:47	Peter Abelard, Friedrich Schleiermacher, Enlightenment and "liberal" movements
Devotional or "pietist"	Through *devotion*, people can enter into Christ's passion and be united with divine love.	Colossians 1:24–25	Thomas à Kempis, mystics, Catholic devotional movements

❀ MEANING OF IHS SYMBOL ❀

This symbol is often found in churches, especially those built with more traditional architecture. It is sometimes said to stand for "In His Service." It originates, however, in the first three letters of the Greek name for Jesus, *Iesous*. It is perhaps more correctly written in Greek small capitals as IHC.

❊ THE WORLD'S ONLY ❊
OFFICIALLY CHRISTIAN NATION

About 4.6 million of Zambia's population of 10 million are Christians. In December 1991, Dr. F. J. T. Chiluba, president of Zambia, declared his nation a Christian state despite the presence of small Muslim and Hindu communities. He saw this declaration as a response to divine intervention in the political transition to the present republic. More important, he believes that the gospel values of love and conscientious living should be the foundation of national life and statecraft. Once a lukewarm Christian, Dr. Chiluba spent time in prison, during which he became immersed in the Scriptures and experienced a reawakening of faith.

❊ RUNNING THE NUMBERS ON KING SOLOMON ❊

- Solomon had 4,000 stalls for his horses (1 Kings 4:26).
- The daily provision for the royal household included 185 bushels of fine flour, 375 bushels of meal, 10 fat oxen, 20 pasture-fed cattle, and 100 sheep and goats (1 Kings 4:22–23).
- He had 12,000 horsemen (1 Kings 4:26).
- He uttered 3,000 proverbs (1 Kings 4:32).
- He composed 1,005 songs (1 Kings 4:32).
- There were 550 chief officers over Solomon's later public works (1 Kings 9:23).
- His seamen brought about 16 tons of gold from Ophir (1 Kings 9:28).
- The queen of Sheba gave Solomon about 4½ tons of gold (1 Kings 10:10).
- Solomon received about 25 tons of gold in a year (1 Kings 10:14).
- He had 1,400 chariots (1 Kings 10:26).
- Solomon could buy chariots from Egypt for about 15 pounds of silver, and horses for about 3¾ pounds, for resale to kings farther north (1 Kings 10:29).
- He had 700 wives (1 Kings 11:3).
- He had 300 concubines (1 Kings 11:3).
- Solomon reigned 40 years over all Israel (1 Kings 11:42).
- Solomon made 200 large shields of beaten gold, each weighing about 7½ pounds, and 300 more shields, each using about 3¾ pounds of gold (1 Kings 10:16–17).

❧ SEVEN RULERS NAMED HEROD ❧

Herod "the Great," a client king within the Roman Empire, had five wives in succession and many children. After his death the Romans divided his kingdom, and his descendants ruled over various parts of it for a century. To make a confusing situation even more so, several of them are sometimes called "Herod II," including one who, apparently, was not a ruler.

Ruler	Territory	Ruled	Comments
Herod the Great	Judea, Samaria, Galilee	39–4 BC	Ruler at the birth of Christ
Herod II Boethius		d. after AD 35	Son of Herod the Great
Herod Archelaus	Judea and Samaria	4 BC– AD 6	Son of Herod the Great; deposed by Rome and banished to Gaul
Herod Antipas	Galilee and Perea	4 BC– AD 39	Son of Herod the Great; executed John the Baptist (Mark 6); later deposed by Rome and banished to Gaul
Herod Philip	"Tetrarchy of Philip"	4 BC– AD 34	Son of Herod the Great; founded Caesarea Philippi
Herod of Chalcis	Chalcis (in Lebanon)	?– AD 48	Grandson of Herod the Great
Herod Agrippa I	Eventually, all former territory of Herod the Great	AD 39–44	Grandson of Herod the Great, brother of Herod of Chalcis
Herod Agrippa II	Chalcis, Tetrarchy of Philip	AD 50–93	Son of Agrippa I; Romans gave him authority to appoint the high priest; Paul made a defense before him (Acts 26)

❦ CHURCH ANNOUNCEMENT "BLOOPERS" ❦

• Miss Charlene Mason sang "I Will Not Pass This Way Again," giving obvious pleasure to the congregation.

• At the evening service tonight, the sermon topic will be "What Is Hell?" Come early and listen to our choir practice.

• The concert held in the Fellowship Hall was a great success. Special thanks are due to the minister's daughter, who labored the whole evening at the piano, which as usual fell on her.

• Eight new choir robes are currently needed, due to the addition of several new members and to the deterioration of some of the older ones.

• The "Over 60 Choir" will be disbanded for the summer with the thanks of the entire church.

• Today's Sermon: "How Much Can a Man Drink?" with hymns from a full choir.

• This being Easter Sunday, we will ask Mrs. Lewis to come forward and lay an egg on the altar.

• For those of you who have children and don't know it, we have a nursery downstairs.

• The church is glad to have with us today as our guest minister the Reverend Green, who has Mrs. Green with him. After the service we request that all remain in the sanctuary for the Hanging of the Greens.

• The sermon this morning: "Jesus Walks on the Water." The sermon tonight: "Searching for Jesus."

• Barbara C. remains in the hospital and needs blood donors for more transfusions. She is also having trouble sleeping and requests tapes of Pastor Jack's sermons.

• During the absence of our pastor we enjoyed the rare privilege of hearing a good sermon when J. F. Scubbs supplied our pulpit.

• The Reverend Merriweather spoke briefly, much to the delight of the audience.

• The pastor will preach his farewell message, after which the choir will sing "Break Forth into Joy."

• The audience is asked to remain seated until the end of the recession.

• This afternoon there will be a meeting in the south and north ends of the church. Children will be baptized at both ends.

• Thursday night—potluck supper. Prayer and medication to follow.

• Remember in prayer the many who are sick of our church and community.

• Due to the Rector's illness, Wednesday's healing services will be discontinued until further notice.

• The peacemaking meeting scheduled for today has been canceled due to a conflict.

• Low Self-Esteem Support Group will meet Thursday at 7 PM. Please use the back door.

• Weight Watchers will meet at 7:00 PM at the First Presbyterian Church. Please use the large double door at the side entrance.

❈ CHURCH ANNOUNCEMENT "BLOOPERS"—CONT. ❈

• The eighth graders will be presenting Shakespeare's *Hamlet* in the church basement on Friday at 7:00 PM. The congregation is invited to attend this tragedy.

• Ladies, don't forget the rummage sale. It is a good chance to get rid of those things not worth keeping around the house. Bring your husbands.

• Next Sunday a special collection will be taken to defray the cost of the new carpet. All those wishing to do something on the new carpet will come forward and do so.

• The outreach committee has enlisted 25 visitors to make calls on people who are not afflicted with any church.

• Irving Benson and Jessie Carter were married on October 24 in the church. So ends a friendship that began in school days.

• Please join us as we show our support for Amy and Alan in preparing for the girth of their first child.

• Don't let worry kill you—let the church help.

• To announce a visit from a missionary: "Come tonight and hear Bertha Belch all the way from Africa."

❈ THE WORLD'S TOP TEN CHRISTIAN NATIONS ❈

This is a list of the world's nations with the largest number of nominal Christians. Of course, in some countries a person might be identified as a Christian only because he or she was baptized in infancy, not because of current participation or practice.

Country	Nominal Christians	Percent of Population
United States	224,457,000	.85
Brazil	139,000,000	.93
Mexico	86,120,000	.99
Russia	80,000,000	.60
China	70,000,000	.5.7
Germany	67,000,000	.83
Philippines	63,470,000	.93
United Kingdom	51,060,000	.88
Italy	47,690,000	.90
France	44,150,000	.98

❀ A FEW OF THE 580 PLACES ❀
NAMED AFTER SAINTS IN QUEBEC

At least 580 placenames begin with "Saint" or "Sainte" in Quebec. This does not include many other names incorporating "Saint," "Sainte," or a saint's name, such as Sault St-Louis, Baie St-Paul, or Cap-de-la-Madeleine (St. Mary Magdalene). Here's a short summary:

Distinction	Name	Comments
Longest names	Ste-Catherine-de-la-Jacques-Cartier St-Jacques-le-Majeur-de-Wolfetown	
Shortest names	St-Pie Ste-Foy	French for St. Pius, Pope Pius V From French for "Holy Faith"
Largest City	St-Laurent	Population 74,240
Most Recreational	St-Ferréol-les-Neiges	Near a ski resort; name means "St. Ferreol of the Snows"
Most Obscure	St-Herménégilde	Population 158. Hermengild (died 585) was a prince of the Visigoths in Spain who was imprisoned by his Arian father because of his conversion to the Catholic faith.
Most Laughable	St-Louis-du-Ha! Ha!	Nowhere near the Ha! Ha! River

❀ THREE ENDINGS TO MARK'S GOSPEL ❀

The oldest manuscripts of the Gospel according to Mark end with 16:8, "for they were afraid," but the final word in Greek, *gar*, is one not used to end a sentence. Something is missing. Perhaps the original ending, written on the outside of the rolled-up document, was damaged in transit.

Verses 9–20, printed in most Bibles, come from later manuscripts. There is an alternate ending in other ancient sources, after verse 8: "But they reported briefly to Peter and those with him all that they had been told. And after this, Jesus himself sent out by means of them, from east to west, the sacred and imperishable proclamation of eternal salvation."

One eighth-century manuscript contains both alternate endings after verse 8.

❋ WHAT'S THE DIFFERENCE BETWEEN ❋ A PURITAN AND A PILGRIM?

The Puritans were a Reformed party within the Church of England in the sixteenth to seventeenth centuries. They sought to restructure and renew the church according to biblical principles. They did not leave the established church but considered themselves the purified Church of England. The Separatists, on the other hand, left the established church and formed their own groups in order to worship according to biblical standards. Because England did not tolerate religious diversity, many Separatists lived in Holland.

The settlers of the Plymouth Colony in 1620 were Separatists. In the nineteenth century they began to be called the *Pilgrims*, but originally they were simply the *first-comers*. A larger group of Puritans established the Massachusetts Bay Colony in nearby Salem and Boston in 1630. The two groups differed in their concept of the church but otherwise had a similar theology and worship. Eventually the two colonies were merged into Massachusetts, and people came to think of all of them as Puritans.

As a sidelight, after these two colonies were established, conditions improved in England for those of the Reformed viewpoint, and immigration to New England slowed till after the American Revolution. As a result, the further settlement of New England occurred through expansion of the original group of colonists, leading to a uniform Puritan culture throughout much of the Northeast. New England was the most settled and prosperous part of colonial America, and its culture was influential in shaping that of the developing nation.

❋ HISTORICALLY AFRICAN-AMERICAN ❋ DENOMINATIONS

Several American denominations have a history of serving the African-American community. In some cases they were formed with the assistance and encouragement of their Caucasian counterparts in order to give African-Americans the opportunity to shape their own church life. While they remain predominantly African-American, these groups now welcome Caucasian or other worshipers as well.

African Methodist Episcopal Church • African Methodist Episcopal Zion Church • Christian Methodist Episcopal Church (formerly Colored Methodist Episcopal Church) • Church of God in Christ • National Baptist Convention of America • National Baptist Convention, USA, Inc. • Progressive National Baptist Association

Two groups are more recently formed:
National Missionary Baptist Convention of America
Full Gospel Baptist Church Fellowship

❧ GOOD-LOOKING MEN AND WOMEN OF THE BIBLE ❧

Women
Sarai, wife of Abraham (Gen. 12:11–14)
Rebecca, wife of Isaac (Gen. 24:16)
Rachel, wife of Jacob (Gen. 29:17)
Abigail, wife of Nabal, then David (1 Sam. 25:3)
Bathsheba, wife of Uriah the Hittite, then David (2 Sam. 11:2–3)
Tamar, daughter of David (2 Sam. 13:1)
Tamar, daughter of Absalom (2 Sam. 14:27)
Abishag the Shunamite, nurse for the aged David (1 Kings 1:1–4)
Esther, queen of Persia (Esther 2)
The daughters of Job (Job 42:15)
The king's bride (Ps. 45:10–11)
The bride in the Song of Solomon (Song 4:1, 7)
Judith (apocryphal Book of Judith 8:7)

Men
Joseph, son of Jacob (Gen. 39:6)
Saul, son of Kish (1 Sam. 9:1–2)
David (1 Sam. 16:11–12)
Absalom, son of David (2 Sam. 14:25–26)
An Egyptian warrior slain by Benaiah (2 Sam. 23:21)
Daniel, Hananiah, Mishael, and Azariah (Dan. 1:3–6)
Adonijah, son of David (1 Kings 1:5–6)
The king as a groom (Ps. 45:2)

❧ DEWEY DECIMAL CODES FOR RELIGION ❧

Dewey Decimal Classification
200 . . . . Religion (General)
210 . . . . Natural religion
220 . . . . Bible
230 . . . . Christian doctrinal theology
240 . . . . Christian moral and devotional
250 . . . . Local churches and religious orders
260 . . . . Social and ecclesiastical theology
270 . . . . History and geography of the church
280 . . . . Christian denominations and sects
290 . . . . Other religions and comparative religion

❀ MOST REPRINTED HYMNS ❀

More than 5,000 different hymnals have been published in the United States—approximately 1,800 by denominations and 3,200 by independent publishers. Studies of Protestant hymnals from the eighteenth to twentieth centuries have suggested the following are the most popular, not counting Christmas or patriotic songs:

1. "All Hail the Power of Jesus' Name"—Edward Perronet, 1780
2. "Jesus, Lover of My Soul"—Charles Wesley, 1740
3. "Alas! And Did My Savior Bleed?"—Isaac Watts, 1707
4. "How Firm a Foundation"—Rippon's Selection, 1787, based on Isaiah 43:1–5
5. "Am I a Soldier of the Cross?"—Isaac Watts, 1724
6. "Come, Thou Fount of Every Blessing"—Robert Robinson, 1758
7. "Guide Me, O Thou Great Jehovah"—William Williams, 1745
8. "On Jordan's Stormy Banks I Stand"—Samuel Stennett, 1787
9. "Rock of Ages, Cleft for Me"—Augustus M. Toplady, 1776
10. "When I Can Read My Title Clear"—Isaac Watts, 1707

Among Catholic hymnals published more recently, the following hymns are most often reprinted:

1. "Faith of Our Fathers"—Frederick W. Faber, 1849
2. "O God, Our Help in Ages Past"—Isaac Watts, 1719 (Ps. 90)
3. "All Hail the Power of Jesus' Name"—Edward Perronet, 1780
4. "Come, Thou Almighty King"—Anonymous, 1757
5. "Amazing Grace"—John Newton, 1779
6. "Joy to the World"—Isaac Watts, 1719 (Ps. 98)
7. "Holy, Holy, Holy! Lord God Almighty"—Reginald Heber, 1826
8. "From All That Dwell Below the Skies"—Isaac Watts, 1719 (Ps. 117)
9. "Love Divine, All Loves Excelling"—Charles Wesley, 1747
10. "Rejoice, the Lord Is King"—Charles Wesley, 1744

❀ STAINED-GLASS WINDOWS IN ❀ THE NOTRE DAME CATHEDRAL

Many Catholic cathedrals are called *Notre Dame*, but the one in Paris is the best known. It has eighty-two stained-glass windows. Most famous is the circular Rose Window in the south transept, which itself has ninety-one sections. It is said to be the largest stained-glass window in the world, but there are other claimants to this honor, including the Great East Window of the York Minster in England, which is as large as a tennis court.

❊ THE PSALMS BY CHAPTER AND VERSE ❊

Catholic Bibles translated from the Latin Vulgate used a different numbering for the Psalms, based on the Septuagint (ancient Greek Old Testament). Protestant Bibles, and newer Catholic Bibles translated from the Hebrew, use the Hebrew numbering. As a result, the familiar Psalm 23 is Psalm 24 in older Catholic Bibles. The numbering differs by one from Psalm 9 to Psalm 113, and from Psalm 117 to Psalm 146, with additional variations.

Protestant	Catholic
1–8	1–8
9 and 10	9
11–113	10–112
114 and 115	113
116	114 and 115
117–146	116–145
147	146 and 147
148–150	148–150

Additionally, the *verse* numbers in the psalms may differ by one between the English and Hebrew versions. Many of the Psalms begin with a superscription (such as a historical note or directions for performance). In the Hebrew text the superscription is verse 1; in the English version, it is unnumbered.

❊ THE FIRST WOMAN BISHOPS ❊

The concept of *apostolic succession* means that a person is a true bishop only if ordained, or consecrated, by another bishop whose ordination goes back through an unbroken succession of bishops to apostolic times. While other churches and denominations have officers called bishops, only those of the historic Eastern and Western churches and the Anglican churches (a division of the Western church) have bishops in the apostolic succession. Using this criterion, the first known woman bishop was Barbara Clementine Harris, an African-American elected in 1989 as a suffragan (assisting) bishop in the Episcopal Diocese of Massachusetts.

If legend is correct, however, the first female to receive Episcopal ordination was Brigid (St. Bride, died around 523), whom St. Patrick converted to Christianity. She founded the first convent in Ireland at Cill-Dara (Kildare), and Bishop Ibor reportedly consecrated her. The Roman Catholic Church discounts the story.

❊ RESTORATION CHURCHES IN AMERICA ❊

The term *restoration churches* refers to groups that have formed to restore what they believed to be the practice of the New Testament church, renouncing all creeds and holding only to the Bible as their authority. The movement began in North America in the early 1800s and is also called the *Christians-only movement*. It had two main thrusts: (1) emulating the New Testament church, and (2) restoring the unity of the church by avoiding denominational structures.

Over time, the movement divided between these two aims. Those stressing early Christian practices largely withdrew from contact with other churches, while those who sought unity with other churches lost many of their "primitive" or early Christian traits. In the process, the movement to end denominationalism resulted in the formation of many new denominations, though most restorationist groups refuse to be considered denominations and avoid organizations that officially link their local churches.

Because many of these churches call themselves *Christian* or *Churches of Christ*, it is often hard to tell which branch of the movement they belong to.

Groups stemming from the "Christians-only" movement include Christian Church (Disciples of Christ), Christian Churches and Churches of Christ (independent), Churches of Christ (noninstrumental), and International Churches of Christ ("Crossroads" or "Boston" movement).

❊ THE LARGEST CHURCHES IN ❊
THE WORLD AND IN THE UNITED STATES

The world's largest church, in terms of membership, is the Yoido Full Gospel Church of Seoul, Korea, with a reported 780,000 members. The largest known church in Africa is the Deeper Life Bible Church of Lagos, Nigeria, with 85,000 members. Compared to these, the eleven largest congregations in the United States are pikers:

Lakewood Church, Houston, TX—25,000
World Changers, College Park, GA—23,100
New Birth Church, Atlanta, GA—23,000
Calvary Chapel of Costa Mesa, Santa Ana, CA—20,000
The Potter's House, Dallas, TX—18,500
Second Baptist Church, Houston, TX—18,000
Southeast Christian Church, Louisville, KY—17,900
First Assembly of God, Phoenix, AZ—17,500
Willow Creek Community Church, South Barrington, IL—17,100
Calvary Chapel of Fort Lauderdale, Fort Lauderdale, FL—17,000
Saddleback Valley Community Church, Lake Forest, CA—15,000

❦ FAMOUS AFRICANS OF CHURCH HISTORY ❦

These are Christian leaders who lived in or came from Africa. Those listed from North or South Africa are not black; Ethiopians also are racially different from black Africans.

Tertullian (160–220), Carthage (in modern Tunisia), first Christian theologian to write in Latin

Commodian (third century), Christian Latin poet of North Africa

Cyprian (died 258), bishop of Carthage and writer of treatises

Ezana, king of Ethiopia (ruled 325–360), converted by the missionary Frumentius (died 380), made Ethiopia one of the world's first Christian nations

Athanasius (296–373), bishop of Alexandria, Egypt; leading opponent of the Arian movement

Donatus (fourth century), leader of a strict Christian sect eventually declared schismatic

Augustine (354–430), bishop of Hippo (in modern Tunisia), influential theologian and Doctor of the Church

Cyril (died 444), patriarch of Alexandria, considered a Doctor of the Church

John Ezzidio (1810–1872), Sierra Leone, former slave, Wesleyan Methodist minister and prominent businessman

Samuel Ajayi Crowther (1806–1891), Yoruba (Nigeria), first African Anglican bishop, 1864

Edward Wilmot Blyden (1832–1912), Liberia, Presbyterian minister and leading African intellectual of the nineteenth century

Andrew Murray (1828–1917), South Africa, Dutch Reformed minister and influential writer in spiritual formation

Haile Selassie (1892–1975), emperor of Ethiopia, styled "King of Kings and Lion of Judah." As emperor he was head of the Ethiopian Church and an opponent of international aggression. His name, which he took at his enthronement, means "Force of Trinity."

David DuPlessis (1905–1987), South African Pentecostal active in the ecumenical movement

Festo Kivengere (1919–1988), Anglican bishop of Kigezi, Uganda, who withstood the dictator Idi Amin

Ndabaningi Sithole (1922–2000), Zimbabwe, Congregational minister and politician

Abel Muzorewa (born 1925), Zimbabwe (Rhodesia), Methodist bishop and first prime minister of Zimbabwe, 1979

❈ THE MAYFLOWER COMPACT ❈

The settlers of Plymouth reached the shores of America in 1620. Before landing, their leaders drew up an agreement that everyone aboard had to sign. It's known as the Mayflower Compact, and it established the basis for a stable government in the new colony, dedicated to the advancement of the Christian faith. This is the original wording of the compact, from William Bradford's handwriting, in which the word *the* is written y^e. All free adult males, and some of the servants, signed the document.

In ye name of God, Amen. We whose names are underwriten, the loyall subjects of our dread soveraigne Lord King James by ye grace of God, of Great Britaine, Franc, & Ireland king, defender of ye faith, &c.

Haveing undertaken, for ye glorie of God, and advancemente of ye Christian faith, and honour of our king & countrie, a voyage to plant ye first colonie in ye Northerne parts of Virginia, doe by these presents solemnly & mutualy in ye presence of God, and one of another, covenant & combine our selves togeather into a civill body politick; for our better ordering & preservation & furtherance of ye ends aforesaid; and by vertue hearof, to enacte, constitute, and frame such just & equall lawes, ordinances, acts, constitutions, & offices, from time to time, as shall be thought most meete & convenient for ye generall good of ye Colonie: unto which we promise all due submission and obedience. In witnes wherof we have hereunder subscribed our names at Cap-Codd ye 11 of November, in ye year of the raigne of our soveraigne lord, King James of England, France, & Ireland ye eighteenth, and of Scotland ye fiftie fourth. An^o: Dom. 1620.

❈ FAVORITE BIBLE VERSIONS IN THE UNITED STATES ❈

A widely reported survey revealed that 34 percent of Protestant pastors in the United States currently favor the New International Version (NIV) Bible. Twenty-four percent say The King James Version (KJV) is their favorite. Pastors ranked the New Revised Standard Version (NRSV) as third, with 17 percent. Ten percent prefer The New King James Version (NKJV), while another 9 percent of pastors use the New American Standard Bible (NASB). More than 2 percent of the 500 pastors surveyed preferred no particular version. (The other 4 percent covers all the versions other than those named, in percentages too small to mention.) Pastors of evangelical or conservative churches prefer the NIV and KJV, with Pentecostal and charismatic pastors heavily favoring the King James. Pastors of mainline or "liberal" churches, on the other hand, prefer the NRSV by a wide margin.

❧ DOCTORS OF THE CHURCH ❧

More than thirty figures from Christian history have been regarded as "doctors of the church" because of their holy lives and the benefit the church has derived from their teaching.

The ancient church of the
West recognized four doctors:
1. St. Gregory the Great
2. St. Ambrose
3. St. Augustine
4. St. Jerome

The Eastern Church
recognized three doctors:
1. St. John Chrysostom
2. St. Basil
3. St. Gregory Nazianzen

St. Thomas Aquinas was added to the list in the sixteenth century, and since then popes have added others, including:

St. Anselm • St. Peter Damian • St. Francis de Sales • St. John of the Cross • St. Teresa of Avila • Most recently named is St. Thérèse of Lisieux, in 1997.

The doctors are often known by distinctive epithets. St. Thomas Aquinas is known as *Doctor angelicus*, the "angelic Doctor"; William of Ockham is known as *Doctor invincibilis*; and St. Albertus Magnus as *Doctor universalis, Doctor venerabilis,* or *Doctor expertus.*

❧ THE LARGEST U.S. DENOMINATIONS ❧

Roman Catholic	50,873,000
Baptist	33,830,000
Methodist/Wesleyan	14,140,000
Lutheran	9,580,000
Presbyterian	5,595,000
Pentecostal/Charismatic	4,407,000
Episcopal/Anglican	3,451,000
Mormon	2,787,000
Churches of Christ	2,503,000
Nondenominational	2,489,000
Congregational/United Church of Christ	1,378,000
Jehovah's Witnesses	1,331,000

❄ CHILDREN OF THE POPES ❄

The Catholic Church traces the origin of the papacy to the apostle Peter, who was married (Jesus healed his mother-in-law, Matt. 8:14–15). Before 1139, when celibacy was made a requirement for Latin Rite clergy, at least four popes and many bishops, priests, and deacons were married. Pope Adrian II (reigned 862–872) was a married layman; a relative of the rival pope Anastasius murdered his wife and daughter. After 1139 Pope Clement IV (1265–1268) was a widower and the antipope Felix V was a married layman. Other clergy married after 1139 despite church policy.

A few popes were sons of popes. Innocent I (reigned 401–417) was the son of Anastasius I, Silverus (536–537) was the son of Hormidas, and John XI (931–935) was the son of Sergius III. Ten other popes were sons of clergymen. Many clergy had children through unmarried alliances both before and after 1139, and at least five popes fathered children after the celibacy rule was issued.

The most famous child of a pope is Lucrezia Borgia, daughter of Pope Alexander VI (Rodrigo Borgia, reigned 1492–1503). Lucrezia was heavily involved in family turmoil and intrigue, though perhaps not as the instigator of it, as she has often been portrayed. Pope Alexander VI had four children by Lucrezia's mother, Vanozza Catanei, and later had a mistress, Giulia Farnese, whom local wags dubbed the "bride of Christ."

❄ THE FIVE POINTS OF CALVINISM ❄

Here are the well-known "five points of Calvinism" and a brief explanation of each.

Total Depravity	People are unable to deliver themselves from bondage to sin.
Unconditional Election	People can do nothing to merit God's choice of them.
Limited Atonement	Christ's death atones for the sin of those whom God has chosen.
Irresistible Grace	Those to whom God has given life find his grace in Christ irresistible.
Perseverance of the Saints	Since salvation is God's gift, the Christian cannot fall away from it.

❋ CHRISTIAN POETS ❋

Edmund Spenser (1552–1599) . . . . English Renaissance poet famous for *The Faerie Queene*, an allegory of the struggle between good and evil

John Donne (1572–1631) . . . . Considered the greatest of the English "metaphysical poets," whose works are marked by an intense and sustained spiritual fervor

George Herbert (1593–1633) . . . . One of the metaphysical poets

John Milton (1608–1674) . . . . English Puritan writer, author of the best-seller *Paradise Lost* and considered one of the greatest poets of the English language

Henry Vaughan (1622–1695) . . . . One of the metaphysical poets

William Cowper (1731–1800) . . . . English poet and hymn writer

William Blake (1757–1827) . . . . Unconventional and obscure English poet and artist, but his work had a great influence on later Romanticism

Emily Dickinson (1830–1886) . . . . Rarely left her home in Amherst, Massachusetts, but came to be considered one of the greatest original poets in American literature

Anna Shipton (died 1901) . . . . English devotional poet of the late 1800s; though little remembered today, she was a favorite of C. H. Spurgeon and D. L. Moody

George MacDonald (1824–1905) . . . . . . Scottish writer influential for C. S. Lewis; much of his fiction has recently been republished in updated versions

Amy Carmichael (1867–1951) . . . . Missionary in India and a prolific writer of devotional books and poetry

Dorothy L. Sayers (1893–1957) . . . . . . Anglican writer recognized for the doctrinal depth of her poetry and other works

Wystan Hugh Auden (1907–1973) . . . . . English poet of probing depth, who adopted a Christian perspective later in life but had gender issues

❈ CHRISTIAN POETS—CONT. ❈

Helen Steiner Rice (1900–1981). . . . . . . Believed to have written several million poems, including greeting-card verse and ten volumes; donated her royalties to her Methodist church in Cincinnati

Vassar Miller (1924–1998) . . . . Considered by some to be the Emily Dickinson of the twentieth century

Madeleine L'Engle (born 1918) . . . . Has written poetry in addition to her popular Christian fiction

❈ PASSAGES OF SCRIPTURE ❈
REPEATED IN SCRIPTURE

Not counting quotations from the Old Testament in the New, many portions of Scripture repeat material found elsewhere. This is a partial list. It is not always certain which of the doubled portions is the "original." Some repeats contain slight alterations.

- Exodus 20:1–17 (the Ten Commandments) is repeated in Deuteronomy 5:6–21.

- Numbers 7:13–17, the list of gifts of the leader of the tribe of Judah, is repeated verbatim eleven times (vv. 18–83) for the gifts of the other eleven tribal leaders.

- Joshua 24:29–32 is repeated in Judges 2:6–9.

- 2 Kings 18:13–20:19 is repeated in Isaiah 36:1–38:11 and 38:21–39:8.

- 2 Chronicles 36:22–23 is repeated in Ezra 1:1–3.

- Psalm 14 is repeated almost verbatim as Psalm 53, with "the LORD" changed to "God."

- Psalm 15:1–4 is repeated in Psalm 24:3–4.

- Psalm 108 is a repeat of Psalms 57:7–11 and 60:5–12.

- Psalm 135 is made up entirely of phrases from other psalms.

- Isaiah 2:2–4 is repeated in Micah 4:1–3. (Joel 3:10 reverses the thought of the last verse.)

- Large portions of the Gospel of Mark are repeated in the Gospels of Matthew and Luke.

- Ephesians 5:18–6:9 is repeated as Colossians 3:16–25.

❈ LITERARY GENRES FOUND IN SCRIPTURE ❈

A literary *genre* is a type of literature, such as a novel, a poem, or a technical manual. These are some of the genres found in the Holy Scriptures, with examples. There are other ways of organizing the classifications, and often the literary forms are mixed. The categories assigned to biblical material do not always reflect the form; for example, the Letter of James is more a sermon than a letter, and the Revelation to John is more a drama than a prophecy.

Poetry Genres

Prophetic Oracle ..... Utterances of "the word of the LORD," throughout the Prophets and in some of the Psalms (e.g., 82, 91)

Hymn .... Many of the Psalms, such as 8, 46, 100, 150, and early Christian hymns in Luke 1–2 or the Revelation to John

Lament .... The majority of Psalms; also found in the Prophets and in Lamentations

Wedding Poetry ...... Psalm 45, the Song of Solomon

Narrative Genres

Story .... A narrative of unfolding events, historical or biographical. This is a major genre found in most parts of the Bible, such as Genesis–Numbers, Joshua–Chronicles, parts of the prophetic books, and the Acts of the Apostles. There are subcategories.

Gospel .... Not a standard history-biography but a specialized proclamation of Jesus as Messiah

Parable .... An illustrative story, developed most fully by Jesus in Matthew–Luke but found elsewhere

Instructional/Wisdom Genres

Law .... Biblical law is more instructional than legal, especially the conditional ("casuistic") law of Exodus

Proverb .... Short instructional sayings, as in the book of Proverbs

Reflection .... Ecclesiastes

Sermon .... Preaching based on law or Christian principles, such as Deuteronomy or the book of James

Epistle Genres

Circular letter ...... The letters of Paul to various churches, or the letters of Revelation 1–3

Official letter ...... Letters to and from officials in the Persian Empire, in the book of Ezra

✵ LITERARY GENRES FOUND IN SCRIPTURE—CONT. ✵

Dramatic Genres
Apocalypse . . . . Daniel and the Revelation to John
Dialogue . . . . The book of Job

Liturgical Genres
Liturgical directives . . . Instructions for performing sacrifices, etc., as in Leviticus
Laws for recitation . . . The Ten Commandments and other groupings ("apodic-
tic" or absolute law)
Festival liturgies . . . . . . Psalms 50, 118

Genealogy
Ancestor or . . . . 1 Chronicles or the genealogies of Jesus in Matthew and
family lists   Luke

✵ HOW A POPE IS ELECTED ✵

The pope, or Holy Father, is the bishop of Rome and is elected by the clergy of his diocese. Because he oversees the Roman Catholic Church worldwide, the priests of the Diocese of Rome (known as the College of Cardinals) are drawn from all across the Catholic Church, most being bishops or archbishops. They are nominally the pastors of churches of the Diocese of Rome, but they normally spend their time administering their own regions or other departments of the church (called *Congregations* or *Dicasteries*).

Pope John Paul II revised the rules for electing a pope. Cardinals must be under eighty years old to take part in the election, and the number of those entitled to vote is limited to 120. When a pope dies, this "conclave" of cardinals spends two to three weeks mourning, then gathers in the Vatican's Sistine Chapel. The electors write the name of their choice on a secret ballot; they are sworn to secrecy about the deliberations and must have no contact with the outside world during the process.

Designated officials tally the ballots. A candidate must receive two-thirds of the eligible votes, but after thirty unsuccessful attempts, a simple majority will elect the new pope. The ballots are burned after each vote as a signal to the outside world, with a substance to turn the smoke white if a new pope has been elected. The new pope chooses the name he will use, and the dean of the College of Cardinals introduces him from the Vatican's main balcony with the words *Habemus Papam*, "We have a pope." An inauguration ceremony follows.

In theory, even a layman can be elected to the papacy, but the last time this happened was in 1059. Since 1378, all popes have been chosen from the College of Cardinals.

❊ THE AMAZING SANTA ❊

Santa Claus, in whatever local disguise is appropriate, is responsible for delivering gifts to good children on the night before Christmas. There are approximately two billion children in the world, but Santa does not handle Muslim, Buddhist, Hindu, Jewish, or Jehovah's Witnesses children or those from other groups that do not celebrate Christmas, leaving him with a clientele of around 378 million.

There is an average of 3.5 children per family, making 108 million homes for him to visit (assuming at least 1 good child in each). Given the rotation of the earth and different time zones, he has 31 hours to work with, making 822.6 visits per second, during each of which he has to pick the correct gifts, descend the chimney, distribute the gifts and fill stockings, eat whatever refreshments have been set out for him, and return to his sleigh. Assuming children are evenly distributed around the earth's landmass, he must travel approximately 75.5 million miles, while working in rest stops and time to change into the appropriate costume for the area visited.

Santa's sleigh must carry approximately a 2-pound gift for each child, of whatever type is the current favorite for boys and girls in the visited regions. Assuming an 85 percent ratio of good children to the total, Santa's sleigh must carry a payload of 321,300 tons, not counting the weight of the massive sleigh nor of Santa himself, who is known to have an obesity challenge (conservative estimates place his weight at 250 pounds).

A standard reindeer can pull about half a ton; assuming that flying reindeer can pull 10 times that amount, 64,620 reindeer are required. The average male reindeer weighs 203 pounds at this time of year, increasing the total weight of cargo and propulsion engine to 327,822 tons. When in motion between visits, Santa and his vehicle are traveling at about 650 miles per second, or 3,000 times the speed of sound. This mass traveling at such a velocity would normally heat up through atmospheric resistance to the point of near-instantaneous vaporization. Moreover, Santa is subjected to centrifugal forces 17,500 times that of gravity, being pinned to the back of his sleigh by around 4,315,000 pounds of force.

It's a miracle that even good children receive any Christmas gifts at all.

❊ THE FIVE POINTS OF ARMINIANISM ❊

These are the "five points of Arminianism."

Destiny for salvation is conditional on our response to God.
All people are offered salvation in the atonement of Christ.
It takes the work of the Spirit to create faith in us.
Saving grace is necessary, but we can resist it.
Yes, it is possible to fall away from God's grace.

❊ WELL-KNOWN WOMEN OF CHRISTIAN HISTORY ❊

Susanna Wesley

Helena (247–327) . . Mother of Emperor Constantine, identified many sites in the Holy Land associated with the life of Christ

Monica (331–387) . . Mother of Augustine, influential in his conversion to Christianity

Héloïse (1095–1164) Mistress and secret wife of Peter Abelard, became head of an abbey of nuns

Hildegard von . . . . . German mystic and Bingen (1098–1179) influential writer, head of a convent

Julian (Juliana) of . . . . English mystic who lived in solitude but was influential Norwich (1342–1413) through her writing

Joan of Arc (1412–1431) . . Visionary and martyr, patron saint of France

Catherine of Aragon . . . . Henry VIII's annulment of their marriage led to the (1485–1536) Church of England's break with Rome

Teresa of Avila . . . . Reformed the Carmelite order, a mystic and authority (1515–1582) on prayer

Elizabeth I (1533–1603) Developed England into the strongest Protestant nation of the time

Susanna Wesley . . . . Mother of John and Charles, influential in their spiritual (1669–1742) formation

Catherine Winkworth . . . Translator of many well-known hymns from German (1829–1878) to English

Catherine Booth . . . . Cofounder of the Salvation Army (1829–1890)

Thérèse of Lisieux . . . . . . French nun and devotional writer, canonized in 1925 (1873–1897)

Fanny Crosby Van . . . . . . Blind poetess of New York City, published more than two Alstyne (1823–1915) thousand hymns, many of which are still in use

Aimee Semple . . . . Evangelist, founder of the Foursquare Gospel Church McPherson (1890–1944)

❊ HISTORIC ORDERS OF THE CATHOLIC CHURCH ❊

In Roman Catholic terminology, the words *religious* and *secular* have special meanings. The *secular* clergy are those assigned to the local churches or parishes, while the *religious* are members of religious orders (monks, nuns, and priests). The religious orders own and operate many of the institutions of the Catholic Church, which in 1992 were said to number 6,200 hospitals or sanitariums; 27,000 homes for the elderly, homeless, or handicapped; 80,600 elementary or primary schools; and 6,400 colleges and universities. The largest orders are the Franciscans, with more than 100,000 members in both men's and women's branches; the Jesuits, with 23,000; and the Salesians, with 17,000.

Common Name	Principal Full Name	Initials	Gender	Founder, Year	Emphases
Augustinians*	Order of St. Augustine	O.S.A.	M, F	Eleventh century	Higher education
Benedictines	Order of St. Benedict	O.S.B.	M, F	Unknown, sixth century	Community life
Carmelites	Order of Our Lady of Mt. Carmel	O.Carm.	M, F	Unknown, around 1150	Many areas of service, including missions
Discalced Carmelites	Order of Discalced Carmelites	O.C.D.	M, F	Teresa of Avila, 1568	Contemplative life
Divine Word Missionaries	Society of the Divine Word	S.V.D.	M	Arnold Janssens, 1875	Missions
Dominicans	Order of Friars Preachers *and many other groups*	O.P.	M, F	Dominic de Guzman, 1205	Doctrine, education
Franciscans	Order of Friars Minor *and many other groups*	O.F.M.	M, F	Francis of Assisi, 1209	Functions include schools, missions, and custody of Holy Land sites
Jesuits	Society of Jesus	S.J.	M	Ignatius Loyola 1540	Higher education

❊ HISTORIC ORDERS OF THE ❊ CATHOLIC CHURCH—CONT.

Common Name	Principal Full Name	Initials	Gender	Founder, Year	Emphases
Lasallians	Brothers of the Christian	F.S.C.	M	Jean-Baptiste de La Salle, 1680	Schools
Marists	Society of Mary	S.M.	M, F	1816	Many areas of service
Missionaries of Charity	Missionaries of Charity	M.C.	M, F	Mother Teresa, 1948	Homes for sick and dying
Paulists	Paulist Fathers	C.S.P.	M	Isaac Hecker, 1858	Education, publishing
Redemptorists	Congregation of the Most Holy Redeemer	C.SS.R.	M	Alphonsus Liguori, 1732	Missions
Salesians	Salesians of Don Bosco			Don Bosco, 1859	Schools
Salvatorians	Society of the Divine Savior	S.D.S.	M, F	Francis Jordan, 1881	Missions
Sisters of Charity**	Sisters of Charity		F	Elizabeth Ann Seton, 1810	Work with the poor
Servites	Order of Friar Servants of Mary	O.S.M.	M	Group, 1240	Many areas of service
Sisters, Servants of Mary	Sisters, Servants of Mary	S.M.	F	Maria Soledad, 1851	Nursing homes
Viatorians	Clerics of Saint Viator	O.S.V.	M	Louis Querbes, 1831	Schools

*The most famous Augustinian is Martin Luther.
**Many groups are called Sisters (or Brothers) of Charity, going back to St. Vincent de Paul, 1633.

❧ THE FOUR HORSEMEN OF THE APOCALYPSE ❧

In chapter 6 of the Revelation to John (called the *Apocalypse*), the Lamb is given a scroll of seven seals, containing the judgments to come upon the land. As each of the first four seals is opened, John sees a horse and rider come forth. The four horsemen are

The Four Horsemen of the Apocalypse

1. A rider on a white horse, with a bow, who is given a crown and rides forth to conquer

2. A rider on a red horse, given a great sword and sent forth to cause people to kill one another

3. A rider on a black horse, holding a balance; a voice describes the impending high cost of food, but with the admonition, "do not harm the oil and wine"

4. Death, riding a pale horse, followed by Hades, given power to kill a fourth of the land's population by sword, famine, pestilence, or wild animals

Some view the "four horsemen" as a picture of judgments yet to occur, others see them as symbolic of ongoing conditions resulting from human sinfulness, and some see in the four horsemen a description of conditions in Judea during the time of the Jewish revolt against Rome and the destruction of Jerusalem and its temple in AD 70.

❧ PRESBYTERIAN BODIES IN NORTH AMERICA ❧

Associate Reformed Presbyterian Church • Bible Presbyterian Church • Cumberland Presbyterian Church • Evangelical Presbyterian Church • Free Presbyterian Church • Korean American Presbyterian Church • Orthodox Presbyterian Church • Presbyterian Church in America • Presbyterian Church (USA) • Reformed Presbyterian Church of North America • Reformed Presbyterian Church (Covenanted) • Second Cumberland Presbyterian Church in the United States

❦ DENOMINATIONS THAT ORDAIN ❦ WOMEN AS PASTORS OR PRIESTS

Paul, in Galatians 3:28, wrote that "there is neither Jew nor Greek, there is neither slave nor free, there is neither male nor female; for you are all one in Christ Jesus." Some Christian groups take this to mean that women may be admitted to the ranks of the ordained ministry. Others, such as the Unitarian Universalist Association, take their cue more from the feminist movement than from Scripture. Churches that ordain women include

> American Baptist Churches in the USA • Assemblies of God • Christian Reformed Church • Church of England and other national Anglican bodies (some bishops do not) • Disciples of Christ • Episcopal Church, USA (some dioceses do not) • "Evangelical Church" (Lutheran) of Germany, Denmark, and other European countries • Evangelical Covenant Church • Evangelical Lutheran Church of America • Holiness groups including the Church of God (Anderson, Indiana) and the Church of the Nazarene • Mennonites • National Association of Congregational Christian Churches • Presbyterian Church (USA) • Salvation Army • Society of Friends (Quakers) • Unitarian Universalist Association • United Church of Canada • United Church of Christ • United Church of Christ in the Philippines (merger of many Protestant bodies) • United Methodist Church

❦ A TYPICAL "SINNER'S PRAYER" ❦

Those making their first commitment as Christians often say the Sinner's Prayer. The prayer has many variations, but they all have the same structure:

1. Acknowledging sin against God
2. Appealing for his forgiveness
3. Affirming belief in Jesus' death and resurrection on one's behalf
4. Asking Jesus to take control of one's life and change it
5. Accepting responsibility for living according to God's will

Based on the above, this could be a typical sinner's prayer:

I need you, Lord Jesus, because I know I have disobeyed God and become separated from him. Forgive my sin and cleanse me. Thank you that you died and rose again to give me new life. Take control of my life and help me live as the person you want me to be. I promise to be God's servant, with the help of his Holy Spirit. Amen.

❋ TWO CHERUBIM OR FOUR? ❋

The ark of the covenant was the symbol of Yahweh's presence with Israel. The *cherubim* were winged figures of hammered gold on the cover of the ark (Exod. 25:18–22). In addition, two cherubim about eighteen feet tall were placed in the inner sanctuary (holy of holies) of the temple of Solomon, where their wings overspread the ark (1 Kings 6:23–28). Thus there were *four* cherubim associated with the presence of the Lord, not counting those carved on the doors of the temple.

The cherubim were not "cherubs" as we know them—the chubby winged children of Michelangelo's painting. They were probably more like the awesome composite guardian figures that have been excavated in the palaces of ancient Assyrian rulers—winged figures with body features of the ox and the lion and the head of a man. They were the symbolic guardians of a royal throne and fulfilled this role in Israel as well: "Thou who art enthroned upon the cherubim, shine forth" (Ps. 80:1).

The prophet Ezekiel was a priest (Ezek. 1:3) and would have had access to the temple's inner sanctuary. The description of the four living creatures in his vision of the Lord's glory (Ezek. 1:5–11) is patterned after the appearance of the cherubim, and the four living creatures of the apostle John's vision (Rev. 4:7) are similar. These four cherubim-like figures became the traditional Christian symbols of the four evangelists or gospel writers: Matthew (winged man), Mark (winged lion), Luke (winged ox), and John (eagle).

❋ LEAST RELIGIOUS STATES IN THE UNITED STATES ❋

Hawaii, Oregon, and Washington are the least religious states in the United States. A 2000 survey indicated that as many as 52 percent of Hawaiians identify with no religion; of the remainder, 29 percent are Christian and the others are divided among non-Christian religions. (Hawaii has a large ethnic Japanese population.) Seventeen percent of Oregonians report themselves to be unaffiliated with any religion. In Washington the figure is 14 percent. One report says the percentage of nonreligious in the U.S. is 7 percent. However, the 2000 survey claimed that 14.1 percent of Americans are "secular," with 76.5 claiming to be Christian. The remaining 9.4 percent are reported to be adherents of non-Christian religions or of unknown preference.

❈ NOTABLE CHURCH ARCHITECTS ❈

Architect	Lived	Style	Example
Abbot Suger	1081–1155	Gothic architecture (pioneer)	Abbey of St-Denis, France
Giacomo della Porta	1532–1604	Classical-Baroque	St. Peter's Basilica, Rome
Christopher Wren	1632–1723	English Baroque	St. Paul's Cathedral and many churches in London
Charles Bullfinch	1763–1844	American classical	St. Stephen's Church, Boston (originally New North Congregational Society)
Henry Hobson Richardson	1838–1886	Romanesque revival	Trinity Church, Boston
William Butterfield	1814–1900	Victorian Gothic	All Saints Church, Margaret Street, London
John Francis Bentley	1839–1902	Victorian Byzantine	Westminster Cathedral (Catholic), London
George Frederick Bodley	1827–1907	Medieval styles	National Cathedral, Washington, D.C
Bertram Grosvenor Goodhue	1869–1924	Modern Gothic, Romanesque	St. Patrick's Cathedral, New York
Antonio Gaudi	1852–1926	Expressionist	La Sagrada Familia, Barcelona
Eliel Saarinen	1873–1950	Art Nouveau or "Modern"	First Christian Church, Columbus, Indiana
Eero Saarinen	1910–1961	"International"	North Christian Church, Columbus, Indiana

❈ THREE CHRISTMAS ISLANDS ❈

The famous Christmas Island of Micronesia in the South Pacific is part of the Republic of Kiribati. Captain James Cook discovered it on December 24, 1777. Another Christmas Island, part of Australia, is in the Indian Ocean. Captain William Mynors discovered it on December 25, 1643. Nova Scotia's Christmas Island is not an island but a village. There are two stories of how it got its name: (1) an Indian chief called Christmas is buried on the small offshore island, (2) a team of surveyors named it after finishing their work on Christmas Day.

❋ THE COLLECT, A PATTERN FOR PRAYER ❋

The *collect* is a short prayer that Anglican, Lutheran, and other liturgical churches use in worship. It is called a *collect* because it "collects" the thoughts of the worshipers into one statement at appropriate points in the service. But collects aren't just random prayers; they have a specific structure. Here is one way a collect could be structured:

1. Address to God
2. Descriptive clause about God, i.e., what it is about God that encourages the purpose of the collect
3. Petition or thanksgiving
4. Reason for, or desired outcome of, prayer
5. Ending

Example:
(1) Almighty God, (2) unto whom all hearts are open, all desires known, and from whom no secrets are hid: (3) Cleanse the thoughts of our hearts by the inspiration of thy Holy Spirit, (4) that we may perfectly love thee and worthily magnify thy holy Name; (5) through Christ our Lord. Amen.

❋ BIRTH ORDERS OF SOME CHRISTIAN LEADERS ❋

Brother Andrew (Andy Van Der Bijl) . . . . Fourth of six
Dietrich Bonhoeffer . . . . Sixth of eight (had a twin sister)
William Carey . . . . Oldest of four
Amy Carmichael . . . . Oldest of seven
Billy Graham . . . . Oldest of four
Pope John Paul II (Karol Wojtyla) . . . . Youngest of three (one died in infancy)
C. S. Lewis (Clive Staples Lewis) . . . . Younger of two
David Livingston . . . . Second of seven
Oral Roberts . . . . Youngest of five
Marion G. "Pat" Robertson . . . . Younger of two
Alexander Solzhenitsyn . . . . Only child
Billy Sunday (William Ashley Sunday) . . . . Younger of two
Corrie ten Boom . . . . Youngest of five
Mother Teresa (Agnes Gonxha Bojaxhiu) . . . . Youngest of four
John Wesley . . . . Fifteenth of nineteen
Charles Wesley . . . . Eighteenth of nineteen
Susanna Wesley (mother of John and Charles) . . . . . . Twenty-fifth of twenty-five

❋ SUPPOSED SAYINGS OF JESUS ❋
NOT FOUND IN SCRIPTURE

Sayings of Jesus exist outside the four Gospels. Paul quoted such a saying in Acts 20:35, "It is more blessed to give than to receive." Jesus also spoke in the Revelation to John. Some editions of the Bible print all the words of Christ in red, highlighting these sayings.

There are, however, other sayings that have come down to us outside the Bible itself, in the writings of the church fathers or in ancient manuscripts. Scholars call these sayings the *agrapha*. Biblical scholars share no universal agreement as to the authenticity of any of them, but a number of prominent scholars consider the following to have the ring of a genuine saying of Jesus.

- Jesus saw a man working on the Sabbath and said to him, "Man, if you know what you are doing you are blessed. But if you don't know, you are cursed and a transgressor against the law."—Codex Bezae (D), in place of Luke 6:5

- "He who is near me is near the fire; he who is far from me is far from the kingdom."—Quoted by Origen

- "No man can obtain the kingdom of heaven, who has not passed through temptation."—Quoted by Tertullian, in the passion narrative before the Garden of Gethsemane

- "I choose for myself the best; the best are those whom my Father in heaven has given me."—Quoted by Eusebius, citing the lost Gospel of the Hebrews

- "Those who are with me have not understood me."—Quoted in the apocryphal Acts of Peter

- "And never be joyful, except when you look upon your brother in love."—Quoted by Jerome, in commenting on Ephesians 5:3–4

- "And pray for your enemies. For he who is not against you is for you, and he who stands far off today will be near you tomorrow."—Oxyrhynchus Papyrus 1224

- "Be approved moneychangers who reject much, but keep the good."—Quoted by Clement of Alexandria in *Stromata*

- "Lift up the stone, and there you will find me; split the wood, and I am there."—Oxyrhynchus Papyrus 1

- "Where one is alone, there I am there also; and where two are, there I am also."—Quoted by Ephraem Syrus

- "Jesus, on whom be peace, has said, 'This world is a bridge. Pass over it, but do not build your dwelling there.'"—On the wall of the ruin of a mosque near Delhi, India, built by Akbar the Great Mogul (1542–1605)

❊ FAMOUS EXCOMMUNICATES ❊

Early Christian leaders deemed heretics were excommunicated (removed from the church). These are some well-known or powerful people who have been excommunicated since the year 1000:

Pope Leo IX and Michael I Cerularius, patriarch of Constantinople—Excommunicated each other in 1054, the official break between the Eastern and Western churches

Henry IV, Holy Roman Emperor—Excommunicated in 1076 for refusing to recognize the authority of Pope Gregory VII and declaring him deposed

Henry VIII of England—Excommunicated in 1533 by Pope Clement VII for annulment of his marriage to Catherine of Aragon and remarriage to Anne Boleyn

Martin Luther, Reformer—Excommunicated in 1521 by Pope Leo X

Elizabeth I of England—Excommunicated in 1570 by Pope Pius V for heresy in claiming to head the Church in England

Giordano (Filippo) Bruno, astronomer—Excommunicated in 1589 by the Lutheran Church of Helmstedt, burned by the Catholic Inquisition in 1593

José María Morelso, priest—Excommunicated around 1813 for leading a Mexican revolt against Spain. He was executed in 1815; a Mexican state is named after him.

Lev Tolstoi, writer—Excommunicated in 1901 by the Russian Holy Synod for departure from Orthodox teaching (We know him as Leo Tolstoy.)

Father Leonard Feeney—Excommunicated in 1953 by Pope Pius XII for refusing to submit to ecclesiastical authority and tone down his harsh, exclusivist teaching

Nikos Kazantzakis, writer—Excommunicated in 1954 by the Greek Orthodox Church for writing the novel *The Last Temptation of Christ*

Juan Perón, Argentine dictator—Excommunicated in 1955 for legalizing divorce and prostitution

Archbishop Marcel Lefebvre—Excommunicated in 1988 by Cardinal Bernardin Gantin for an irregular consecration of bishops and opposition to Vatican II changes

❈ CHRISTIAN HUMANITARIANS ❈

A humanitarian is a person who promotes human welfare and social reform. Christian faith has motivated many humanitarians of the Western world. These are a few of them.

William Wilberforce (1759–1833) . . . . . British Member of Parliament who secured the abolition of slavery and promoted missions and the Bible Society

George Mueller (1805–1898) . . . . Founder of children's homes in England and leader of the Brethren movement

William (1821–1912) and . . . . Evangelists with an outreach to the poor
Catherine (1829–1890) Booth of England; they founded the Salvation Army

Florence Nightingale (1820–1910) . . . . . English pioneer of nursing and modern hospitals; she described her nurses as "handmaidens of the Lord"

Clara Barton (1821–1912) . . . . Organizer of the American Red Cross. She was a Universalist, which was originally not a Unitarian movement.

Dorothy Day (1897–1980) . . . . Convert to Catholicism, she became an advocate for workers, the poor, and pacifism, making New York her base.

Mother Teresa (1910–1997) . . . . Macedonian-born nun who spent her life operating a home for the dying in Calcutta, India

Martin Luther King Jr. (1929–1968) . . . . Baptist minister who led the civil-rights movement; won the Nobel Peace Prize in 1966

Millard Fuller (1935–) . . . . Founder and president of the ministry Habitat for Humanity International, which provides housing for needy families worldwide

❧ ST. PATRICK'S BREASTPLATE ❧

According to legend, St. Patrick wrote this hymn on his breastplate, or *lorica*, to protect himself from an ambush, and when he and his companions passed by their enemies, they appeared to be deer. It is sometimes called the *Deer's Cry.*

I bind unto myself today
The strong Name of the Trinity,
By invocation of the same
The Three in One and One in Three.

I bind this today to me forever
By power of faith, Christ's incarnation;
His baptism in Jordan river,
His death on Cross for my salvation;
His bursting from the spicèd tomb,
His riding up the heavenly way,
His coming at the day of doom
I bind unto myself today.

I bind unto myself the power
Of the great love of cherubim;
The sweet "Well done" in judgment hour,
The service of the seraphim,
Confessors' faith, Apostles' word,
The Patriarchs' prayers, the prophets' scrolls,
All good deeds done unto the Lord
And purity of virgin souls.

I bind unto myself today
The virtues of the star lit heaven,
The glorious sun's life giving ray,
The whiteness of the moon at even,
The flashing of the lightning free,
The whirling wind's tempestuous shocks,
The stable earth, the deep salt sea
Around the old eternal rocks.

I bind unto myself today
The power of God to hold and lead,
His eye to watch, His might to stay,
His ear to hearken to my need.
The wisdom of my God to teach,
His hand to guide, His shield to ward;

The word of God to give me speech,
His heavenly host to be my guard.
Against the demon snares of sin,
The vice that gives temptation force,
The natural lusts that war within,
The hostile men that mar my course;
Or few or many, far or nigh,
In every place and in all hours,
Against their fierce hostility
I bind to me these holy powers.

Against all Satan's spells and wiles,
Against false words of heresy,
Against the knowledge that defiles,
Against the heart's idolatry,
Against the wizard's evil craft,
Against the death wound and the burning,
The choking wave, the poisoned shaft,
Protect me, Christ, till Thy returning.

Christ be with me, Christ within me,
Christ behind me, Christ before me,
Christ beside me, Christ to win me,
Christ to comfort and restore me.
Christ beneath me, Christ above me,
Christ in quiet, Christ in danger,
Christ in hearts of all that love me,
Christ in mouth of friend and stranger.

I bind unto myself the Name,
The strong Name of the Trinity,
By invocation of the same,
The Three in One and One in Three.
By Whom all nature hath creation,
Eternal Father, Spirit, Word:
Praise to the Lord of my salvation,
Salvation is of Christ the Lord.

❧ CHRISTIAN PICKUP LINES ❧

"Hi, my name's Will
. . . God's will."

"Hey, baby, you wanna take the
church van for a spin?"

"Has anyone ever told you
your eyes are like doves and
your neck is like the tower
of David?"

"So . . . what's your favorite
Bible verse?"

"That *Strong's Exhaustive
Concordance* looks pretty heavy.
Could I carry it for you to
your next class?"

"I think God was showing off
when he made you."

"Nice WWJD bracelet!
'Who would Jesus date?'—uh,
I mean, 'What would Jesus do?'"

"I don't see it myself, but people
tell me I look like Michael
W. Smith."

"Did I tell you my great uncle
was a personal friend of
Billy Graham?"

"Would you like to come over to
my place and see my collection
of C. S. Lewis books?"

❧ HOW TO BENEFIT FROM A LECTIONARY ❧

Many Christians follow a personal plan for reading through the Bible in a year, but what about the Bible passages chosen for reading in their church's worship services? Lectionaries are lists of Scripture readings to be read throughout the year in Christian worship. Believers have used lectionaries since the fourth century, but the Protestant Reformers largely abandoned them in favor of preaching straight through the books of the Bible. In the 1960s a group called the *Consultation on Common Texts* began to develop a lectionary that Catholic, Anglican, and other Protestant churches in North America could use.

The *Revised Common Lectionary* arranges the Scripture readings in a three-year cycle: A, B, and C. For each Sunday there are readings from the Old Testament, Psalms, Epistles, and Gospels, with occasional readings from the Apocrypha (an alternate Old Testament reading is supplied). Each denomination using the *Revised Common Lectionary* has its own minor variations to accommodate its special worship needs, but on a given Sunday the readings are likely to be much the same. Year A begins with the Advent season in November 2004, 2007, 2010, and so on.

Using a lectionary helps to coordinate the seasons of the church year with God's history of salvation, especially the gospel story of Christ. It also encourages preachers not to overemphasize their favorite passages while neglecting others.

❦ BIBLE RECIPES ❦

Unleavened Bread
2 cups whole wheat flour
1 tablespoon cooking oil
½ teaspoon salt

Adding enough warm water, mix the ingredients into a smooth dough. Let the mixture rest for at least a half-hour. Then roll out portions (about the size of a golf ball) on a floured board to about the size of a saucer. Place the cakes on a hot plate or skillet till they begin to blister, then turn them over and do the other side. A covered grill can also be used. Any grain flour may be substituted for wheat.

Boiled Leeks
3 large leeks
1¼ teaspoons toasted mustard seed
1 tablespoon red wine vinegar
2 tablespoons olive oil
Salt and pepper to taste

Rinse the leeks under running water. Trim the ends and cut them crosswise into 1/2-inch slices. Bring a pot of water to a boil, add the leeks, and cook 20–25 minutes until very soft. Drain, and then place in a serving dish. Finely grind 1 teaspoon of the toasted mustard seeds. Blend the vinegar and ground mustard seed. Slowly whisk in the olive oil and season with salt and pepper. Spoon this mixture over the leeks. Sprinkle the remaining 1/4 teaspoon whole mustard seeds over the leeks and serve at room temperature. Recipe serves 4.

Esau's Pottage
1 cup uncooked barley
1 cup uncooked lentils
1 large onion, chopped
½ cup celery, chopped
1 clove of garlic, minced or pressed
1 teaspoon salt

Combine all ingredients in a covered pot. Bring to a boil, then reduce heat and simmer until done (may be baked for 45 minutes at 350 degrees). Serve with bread. Recipe serves 8.

❧ HYMNS BASED ON THE PSALMS ❧

Psalm 8 . . . . "O How Glorious, Full of Wonder" (Curtis Beach, 1940s)

Psalm 19 . . . . "The Spacious Firmament on High" (Joseph Addison, 1712)

Psalm 23 . . . . "The King of Love My Shepherd Is" (Henry W. Baker, 1868)

Psalm 23 . . . . "The Lord's My Shepherd, I'll Not Want" (Scottish Psalter, 1650)

Psalm 34   "Through All the Changing Scenes of Life"
(Tate and Brady, 1696)

Psalm 46 . . . . "A Mighty Fortress Is Our God" (Martin Luther, 1529)

Psalm 72 . . . . "Hail to the Lord's Anointed" (James Montgomery, 1821)

Psalm 72 . . . . "Jesus Shall Reign" (Isaac Watts, 1719)

Psalm 84 . . . . "How Lovely Is Thy Dwelling Place" (Scottish Psalter, 1650)

Psalm 87 . . . . "Glorious Things of Thee Are Spoken" (John Newton, 1779)

Psalm 90 . . . . "O God, Our Help in Ages Past" (Isaac Watts, 1719)

Psalm 97 . . . . "Rejoice, the Lord Is King" (Charles Wesley, 1744)

Psalm 98 . . . . "Joy to the World! the Lord Is Come" (Isaac Watts, 1719)

Psalm 100 . . . . "Before Jehovah's Awful Throne" (Isaac Watts, 1707)

Psalm 103 . . . . "O My Soul, Bless God the Father" (Presbyterian Book of
Psalms, 1871)

Psalm 104 . . . . "O Worship the King" (Robert Grant, 1833)

Psalm 117 . . . . "From All That Dwell Below the Skies" (Isaac Watts, 1719)

Psalm 148 . . . . "Praise the Lord! O Heavens, Adore Him" (Founding Hospital
Collection, 1796)

❧ THE FAMOUS WESLEYAN QUADRILATERAL ❧

The phrase *Wesleyan Quadrilateral* has come into use to denote four principal factors that John Wesley believed would help in understanding Christian faith. Many theologians take it as a good paradigm for doing theological work.

1. *Scripture* is the primary source and standard for Christian teaching.

2. *Tradition* is the witness to the development of the faith through the history of the church.

3. *Reason* is discerning, consistent thinking about the truths of the faith and its logical exposition.

4. *Experience* is the believer's living out of his or her faith.

❋ NORTH AMERICAN TOWNS WITH BIBLICAL NAMES ❋

To list all the places in North America with names from the Bible would fill several pages. We can mention only some of the most often used or interesting names and the larger cities. Bible names in Canada and the United States come in two categories: places named for people in the Bible and places named for biblical locations.

Places with names of apostles or gospel writers include

Paul—St. Paul, Alberta and KS; San Pablo, CA; South St. Paul, MN

Peter—Petersburg, VA; Pierre, SD; San Pedro, CA

Matthew—St. Matthews, KY; San Mateo, CA

Mark—San Marcos, CA and TX

Luke—Lucas, TX; Lucasville, OH. Toledo, OH, is in Lucas County.

James—Jamestown, NY, ND, and VA; St-Jacques, Quebec

John—Johnstown, NY and PA; St. Johns, MI; St. Johnsbury, VT; St-Jean, Quebec; San Juan, TX

Thomas—Thomas, WV; St. Thomas, Ontario; Thomasville, GA and NC; Thomaston, GA

Philip—Philipsburg, PA; Phillipsburg, KS

These are some other interesting names:

Babylon and West Babylon, NY

Beulah, ND

Dothan, AL

Emmaus, PA

Fair Haven, VT

Gahanna, OH

Jericho, NY and VT

Mars Hill, ME

Moab, UT

Nazareth, PA

Palestine, TX; East Palestine, OH

Paradise, CA

Philippi, WV

Pisgah, AL and OH

Rehoboth, MA; Rehoboth Beach, DE

Sardis, MS

Sidon, MS

Sodom, ME

Tekoa, WA

Zarephath, NJ

Zion and Mt. Zion, IL

❀ WOMEN IN THE LIFE OF PAUL ❀

Some have accused the apostle Paul of downplaying the role of women in the church, but in fact a number of women were involved in his ministry or played a part in his story. They are mentioned in his letters, in the book of Acts, or in apocryphal sources.

- Paul's mother is not mentioned in the Bible, though she must have lived in Paul's home city of Tarsus (Acts 21:39). Paul was both a Jew and a Roman citizen. His citizenship could have come from his father's status. Probably both his parents were Jewish; but if his father was not, by Jewish custom Paul would have been considered a Jew through his mother.

- Paul's sister apparently lived in Jerusalem; her son warned Paul of an ambush (Acts 23:16).

- Lydia was a businesswoman of Thyatira who provided hospitality for Paul and the apostles (Acts 16:14–15).

- A slave girl, out of whom Paul cast a spirit of divination (Acts 16:18), became the cause of a disturbance in Philippi that led to Paul's imprisonment and the salvation of the jailer and his family.

- Prisca (Priscilla) and her husband, Aquila, labored with Paul in Corinth and Ephesus, both in evangelism and in their craft of leatherworking (tentmaking), and at one point they even saved his life (Rom. 16:4).

- Phoebe was a deaconess in the church of Cenchreae, whom Paul commended to the church in Rome (Rom. 16:1).

- Mary was a hard worker in the Roman congregation (Rom. 16:6).

- Tryphaena, Tryphosa, and Persis were workers Paul knew in the church in Rome (Rom. 16:12).

- Rufus's mother was like a mother to Paul (Rom. 16:13).

- Julia and the unnamed sister of Nereus were also members of the congregation in Rome (Rom. 16:15).

- Euodia and Syntyche were fellow workers with Paul in the church in Philippi; Paul urged them to settle their quarrel, whatever it was (Phil. 4:2).

- Nympha made her house available for church gatherings, apparently in Laodicea (Col. 4:15).

- Apphia was the wife either of Philemon or Archippus, and apparently the church in Colossae met in her home (Philem. 1:2).

- Lois and Eunice were Timothy's grandmother and mother, whom Paul respected for their faith (2 Tim. 1:5).

- Thecla was said to be a girl from Iconium who broke her engagement when converted, joined Paul in his missionary work, and was martyred in her old age (apocryphal Acts of Paul).

❈ CHRISTIAN QUOTABLES ❈

"Thou hast made us for Thyself, and our hearts are restless until they find their rest in Thee." —Augustine of Hippo

"The Christian ideal has not been tried and found wanting; it has been found difficult and left untried." — G. K. Chesterton

"Worship is the normal employment of moral beings." —A. W. Tozer

"No man is a fool to exchange what he cannot keep for that which he cannot lose." —attributed in several forms to Jim Elliot

"Never forget that only dead fish swim with the stream."—Malcolm Muggeridge

"I believe in Christianity as I believe in the rising sun; not because I see it, but by it I can see all else." —C. S. Lewis

"I have had more trouble with myself than with any other man." —D. L. Moody

"Going to church doesn't make you a Christian any more than going to the garage makes you a car." — attributed to several, including Moshe Rosen and Laurence J. Peter

"There are many of us that are willing to do great things for the Lord, but few of us are willing to do little things." —D. L. Moody

"Cleanliness is indeed next to godliness." —John Wesley

"I know God will not give me anything I can't handle. I just wish that he didn't trust me so much." —Mother Teresa

"Anything worth doing is worth doing poorly."—attributed to G. K. Chesterton

"Whoever acknowledges the leading truths of Christianity, and conforms his life to that acknowledgement, we esteem a Christian." —Barton W. Stone

"If we cannot believe God when circumstances seem to be against us, we do not believe Him at all." — Charles H. Spurgeon

"If a man hasn't discovered something that he would die for, he isn't fit to live."—Martin Luther King Jr.

"Worry does not empty tomorrow of its sorrow; it empties today of its strength." —Corrie ten Boom

"Do all the good you can by all the means you can in all the places you can at all the times you can to all the people you can as long as ever you can." —John Wesley

❉ CHRISTIAN QUOTABLES—CONT. ❉

"Evidence of our hardness is that we are more concerned about our sufferings than our sins." —Matthew Henry

"My temptations have been my masters in divinity." —Martin Luther

"This life was not intended to be the place of our perfection, but the preparation for it." —Richard Baxter

"The world is my parish." —John Wesley

"Faith isn't believing what you know isn't true." —Donald T. Rowlingson

"Go into all the world and preach the gospel, and if necessary, use words."—Francis of Assisi

❉ FAMOUS MARTYRS ❉

The word *martyr* comes from a Greek word meaning "witness," and it applies to people who have died because of their Christian belief, practice, and testimony. This is a short list that includes both some slain for being Christians and some executed for advocating reform in the church. The apostle Paul and Jesus' disciples, all of whom are said to have been martyred except John, are not listed.

Stephen, the first martyr, around AD 34

Polycarp, bishop of Smyrna, around 160

Justin Martyr, apologist, around 165

Perpetua and Felicitas, women of Carthage, 203

Cyprian, bishop of Carthage, 258

George, Christian of Asia Minor, fourth century (the "great martyr" of the Eastern churches)

Thomas à Becket, archbishop of Canterbury, 1170 (the "holy blissful martyr" of Chaucer's *Canterbury Tales*)

Jan Hus, Bohemian reformer, 1415

Joan of Arc, French visionary and nationalist, 1431

William Tyndale, English Bible translator, 1536

John Philpot, English Protestant cleric, 1553

John Bradford, English Protestant scholar, 1555

Thomas Cranmer, archbishop of Canterbury, 1556

Dietrich Bonhoeffer, German theologian, 1945

Jim Elliot, American missionary to Auca Indians of Ecuador, 1956

❉ GROWTH OF MAJOR RELIGIOUS GROUPS ❉ IN THE UNITED STATES, 1650-1950

Groups are listed in order of the number of congregations in 1950. If no number appears, the movement had not been established in what is now the United States in the applicable year. Today's evangelical and Pentecostal churches were not present as denominational groups in 1850.

Denomination	1650	1750	1850	1950	Percent Growth 1850–1950
Baptist	2	132	9,375	77,000	721
Methodist			13,820	54,000	291
Lutheran	4	138	1,217	16,403	1,248
Roman Catholic	6	30	1,221	15,533	1,172
Presbyterian	4	233	4,824	13,200	174
Anglican/Episcopal	31	289	1,459	7,784	434
Christian/Disciples of Christ			1,898	7,769	309
Congregational	62	465	1,706	5,679	233
German Reformed		90	338	2,754	715
Mormon			16	2,693	16,731
Jewish		5	30	2,000	6,567
Dutch Reformed	3	79	330	763	131
Quaker	1	250	654	726	11

❉ A SHORT HISTORY OF THE CHRISTMAS TREE ❉

The origins of the Christmas tree go back to antiquity. It is said that ancient Egyptians, for example, hung green palm branches in their homes on the shortest day of the year, symbolizing the triumph of life over death. Trees that stay green all year were thought to ward off illness and evil spirits, and people hung branches over their doors and windows. The Romans used evergreens as decorations during Saturnalia, their winter festival. Druid priests decorated oak trees with apples during their celebration of the winter solstice. By the Middle Ages the custom of decorating evergreens had crept into Christian practice with the "Paradise tree," hung with apples, that was used on the Feast of Adam and Eve, December 24. A legend holds that a seventh-century English monk used the triangle-shaped fir tree to teach Germans about the Holy Trinity.

❀ A SHORT HISTORY OF THE CHRISTMAS TREE—CONT. ❀

Martin Luther is said to have decorated a small tree with candles for his children. In Strasbourg in the 1600s, trees were decorated with sweets and colored paper flowers, and tinsel began to be used in Germany. In 1714 England took on a German ruler, George I from Hanover, and German merchants living in England began to use the Christmas tree. When pictures of Queen Victoria and her German husband, Prince Albert, appeared in London newspapers, showing them with their children around a Christmas tree, the tree became fashionable in English and East Coast American society. Some of the German Hessians who fought in the Revolutionary War had remained in America and had already introduced the tree in their communities. After Queen Victoria, the use of the tree went into decline but was revived in the 1930s when Charles Dickens's writings popularized it again in Britain and North America. In Catholic countries of southern Europe, however, the crèche or manger scene has been more popular.

❀ THE "CURSING" PSALMS ❀

Some of the Psalms are called *psalms of imprecation,* or cursing, because they call upon the Lord to avenge the speaker's enemies. An example is this passage from Psalm 109:

> May his days be few;
>   may another seize his goods!
> May his children be fatherless,
>   and his wife a widow!
> May his children wander about and beg;
>   may they be driven out of the ruins they inhabit!
> May the creditor seize all that he has;
>   may strangers plunder the fruits of his toil!
> Let there be none to extend kindness to him,
>   nor any to pity his fatherless children! (vv. 8–12)

Other psalms that might be called psalms of imprecation are 35, 55, 69, 73, 79, 137; many others mention the speaker's enemies without actually calling for bad things to happen to them. When John Wesley prepared a collection of psalms for the use of American Methodists, he removed these "cursing psalms," regarding them as unfit for the lips of Christian worshipers.

The speaker in these psalms never threatens to attack his enemies himself. Instead, he appeals to God to vindicate him, for he sees himself as the Lord's servant and the Lord's enemies as his own.

❄ PHONY FEASTS AND FUNNY FESTIVALS ❄

The Feast of Fools took place around New Year's Day in France and England, during the twelfth to fourteenth centuries. Subdeacons organized the festivals, which included buffoonery and humorous mock church services. The event was sometimes called the Feast of Asses and related to Balaam's donkey (Num. 22), as well as the flight of Jesus' family into Egypt after his birth. The Feast of Fools was suppressed in the fifteenth century.

Plough Monday, the first Monday after the twelve days of Christmas, was an English festival. Plowmen blackened their faces and took their decorated plows around town asking for money, accompanied by someone costumed as "the Fool."

Mardi Gras, the day before Ash Wednesday, developed in Europe as a time of extravagance before the austerity of Lent. In New Orleans it has been carried to a modern extreme.

Hallowe'en or the Eve of All Hallows (All Saints' Day) may have originated in a "memorial day" for Christian martyrs, when worshipers dressed as saints who had given their lives for the faith. Other theories suggest Jewish or pagan origins for the day and its practices. In modern times the festival has been commercialized and, to a degree, related to imagery of satanism and the occult, and many Christian families minimize it or steer clear of it entirely.

The Grimaldi Memorial Service, or Clown Sunday, is held the first Sunday of February at Holy Trinity Church in London, England. Clowns from around the world gather in full costume to honor Joseph Grimaldi (1778–1837), the father of modern clowning.

The Hare Pie (now beef) is served—actually, tossed—each year to crowds at Hallaton in Leicestershire, England, because of a bequest made centuries ago by a woman whose life was saved when a rabbit diverted her from the path of a bull. After the pie, partyers play a game in which teams try to get three barrels across goal lines a mile apart, between Hallaton and a neighboring town.

The Christian Jugglers Association participates in events such as the Groundhog Day Jugglers' Festival.

❄ THE SEVEN DEADLY SINS ❄

The traditional list of the tendencies and traits to avoid:

1. Pride (vanity)
2. Envy
3. Gluttony
4. Lust
5. Anger (wrath)
6. Greed (avarice, covetousness)
7. Sloth

❊ THE TEN COMMANDMENTS IN THE NEW TESTAMENT ❊

Jesus referred to several commandments in Matthew 15:19: "For out of the heart come evil thoughts, murder, adultery, fornication, theft, false witness, slander." He repeated several commandments in Luke 18:20: "You know the commandments: 'Do not commit adultery, Do not kill, Do not steal, Do not bear false witness, Honor your father and mother.'" Paul listed several in Romans 13:9: "The commandments, 'You shall not commit adultery, You shall not kill, You shall not steal, You shall not covet,' and any other commandment, are summed up in this sentence, 'You shall love your neighbor as yourself.'"

"You shall have no other gods before me" (Exod. 20:3).

"You shall love the Lord your God with all your heart, and with all your soul, and with all your mind" (Matt. 22:37, actually quoting Deut. 6:5).

"You shall not make for yourself a graven image, or any likeness of anything that is in heaven above" (v. 4).

"They exchanged the truth about God for a lie and worshiped and served the creature rather than the Creator" (Rom. 1:25).

"You shall not take the name of the LORD your God in vain" (v. 7).

"Not every one who says to me, 'Lord, Lord,' shall enter the kingdom of heaven, but he who does the will of my Father who is in heaven" (Matt. 7:21).

"Remember the sabbath day, to keep it holy" (v. 8).

"The sabbath was made for man, not man for the sabbath; so the Son of man is lord even of the sabbath" (Mark 2:27–28).

"Honor your father and your mother" (v. 12).

"'Honor your father and mother' (this is the first commandment with a promise), 'that it may be well with you and that you may live long on the earth'" (Eph. 6:2–3).

"You shall not kill" (v. 13).

"You have heard that it was said to the men of old, 'You shall not kill; and whoever kills shall be liable to judgment.' But I say to you that every one who is angry with his brother shall be liable to judgment" (Matt. 5:21–22).

"You shall not commit adultery" (v. 14).

"You who say that one must not commit adultery, do you commit adultery?" (Rom. 2:22).

"You shall not steal" (v. 15).

"But let none of you suffer as a murderer, or a thief, or a wrongdoer, or a mischief-maker" (1 Pet. 4:15).

"You shall not bear false witness" (v. 16).

"Rob no one by violence or by false accusation, and be content with your wages" (Luke 3:14).

"You shall not covet" (v. 17).

"I should not have known what it is to covet if the law had not said, 'You shall not covet'" (Rom. 7:7).

❃ REFORMERS BEFORE THE REFORMATION ❃

Peter Waldo (died 1217) of Lyons, France, protested the worldliness of the church. His followers organized a separate movement in pockets through southern and central Europe. Despite persecution until the Reformation, the Waldensian church still exists with about fifty thousand members in Italy and Latin America.

Jan Hus (1373–1415) of Bohemia refused to stop preaching when ordered to do so, and he opposed the sale of indulgences. He was excommunicated in 1412 and burned at the stake three years later.

John Wycliffe (1329–1384), English scholar, denied the Catholic doctrine of transubstantiation (the elements of the Mass actually become the body and blood of Christ) and began translating the Bible from Latin into English.

Girolamo Savonarola (1452–1498), Dominican monk and preacher, instituted a moral reform in Florence, Italy, and denounced the corruption of the papal court; he was executed as a heretic.

❃ THE COUNTER REFORMATION ❃

The Counter Reformation was a sixteenth-century movement for reform and missionary outreach in the Roman Catholic Church, partly as a response to the Protestant Reformation. New religious orders were established to revive the ideals of charitable work and evangelism Francis of Assisi established. Chief among these was the Society of Jesus (Jesuits), founded by Ignatius Loyola and others, which became a powerful anti-Protestant force. A revival of Catholic devotion took place through the work of figures such as Teresa of Avila, John of the Cross, and Francis of Sales. The Council of Trent (1545–1563) reformed the structure of the church and reaffirmed Catholic teaching in opposition to Protestant views. The power of the papacy was strengthened and the Latin Mass was standardized to the form known in Rome, known today as the *Tridentine Mass* after the Council of Trent.

❃ THE CHRISTMAS CACTUS ❃

The Christmas cactus (*Schlumbergera bridesii* and other varieties) is native to southeastern Brazil. The scientific name comes from Frederick Schlumberger, a Belgian explorer and horticulturist, who discovered the genus in the 1800s. The Christmas cactus is not a true cactus and requires more frequent watering than its name implies. It derives its popular name from its tendency to bloom at the beginning of winter, but some varieties bloom at other times.

❋ SOME LUTHERAN BODIES IN NORTH AMERICA ❋

American Association of Lutheran Churches • Apostolic Lutheran Church of America • Association of Free Lutheran Congregations • Canadian Association of Lutheran Congregations • Church of the Lutheran Brethren of America • Church of the Lutheran Confession • Concordia Lutheran Conference • Estonian Evangelical Lutheran Church • Evangelical Catholic Church • Evangelical Community Church—Lutheran • Evangelical Lutheran Church in America • Illinois Lutheran Conference • Independent Lutheran Congregations • International Lutheran Fellowship • Laestadian Lutheran Church • Latvian Lutheran Church • Lithuanian Evangelical Lutheran Church in Diaspora • Lutheran Confessional Synod • Lutheran Congregations in Mission for Christ • Lutheran Ministerium and Synod—USA • Wisconsin Evangelical Lutheran Synod

❋ U.S. PRESIDENT WHO WAS A MINISTER ❋

James A. Garfield (1831–1881) of Ohio, the twentieth president of the United States, was a lay minister of the Disciples of Christ. He was baptized in 1850 and became a fervent preacher, though like most preachers of the Churches of Christ movement, he was never officially ordained. After serving in the Ohio Senate and the Union Army, he was elected to Congress in 1863, then to the U.S. Senate, and in 1880 was elected president.

As president, Garfield opposed the system of patronage in which U.S. senators controlled political appointments in their states. As a result, he angered many who were seeking such appointments. A disgruntled office-seeker shot Garfield in July 1881, and after lingering several months, he died in September.

❋ THE FIRST AND ONLY ENGLISH POPE . . . ❋ AND THE MAN WHO NEARLY BECAME THE SECOND

Only one pope spoke a form of English as his native language. Nicholas Brekespear reigned as Pope Adrian IV from 1154 till 1159. Another Englishman, however, came close to being elected pope. Reginald Pole, a scholar, spent most of his time in Rome and other parts of Europe, and he partially avoided being involved in the controversies over the marriages of Henry VIII. He was regarded as a favorite to succeed Pope Paul III, who died in 1549, but he had not yet been ordained a priest and did not push his own candidacy. When Mary I ("Bloody Mary") became queen of England, she had Pole ordained and made him archbishop of Canterbury, succeeding the martyred Thomas Cranmer.

❈ RELIGIOUS WORDS TURNED SECULAR ❈

Word	Original Religious Usage	Common Secular Meaning
Bedlam	A corruption of *Bethlehem*, from a London insane asylum called the Hospital of St. Mary of Bethlehem	A state of uproar or confusion
Crusade	One of a series of medieval expeditions to recover the Holy Land for Christianity	A zealous and sustained effort to achieve a goal or remedy some undesirable situation
Dogmatic	Dogmatic theology, or *dogmatics*, is the discipline that interprets the teachings of a religious faith	Asserting an opinion, often arrogantly or without sufficient evidence
Enthusiasm	Filled with religious fervor, from a Greek word based on *theos*, "God"	Strong excitement or feeling for a cause or activity
Good-bye	Shortened form of *God be with you*	Simple indication of leaving or parting
Heretic	From a Greek word meaning the action of choosing or taking; one who holds a view that contradicts established church teaching	A person who dissents from the generally accepted thinking on any subject
Kosher	Permitted by the Jewish dietary laws of *Kashrut*	Being proper, acceptable, or satisfactory
Martyr	From the Greek word for "witness"; a person who is killed for his or her religious stance	Any person who incurs loss or death for a cause or principle
Ordinary	A church official, especially a bishop, having responsibility for a specified territory or group; also the part of the Mass that does not vary with days or seasons of the liturgical year	The usual condition or course of things, i.e., "nothing out of the ordinary"; in Britain, an eating house serving set meals
Orientation	Facing or pointing toward the East or Orient; used of temples or churches where the altar is placed at the east end	Making someone familiar with an existing environment or situation, as "new member orientation," or directing something toward a particular group
Orthodox	From Greek elements meaning "correct opinion" or "right	Conforming to established or conventional ideas; a different

❧ RELIGIOUS WORDS TURNED SECULAR—CONT. ❧

Word	Original Religious Usage	Common Secular Meaning
	thinking." The term is used theologically to refer to the Eastern churches and to generally accepted Christian belief as opposed to that of splinter groups ("heterodox").	way of doing something might be called *unorthodox*
Pall	A cloth draped over a casket or a stiffened linen placed over the Communion chalice	An overspreading atmosphere of gloom or dismay
Placebo	From Latin for "I shall please," a name for the Roman Catholic vespers for the dead	Something intended to soothe, or a substance having no effect used as a control in testing medications
Proselyte	From Greek words meaning "an alien resident"; a new convert to a religious group, especially to Judaism	A person who comes to accept a new, perhaps controversial, idea
Passion	From a Latin root referring to suffering, or being acted upon; the suffering of Christ leading to the crucifixion	Enthusiasm or deep conviction for something, or romantic and erotic emotions
Pontificate	(Noun) The office or term of a pope, or *pontiff*	(Verb) To make pompous or dogmatic statements
Regular	From the Latin word for "rule"; denoting a member of a religious order that follows its particular *rule* or lifestyle	Formed or ordered according to some generally accepted pattern, arrangement, or usage; formed or functioning in a fixed or uniform way
Scapegoat	The goat driven into the wilderness on the Day of Atonement, bearing the sin of the people (Lev. 16:10)	A person punished for wrongdoing by others or made the object of hostility for no reason.
Set in stone	Refers to the giving of the Ten Commandments on stone tablets (Exod. 24:12)	Unchangeable

❋ AMERICAN RELIGIOUS MOVEMENTS ❋ STARTED BY WOMEN

Christian Science—Grew from a church founded in 1879 in Boston by Mary Baker Eddy (1821–1910) and is still based on her writings, especially *Science and Health with Key to the Scriptures* (1875)

Holiness Groups—Denominations originating in the holiness movement, such as the Church of God (Anderson, Indiana) and the Church of the Nazarene, trace their origins to Phoebe Palmer (1807–1874), a Methodist woman who began holding meetings for the promotion of holiness in New York in 1840.

International Church of the Foursquare Gospel—Incorporated by evangelist Aimee Semple McPherson (1890–1944) in 1927 in Los Angeles

Mount Sinai Holy Church of America—Founded in 1924 by Ida Robinson

Salvation Army—Founded in London in 1878 by Catherine Booth and her husband, William Booth

Seventh-Day Adventists—Formed around 1850 largely through the influence of prophetess and writer Ellen G. White (1827–1915)

Shakers—Founded in England by Mother Ann Lee (died 1784); now almost extinct

Theosophical Society—A society advocating a Hindu-like humanist philosophy, founded in 1875 in New York by Ukrainian-born Helena P. Blavatsky (1831–1891) and others. Annie Besant (1847–1933) was a later leader of the movement. The American headquarters of the Theosophical Society are located, paradoxically, in Wheaton, Illinois, a major center for Christian organizations.

❋ A WORD THAT CHANGED CHURCH HISTORY ❋

The Nicene Creed, as used in the churches of the West (Anglican, Catholic, Lutheran, and others), contains the statement, "We believe [*or* I believe] in the Holy Spirit, the Lord, the giver of life, who proceeds from the Father and the Son." In Latin the phrase "and the Son" is one word: *filioque*. The word was not in the original creed as it came from the councils of Nicaea and Constantinople, but churches began to add it around the time of the Third Council of Toledo (Spain) in 589. Eastern (Orthodox) churches retain the original wording, "who proceeds from the Father," period. Support for the concept of the "double procession of the Holy Ghost" is found in New Testament passages such as John 16:14, where Jesus said the Spirit "will take what is mine and declare it to you," but Orthodox theologians have objected that there must be only one "fount of divinity" in the Godhead. The *filioque* issue has never been resolved and remains a major theological factor that keeps the Eastern and Western churches from reunification.

❊ THE MYSTERIOUS "Q": FACT OR FICTION? ❊

The first three gospels—Matthew, Mark, and Luke—cover a lot of the same material about Jesus' life and ministry, while John follows its own scheme. Scholars call the first three the *synoptic Gospels*, from Greek words that mean "seeing from the same viewpoint." How do they explain the fact that Mark is missing many of Jesus' teachings that appear in Matthew and Luke, yet wherever Mark covers the same ground, his story is a bit longer? One widely held theory is that Matthew and Luke both used Mark as a source, as well as an unknown source scholars call Q, from the German word *Quelle*, "source." (Luke himself seemed to admit he based his work on that of others: Luke 1:1–4.) "Q" was probably not a written document, but a collection of Jesus' teachings that had been handed down by word of mouth. It's only a theory, but it looks like this:

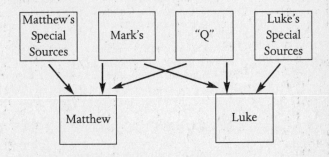

❊ MODERN MORALITY ❊

In a recent poll, Americans declared the following to be morally wrong:

Polygamy . . . . 91 percent
Married men and women having an affair . . . . 91 percent
Suicide . . . . 79 percent
Homosexual behavior . . . . 54 percent
Abortion . . . . 50 percent
Having a baby outside marriage . . . . 45 percent
Sex between an unmarried man and woman . . . . 36 percent
Buying and wearing clothing made of animal fur . . . . 31 percent
Gambling . . . . 30 percent
Death penalty . . . . 28 percent
Divorce . . . . 26 percent

❋ PROVERBS NOT FOUND IN THE BIBLE ❋

Some of these sayings may have a foundation in Scripture, and some are fragments of a biblical statement. But in these forms, they do not appear in the Bible.

Waste not, want not.
If the shoe fits, wear it.
Practice makes perfect.
Time heals all wounds.
Once saved, always saved.
Money is the root of all evil.
Cleanliness is next to godliness.
Spare the rod, and spoil the child.
You can't judge a book by its cover.
God said it, I believe it, that settles it.
God helps those who help themselves.
You can't teach an old dog new tricks.
An apple a day keeps the doctor away.
Children should be seen and not heard.
All good things come to those who wait.
If at first you don't succeed, try, try again.

❋ CHURCHES THAT WON'T USE INSTRUMENTS ❋

Early Christian worshipers did not use instruments. At first this was for practical reasons: the church was a small minority group in a hostile culture and without significant musical resources. Later on some of the church fathers justified the exclusion of instruments on theological grounds. Churches began using the organ around the seventh century, but some Protestant Reformers objected to the use of instruments in worship because they were not mentioned in the New Testament. The famous Baptist preacher C. H. Spurgeon (1834–1882) did not permit them in his church. Some groups that do not use instruments today include

- The Eastern Orthodox churches (with a few exceptions)
- The Coptic churches
- The Churches of Christ (but related groups of "Christian" churches do use instruments)
- The Reformed Presbyterian churches in North America and similar groups
- Some Quaker groups
- Primitive Baptist churches

❧ TERMS USED IN THE STUDY ❧ OF BIBLICAL MANUSCRIPTS

The study of ancient biblical manuscripts is an exacting discipline. Scholars who work with these documents and write about them use a specialized vocabulary.

Apparatus . . . . The layout of a printed edition of a text, with its footnotes and references, and the *sigla* or symbols and abbreviations (often in Latin) that indicate ancient versions, variant readings, conjectural emendations or reconstructions, other printed editions, or the various manuscript sources and their families

Codex . . . . A manuscript in book form, as opposed to a roll

Dittography . . . . An error made by repeating material while copying

Harmonization . . . . . . Similar to conflation; a copyist makes one text conform to another, e.g., inserts "missing" words in Mark by taking them from another gospel

Hand . . . . The handwriting style of a particular scribe

Lacuna . . . . A gap in the text caused by deterioration of the manuscript or other damage

Minuscule . . . . A manuscript written in a smaller cursive hand, as opposed to an uncial manuscript

Palimpsest . . . . A manuscript that has had the original writing scraped off and another text written over it. Invariably it is the older text that is of more interest to biblical scholars.

Papyrus . . . . Writing material made from reeds flattened and pressed together

Parchment . . . . Writing material made of sheepskin or goatskin

Points . . . . In a Hebrew text, the signs over, under, and within letters that represent the vowel sounds

Scripta defectiva . . . . The writing in a Hebrew or other Semitic language text in which there are no letters representing vowel sounds

Scripta plene . . . . The writing in a Hebrew text in which vowel sounds are represented by some of the consonant letters. In Hebrew there are, strictly speaking, no vowel letters, but certain consonants double as vowels in later texts.

Scriptorium . . . . A room set aside for the use of scribes or copyists

Uncial . . . . A manuscript written in all capital letters, with no word separation. The oldest New Testament manuscripts are uncials.

Vellum . . . . A fine-quality writing material made from lambskin, kidskin, or calfskin

Verso . . . . The back of a codex page, i.e., the page on the left

❋ TRADITIONAL CLERGY AND WORSHIP GARB ❋

The Geneva gown came into use for preaching during the Protestant Reformation. It is an academic garment university professors and students originally wore. It had three purposes: (1) to provide warmth in cold buildings, (2) to conceal the wearer's clothing that revealed whether he was wealthy or poor, and (3) to carry one's lunch or other items in the wide sleeves. The clerical collar was not originally a clergy garment, but something all prosperous gentlemen wore. When styles changed, the clergy were too poor to afford new clothing, and the old-style collar came to identify them. In Reformed or Anglican usage, preachers sometimes wear "preaching tabs" extending down from the collar.

Alb with cincture (cord), worn by a variety of worship leaders

Cassock, worn by clergy alone or under other vestments

Cassock with amice, worn under other vestments

Surplice with stole, over cassock

Chasuble over alb

Geneva gown with stole

Collar and Rabat (frontal or "dickey") worn by ordained clergy as everyday garb

Cotta, worn over cassock by singers or acolytes

❋ NUMBER OF LANGUAGES THE BIBLE ❋
HAS BEEN TRANSLATED INTO

The Holy Bible has been translated into at least 2,018 languages, with countless additional translations of portions of the Scriptures. There are also many recorded audio translations for unwritten languages. By comparison, the works of Shakespeare, whom many consider to be the master writer of the English language, have been translated into only 50 languages.

❊ A MOTLEY CREW: ISRAEL'S JUDGES ❊

The "judges" were not legal officials but local warriors or military leaders during a period of turmoil after the death of Joshua. The ending of the book of Judges summarizes this period: "In those days there was no king in Israel; every man did what was right in his own eyes" (Judg. 21:25). The era of the judges phased out with the rise of the prophet Samuel and the anointing of Saul, Israel's first king.

Here are descriptions of some of Israel's most colorful kingly characters.

Othniel . . . . Delivered Israel from Cushan-rishathaim of Mesopotamia

Ehud . . . . Was left-handed; he assassinated Eglon, the obese king of Moab, and freed Israel

Shamgar . . . . Killed six hundred Philistines with an ox goad

Deborah . . . . Urged Barak to throw off Israel's Canaanite masters

Gideon (Jerubbaal) . . . . . . Gathered a commando force that defeated the Midianites, then turned down Israel's offer to make him king

Jair the Gileadite . . . . Had thirty sons who rode on thirty donkeys

Jephthah . . . . Defeated the Ammonites but had to sacrifice his daughter due to a rash vow

Ibzan of Bethlehem . . . . . . Had thirty daughters

Abdon . . . . Had forty sons and thirty grandsons

Samson . . . . A Nazirite who turned away from his vow because of his interest in women; Delilah tricked him so that he was taken prisoner by the Philistines and blinded. In his last performance, he "brought down the house."

❊ THREE EXTRA FRUIT OF THE SPIRIT ❊ FOUND IN THE VULGATE

In Galatians 5:22–23, Paul listed the "fruit of the Spirit" in the believer's life:

love • goodness • joy • faithfulness • peace • gentleness (meekness) • patience (long-suffering) • self-control (temperance) • kindness

The Latin Vulgate of Jerome adds three more:

modesty • continence • chastity

Thomas Aquinas, the great Catholic theologian, defended twelve as the correct number on theological grounds, though the oldest Greek manuscripts have only nine.

❊ THE APOSTOLIC FATHERS ❊

The *Apostolic Fathers* is a collection of the very earliest Christian writings after the New Testament.

1 Clement (a letter from the Romans to the Corinthians)
2 Clement (an early Christian sermon)

The Letters of Ignatius, bishop of
Antioch:

The Letter of Polycarp
to the Philippians

To the Ephesians
To the Magnesians
To the Trallians
To the Romans
To the Philadelphians
To the Smyrneans
To Polycarp

The Didache (Teaching of the Twelve
Apostles)
The Epistle of Barnabas
The Shepherd of Hermas
The Epistle to Diognetus
The Fragments of Papias

❊ CLASSIC ATTRIBUTES OF GOD ❊

These are some of the classic terms used in discussing the attributes of God.

Aseity . . . . God is self-existent, or pure, not being called into existence by anything else.

Impassibility . . . . God has no passions, that is, desires for what he does not have.

Immanence . . . . God fills all space, even if he is not spatial.

Immensity . . . . God is not limited by space.

Immutability . . . . As a perfect Being, God does not change.

Incomprehensibility . . . It is impossible for beings in God's creation to comprehend the Creator.

Infinity . . . . God cannot be encompassed or understood by finite intelligence.

Noncontingency . . . . . It is necessary that God exist; it is impossible for him not to be.

Nontemporality . . . . . . God is eternal, beyond the framework of time.

Omnipotence . . . . God has all power.

Omniscience . . . . God knows all things.

Relatability . . . . God is related to his creation but not dependent on it.

Simplicity . . . . God has no parts into which he can be divided.

Transcendence . . . . God is beyond his creation, not part of it.

Ubiquity . . . . God is present in every place, or omnipresent.

Unity . . . . God is one; if he were more than one, the parts would lack what the other parts have.

❧ KOSHER REGULATIONS ❧

The word *kosher* comes from a Hebrew word meaning "fit" or "proper." Jewish kosher food laws are an extension of the commandment in Exodus 23:19, "You shall not boil a kid in its mother's milk" and the list of prohibited foods in Leviticus 11. These regulations are complex, and this is only a summary.

1. Only animals that chew their cud and have divided hooves may be eaten. (This rules out meat from pigs and many other animals.)
2. There are twenty-four specifically forbidden species of birds, but kosher observers usually limit fowl to chicken, turkey, duck, and goose.
3. Meat and poultry must be slaughtered in a particular way. Trained and certified slaughterers sever the trachea and esophagus with a special knife, then inspectors make sure the internal organs have no abnormalities.
4. No blood may be consumed, so before meat is eaten, the blood must be removed by salting or broiling.
5. Fish must have fins and scales that are easily removed, and they must be visible to the consumer when purchased. All shellfish are prohibited. Fish and meat must not be eaten together.
6. Meat and milk must never be cooked or eaten together, and as a safeguard they must not be prepared or served with the same equipment or dishes. A kosher kitchen must have two sets of utensils, one for meat and poultry and the other for dairy foods. Cheese must be certified to make sure it has been processed in a kosher manner.
7. Bread containing dairy ingredients cannot be eaten, since bread is served with most meals and one could accidentally eat dairy bread with a meat meal.
8. Food containing neither meat nor dairy products or processed with the same equipment is called *pareve*, and it may be eaten with either meat or dairy meals.

❧ *SELAH* IN THE PSALMS ❧

The term *selah* occurs seventy-one times in thirty-nine of the Psalms. No one is sure what it means. Some think of it as a reminder to meditate on what has been said. More likely, however, it comes from the verb *salal*, to "lift up" a song. It might indicate a place where instruments play an interlude. Or it could designate a point where free-flowing vocal and instrumental praise occurred, perhaps using a familiar refrain such as "O give thanks to the LORD, for he is good, / for his steadfast love endures for ever" (Ps. 136:1).

❈ WAYS TO SING THE PSALMS ❈

Psalm singing has been a feature of Christian worship from the beginning (Eph. 5:19), and in some Christian communities it has been the only type of music permitted in worship. These are some historic ways of singing the Psalms.

Plain Chant . . . . Psalms are sung according to conventional rules, using set "tones" or melodies. Parts are sometimes added to support or augment the melody.

Metrical Psalms . . . . Composers wrote measured tunes that could be used with the Psalms, in the local language. This sometimes required rearranging the words of Scripture in either a "close-fitting" or "loose-fitting" manner. A collection of these metrical psalms is called a *psalter*. "The Lord's My Shepherd, I'll Not Want" (Ps. 23, *Scottish Psalter* of 1650) is an example of a "loose fitting" and rhymed metrical psalm.

Anglican Chant . . . . This is a nonmetrical form of singing, in which it is not necessary to alter the form of the Bible text. The first part of a line is sung on a sustained pitch with supporting harmony, and the final syllables resolve in a short series of chords.

Psalm Paraphrase . . . . . . Isaac Watts departed from the tradition of metrical psalm singing in his *Psalms of David* of 1719. He wrote new, rhymed poetry based on the Psalms but often introduced Christ and the gospel into the text. Psalms of this type have become familiar hymns, such as "O God, Our Help in Ages Past" (Ps. 90).

Responsorial Psalms . . . . In this type of psalm singing, one verse serves as a refrain (antiphon) to be sung by the congregation, and a cantor sings the other verses. Sometimes the psalm is paraphrased.

Taizé Psalms . . . . In the latter half of the twentieth century, the ecumenical Taizé community of France introduced a simple form of singing for its own worship that has spread throughout the Christian world. Some of the texts used are from the Psalms.

Pointed Psalms . . . . Psalm texts are printed with symbolism, allowing them to be sung to a set of psalm tones in a style similar to Anglican chant. A Lutheran hymnal introduced this style in 1978.

Scripture Songs . . . . Some contemporary worship choruses or "Scripture songs" are psalm paraphrases. "Let Us Exalt His Name" by Stuart Dauermann is a version of Psalm 34.

❧ NOVELS BASED ON THE BIBLE ❧

Novelists have written hundreds of books based on biblical characters or events.
The following is only a sampling of those published between 1880 and 1980.

Title	Author	Published in English
Ben-Hur: A Tale of the Christ	Lew Wallace	1880
Onesimus	Edwin Abbott	1882
Quo Vadis?	Henryk Sienkiewicz	1897
Paul of Tarsus	Robert Bird	1900
She Stands Alone: The Story of Pilate's Wife	Mark Ashton	1901
Balthazar	Anatole France (Jacques Anatole Thibault)	1909
The Tales of Jacob*	Thomas Mann	1933
Young Joseph*	Thomas Mann	1935
Joseph in Egypt*	Thomas Mann	1938
The Nazarene	Sholem Asch	1939
The Robe	Lloyd C. Douglas	1942
The Apostle	Sholem Asch	1943
The Hour of Barabbas	Otto Michael	1943
Joseph the Provider*	Thomas Mann	1944
The Big Fisherman	Lloyd C. Douglas	1948
Mary	Sholem Asch	1949
Prince of Egypt	Dorothy Clarke Wilson	1949
First the Blade	Drayton Mayrant	1950
Moses	Sholem Asch	1951
The Road to Bithynia	Frank G. Slaughter	1951
The Silver Chalice	Thomas B. Costain	1952
Salome, Princess of Galilee	Henry Denker	1953
Lot's Wife	Maria Ley-Piscator	1954
Daughter of Nazareth	Florence Marvyne Bauer	1955
The Prophet	Sholem Asch	1955
If I Forget Thee	Robert De Ropp	1956
Dear and Glorious Physician	Taylor Caldwell	1959
Pontius Pilate	Paul L. Maier	1968
Judas, My Brother	Frank Yerby	1968
Great Lion of God	Taylor Caldwell	1970
Justus	Arthur L. Lapham	1973
Lydia	Lois T. Henderson	1979

*The four novels by Thomas Mann were published together as *Joseph and His Brothers.*

❄ WOMEN EVANGELISTS ❄

Selina Hastings, Countess of Huntingdon (1707–1771)—While not a preacher herself, she used up her wealth in supporting the Methodist revival in England.

Sojourner Truth (Isabella Baumfree, 1797–1888)—Escaped slave who walked through Long Island and Connecticut preaching; she became a speaker for the abolition of slavery

Jarena Lee (1783–after 1850)—African-American widow from New Jersey who preached in the African Methodist Episcopal Church

Catherine Booth (1829–1890)—Preached along with her husband, William, and with him founded the Salvation Army and worked for improvement of conditions for the poor in England

Amanda Berry Smith (1837–1915)—African-American evangelist and temperance promoter

Maria Woodworth-Etter (1844–1924)—Holiness evangelist who pioneered in the Pentecostal revival

Aimee Semple McPherson (1890–1944)—Canadian-born, she preached the "foursquare gospel," opened Angelus Temple in California, and founded the Foursquare Gospel Church.

Kathryn Kuhlman (1907–1976)—Had a prominent healing ministry based in Pittsburgh, Pennsylvania

❄ RULES FOR THE BANNS OF MARRIAGE ❄

In Anglican, Catholic, and other churches, it is traditional to publish the *banns*, or announcement, of a forthcoming marriage in the parish. The purpose in doing so, in an earlier era, was to make sure the prospective bride and groom were not related too closely to be married. People who knew their family histories heard about the marriage in time to report any problem to the parish priest. Obtaining a marriage license is considered the equivalent of the banns, but many churches still follow the traditional procedure. These are the standard Anglican procedures:

1. The banns must be published in an audible manner in the parish church on three Sundays before the marriage. (Today the banns are often printed in the church bulletin.)

2. If the persons being married live in different parishes, the banns must be published in both.

3. The clergyman must be notified at least seven days before the first announcement is to be made.

4. If the couple delays marriage more than three months, the banns must be published again.

❊ THREE VIEWS OF THE MILLENNIUM ❊

Theologians offer diverging pictures of "last days" or end-time events, usually described as *millennial* views. The term *millennium* is derived from Latin for "thousand years," a period mentioned in Revelation 20. The differing views are often labeled depending on how the timing of Christ's return (his second coming or second advent) is related to this thousand-year period.

1. *Premillennialism*—Christ returns before the millennium to inaugurate it as his kingdom. Most premillennialists look for a seven-year period of "tribulation" or cataclysmic events preceding the appearance of Christ. There are subcategories of premillennialism, based on the timing of the "rapture" or "catching up" of Christians suggested in 1 Thessalonians 4:17: (a) *Pretribulationism*—the church is raptured before the Tribulation; (b) *Posttribulationalism*—the church is raptured after the Tribulation; (c) *Midtribulationism*—the church is raptured during the Tribulation. This view came to the forefront among evangelicals beginning around 1900.

2. *Postmillennialism*—The millennium is a period of righteousness, peace, and blessing brought about by the steady advance of the gospel of Christ and the growing influence of the principles of God's kingdom. At the end of the millennium, Christ returns for the general resurrection and judgment. This view has been common in historic Protestant denominations.

3. *Amillennialism*—The term means "nonmillennialism." In this view, the millennium is a symbolic concept that describes the present rule of Christ through his Word and Spirit in the church. The "last days" began with Jesus' resurrection and ascension, and the "tribulation" refers to the events of the first century that led to the destruction of Jerusalem and its temple. Christ will return for judgment after his present reign, but believers enter the kingdom through new life in Christ now and at their death. This is the "classic" view that the majority of theologians held until the nineteenth century.

❊ METHODIST DENOMINATIONS IN THE UNITED STATES ❊

African Methodist Episcopal Church • African Methodist Episcopal Zion Church • Christian Methodist Episcopal Church • Congregational Methodist Church • Evangelical Methodist Church • Free Methodist Church of North America • Independent Methodist Churches • Primitive Methodist Church in the USA • Southern Methodist Church • United Methodist Church • The Wesleyan Church (originally Wesleyan Methodist Church, merged with Pilgrim Holiness Church)

❈ MANY NAMES FOR "MEN OF THE CLOTH" ❈

ARCHDEACON—A deacon who assists the bishop or who has a leading position among the other deacons of a group of churches

BISHOP—Often applied to the local pastor in Pentecostal or African-American churches

BROTHER—In Pentecostal churches, a form of address for a pastor, as in "Brother Jukes is our preacher today"; also used for respected laymen

DEACON—As a title for ordained clergy, it can designate (1) a person in process toward the priesthood or fully ordained ministry, or (2) a permanent deacon with particular assignments in the church. In some churches deacons have specific roles in the liturgy, such as reading the gospel lesson, preparing the altar for Communion, or pronouncing the dismissal.

CANON—A clergyman on the staff of a cathedral; the canons collectively are called a *chapter*

DEAN—The head of a cathedral chapter or a priest appointed as leader of a group of churches within a diocese (deanery)

DOMINIE—Traditional Dutch Reformed title for a minister

FATHER—Respectful address for a priest but not universal among Anglicans

INCUMBENT—Anglican term for the priest of a particular parish

MINISTER—General term for a clergyman but used less often in evangelical churches, and used in the Catholic Church mostly for laypeople who assist in serving Holy Communion

MONSIGNOR—Traditional title of honor conferred on a veteran Catholic priest

MR.—In classic Episcopal or other Protestant usage, the proper form of address or reference for a clergyman, i.e., "This is Mr. Bottomly, our curate."

PASTOR—Its use as a title and form of address for a local clergyman is favored in Lutheran and many evangelical and Pentecostal churches. Where not used as a form of address or title, it can designate the chief clergyman of any local church, i.e., the main priest of a Catholic parish is its pastor.

PREACHER—Often used synonymously with pastor in evangelical and Pentecostal churches

❊ MANY NAMES FOR "MEN OF THE CLOTH"—CONT. ❊

PREACHING ELDER—Title given to the main pastor or preacher in a "Christian" or "Churches of Christ" congregation

PRIEST—In the Catholic, Orthodox, or Anglican communities, a fully ordained clergy person who is authorized to preside at the Eucharist

RECTOR—Anglican or Episcopal title for the head pastor of a local parish

REVEREND—Strictly speaking, not a title but an honorific adjective. It is not correct to say "Reverend Crawford" but "the Reverend Mr. Crawford" (or "Dr." if applicable).

TEACHING ELDER—In Presbyterian usage, an elder who is a clergyman in contrast to a lay or "ruling" elder

VICAR—In Anglican usage, the pastor of a local parish; strictly speaking, it applies to the pastor of a parish that is under the direct supervision of the bishop for whom the local clergyman acts vicariously.

❊ CRUCIFIXION SURVIVOR ❊

Crucifixion was an agonizing, prolonged method of executing people considered threats to Roman rule.

A man survived the cross some forty years after the death of Christ, during the Jewish Revolt against Rome. The Jewish historian Flavius Josephus (AD 37–100), who had gone over to the Roman side, described how this happened.

> And when I was sent by Titus Caesar with Cerealius, and a thousand horsemen, to a certain village called Thecoa, in order to know whether it were a place fit for a camp, as I came back, I saw many captives crucified, and remembered three of them as my former acquaintance. I was very sorry at this in my mind, and went with tears in my eyes to Titus, and told him of them; so he immediately commanded them to be taken down, and to have the greatest care taken of them, in order to their recovery; yet two of them died under the physician's hands, while the third recovered. (*The Life of Flavius Josephus*, chapter 75)

We don't know this survivor's name or what happened to him afterward. But he lived because the right person—his friend—happened to find him and his companions.

❋ ARAMAIC AND HEBREW WORDS ❋ IN THE NEW TESTAMENT

Aramaic, the language of some parts of the Old Testament (portions of Daniel and Ezra), is a sister language of Hebrew. It was the ordinary language of Judea and Galilee in the first century, and it is sometimes called "Hebrew" in the New Testament. Jesus probably could speak some Greek, as there were Greek-speaking cities in Galilee, and he conversed with a Greek-speaking Syrophoenician woman (Mark 7:24–30). Since Jesus mainly taught the common people, though, Aramaic was his language and that of the earliest Christians.

Some Aramaic words are preserved in the Greek New Testament:

abba	Father
akeldama	"field of blood," perhaps a proper name (Acts 1:19)
Eloi, Eloi, lama sabachthani	"My God, my God, why have you forsaken me?" (Mark 15:34, after Ps. 22:1)
ephphatha	"Be opened" (Mark 7:34)
korbanas	The temple treasury (Matt. 27:6)
mammonas	"Mammon," "riches" (Matt. 6:24)
maranatha	"Our Lord has come" or "Our Lord, come!" (1 Cor. 16:22)
talitha koumi	"Little girl, arise!" (Mark 5:41)
rabbi	"My Master" or "My great one" (rabboni in John 20:16)
raca	"You fool" (Matt. 5:22)

Other words are actually Hebrew, though transmitted through Aramaic:

Alleluia	"Praise Yahweh"
amen	"Truly, reliably"
korban	"Dedicated offering" (Mark 7:11)
pascha	Passover
geenna	Gehenna, from *gei hinnom*, or Valley of Hinnom, the Jerusalem city dump
manna	Manna, literally, "What is it?"
sabaoth	From Hebrew meaning "hosts, armies" (Rom. 9:29; James 5:4)
sabbaton	Sabbath
satanas	Satan, or "the adversary"

❧ POPULAR HYMNS OF CHARLES WESLEY ❧

Charles Wesley (1707–1788) wrote more than six thousand hymns. These are some of the ones most often sung today.

"And Are We Yet Alive" (1749)

"And Can It Be That I Should Gain?" (1738)

"Blow Ye the Trumpet, Blow" (1750)

"A Charge to Keep I Have" (1762)

"Christ the Lord Is Risen Today" (1739)

"Christ, Whose Glory Fills the Skies" (1740)

"Come, Holy Ghost, Our Hearts Inspire" (1740)

"Come, Let Us Join Our Friends Above" (1759)

"Come, O Thou Traveler Unknown" (1742)

"Come, Sinners, to the Gospel Feast" (1747)

"Come, Thou Long Expected Jesus" (1744)

"Forth in Thy Name, O Lord, I Go" (1749)

"Hark, the Herald Angels Sing" (1739)

"How Can a Sinner Know?" (1749)

"How Happy Every Child of Grace (1759)"

"I Know That My Redeemer Lives" (1741)

"Jesus, Lover of My Soul" (1740)

"Jesus! the Name High over All" (1749)

"Jesus, Thine All-Victorious Love" (1740)

"Jesus, United by Thy Grace" (1740)

"Love Divine, All Loves Excelling" (1747)

"O Come and Dwell in Me" (1762)

"O for a Heart to Praise My God" (1742)

"O for a Thousand Tongues to Sing" (1739)

"O Thou Who Camest from Above" (1762)

"Rejoice, the Lord Is King" (1744)

"Sing to the Great Jehovah's Praise" (1750)

"Talk with Us, Lord" (1740)

"Thou Hidden Source of Calm Repose" (1749)

"'Tis Finished! The Messiah Dies" (1762)

"Where Shall My Wondering Soul Begin?" (1739)

"Ye Servants of God, Your Master Proclaim" (1744)

❧ CATHOLIC SAINTS OF THE TWENTIETH CENTURY ❧

The Catholic Church has canonized (declared saints) at least twenty-four people who lived in the twentieth century. Among them:

Pope Pius X . . . . Giuseppe Melchiorre Sarto (1835–1914) reformed the liturgy, fought Modernism, reorganized the Roman curia, and otherwise encouraged renewal in the church. Canonized by Pope Pius XII in 1954.

Frances Xavier Cabrini . . . . . . Known as Mother Cabrini, she founded Missionaries (1850–1917) of the Sacred Heart with clinics and homes in New York, Latin America, and elsewhere. Canonized by Pope Pius XII in 1946.

Teresa de los Andes . . . . Juana Fernandez Solar, a nun, the first Chilean to be (1900–1920) declared a saint. Canonized by Pope John Paul II in 1993.

Ivan Merz (1896–1928). . . . . . Croatian layman who took a vow of celibacy and worked for evangelism and revival in the church. Canonized by Pope John Paul II in 2003.

László Batthyány- . . . . Hungarian physician who turned an inherited family Strattmann (1870–1931) castle into a hospital for the poor. Canonized in 2003 by Pope John Paul II.

Maximilian Kolbe . . . . Raymond Kolbe, Polish Franciscan priest who was (1894–1941) executed at Auschwitz. Canonized by Pope John Paul II in 1982.

Teresa Benedicta of . . . . Edith Stein, convert from Judaism who became a the Cross (1891–1942) nun and died in the Auschwitz gas chambers. Canonized by Pope John Paul II in 2003.

Katharine Drexel . . . . American nun who founded the Sisters of the (1858–1955) Blessed Sacrament for work among Native Americans and African-Americans. Canonized by Pope John Paul II in 2000.

Maria of Jesus Crucified . . . . Croatian nun who founded the Congregation of the Petkovic (1892–1966) Daughters of Mercy. Canonized by Pope John Paul II in 2003.

❈ FAMOUS LAST WORDS ❈

Stephen, AD 36
Lord, do not hold this sin against them.

St. Lawrence (martyr), 258
Turn me. I am roasted on one side.

Thomas à Becket, 1170
I commend myself to God, the Blessed Mary, St. Denis, and the patron saints of this Church . . . Father, into your hands I commend my spirit.

Jan Hus, 1415
O, holy simplicity!

Joan of Arc, 1431
Hold the cross high so I may see it through the flames!

Martin Luther, 1546
Father, into your hands I commit my spirit; you have redeemed me, O Lord, God of truth.

Hugh Latimer, 1555
Be of good comfort, Master Ridley, and play the man; we shall this day, by God's grace, light such a candle in England as I trust shall never be put out.

Thomas Cranmer, 1556
I see Heaven open and Jesus on the right hand of God.

Cotton Mather, 1728
Is this dying? Is this all? Is this what I feared when I prayed against a hard death? Oh, I can bear this! I can bear this!

Susanna Wesley, 1742
Children, when I am gone, sing a song of praise to God.

Selina Hastings, Countess of Huntingdon, 1771
My work is done; I have nothing to do but go to my Father.

John Wesley, 1791
The best of all: God is with us!

Catherine Booth, 1890
The waters are rising, but so am I. I am not going under, but over. Do not be concerned about dying. Go on living well; the dying will be right.

Dwight L. Moody, 1899
This is my coronation day. If this is death, it is sweet!

❈ BIBLE STORIES YOU KNOW AND LOVE— ❈ AS SEEN ON THE BIG SCREEN

Joseph in the Land of Egypt (1914) ● *The Chosen Prince* or *The Friendship of David and Jonathan* (1917) ● *Lot in Sodom* (1933) ● *Samson and Delilah* (1949) ● *Quo Vadis?* (1912, 1932, 1951) ● *David and Bathsheba* (1951) ● *Demetrius and the Gladiators* (1954 sequel to *The Robe*) ● *The Ten Commandments* (1923, 1956) ● *Ben-Hur* (1907, 1925, 1959) ● *The Big Fisherman* (1959) ● *Solomon and Sheba* (1959) ● *Esther and the King* (1960) ● *Barabbas* (1961) ● *Sodom and Gomorrah* (1962) ● *The Bible* (1966) ● *King David* (1985) ● *A.D.* (1985 miniseries) ● *The Prince of Egypt* (1998) ● *Abraham* (TV, 1994) ● *Jacob* (TV, 1994) ● *David* (TV, 1997) ● (See also *Jesus Goes to Hollywood: Movies about the Life of Christ*)

❧ THE TRADITIONAL SECTIONS ❧
OF A CHURCH BUILDING

Churches vary in architectural style, but these are some terms applied to the parts of a traditional church.

Altar—The table where the Mass or Eucharist is consecrated. In Protestant churches with a different theology, the proper term is *Communion table*. In evangelistic churches, the term *altar* may refer to the area at the foot of the chancel where worshipers kneel for prayer.

Ambo—A stand that combines the functions of pulpit and lectern; from the Latin prefix meaning "both." Often the ambo is called a *pulpit*.

Ambulatory—In a larger church, the area surrounding the altar where worshipers can walk; from a Latin word that refers to walking

Apse—A semicircular area in some churches where the altar is placed, projecting from the wall of the church. This end of the church is called the *east*, regardless of the actual geographical positioning of the building.

Chancel—The area from which the worship service is led. A chancel with a pulpit on one side, a lectern on the other, and the altar or Communion table in the center is sometimes called a *divided chancel*.

Choir—One of the "arms" of a cross-shaped ("cruciform") church, where the singers originally sat; if not a cruciform

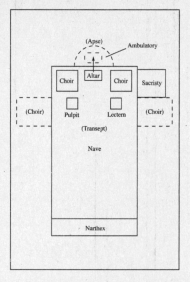

church, the choirs may be at the sides of the chancel.

Lectern—A stand for reading the Scriptures

Narthex—An area behind the nave, leading to the outside doors

Nave—The area where the congregation sits or stands; from the Latin word for "ship" because it resembles the upside-down hold of a sailing vessel. The side opposite the pulpit is called the *Gospel side*, and the side opposite the lectern is called the *Epistle side*. In churches that focus on preaching, the nave is sometimes called the *auditorium*.

❈ THE TRADITIONAL SECTIONS ❈
OF A CHURCH BUILDING—CONT.

Prayer-desk—Also called a *prie-dieu* (French for "pray God"), placed in the chancel for the use of worship leaders

Pulpit—The stand from which the sermon is preached

Sacristy—A room where the sacrament (Eucharist, Communion) is prepared; also used for vesting of clergy and others if there is no separate vestry

Sanctuary—The area around the altar, from the Latin word for "holy." In Protestant usage the term is often applied to the entire worship space, synonymous with *auditorium*.

Transept—In a cross-shaped church, the area where the arms come together; also applied to the projecting areas on either side (see *Choir*)

Vestry—A separate room where clergy or other worship functionaries put on their vestments (robes); in some churches the term refers to a fellowship hall, often in the basement.

❈ HISTORIC CHURCH CONFESSIONS ❈

In addition to the ancient creeds of the church (Apostles', Chalcedonian, Nicene, Athanasian), Protestant groups have formulated historic confessions, or statements of faith. These confessions reveal the issues churches were dealing with at various times and guide theological discussion up to the present. These are some of the historic confessions.

AUGSBURG CONFESSION (1531)—This confession, largely the work of Philipp Melanchthon, is a moderate statement of essential Lutheran doctrines such as justification by faith, with an appeal for correction of abuses in the Catholic Church.

BELGIC CONFESSION (1561)—This Reformed confession was originally drawn up in French as a repudiation of Anabaptist teachings. It was adopted as authoritative for the Netherlands in 1566 and reaffirmed by the Synod of Dort (Dordrecht) in 1619.

HEIDELBERG CATECHISM (1563)—This confession was drawn up in Heidelberg as a standard for the Palatinate, a German state.

❋ HISTORIC CHURCH CONFESSIONS—CONT. ❋

THE THIRTY-NINE ARTICLES (1571)—This document was finalized during the reign of Elizabeth I as a statement of the position of the Church of England on major theological issues of the time.

WESTMINSTER CONFESSION (1648)—This is the major confession of the Presbyterian churches, formulated by the Westminster Assembly of Divines (theologians) and ratified by the English Parliament during the Puritan Commonwealth.

SAVOY DECLARATION (1658)—This is a reaffirmation of most of the Westminster Confession, but it adds a "platform of discipline" affirming the congregational form of church government.

DECLARATION AND ADDRESS (1809)—A statement Thomas Campbell composed that advocated "simple evangelical Christianity, free from all mixture of human opinions and inventions of men."

BARMEN DECLARATION (1934)—This declaration, written largely by theologian Karl Barth (1886–1968), was issued by a group of Protestant leaders in response to the "German-Christian" movement, which was trying to reconcile the understanding of the church with conditions during the Hitler era.

❋ PROTESTANT "SAINTS" OF ❋ THE TWENTIETH CENTURY

All faithful Christians are "saints," or people called to be set apart as God's (1 Cor. 1:2). Therefore Protestants have no official process or agency to recognize anyone as a special saint. In the history of the Reformation, however, some have been widely recognized as martyrs, or witnesses who died for the faith, through such media as John Foxe's *Book of Martyrs* (first published in 1563). A list of twentieth-century saints in the Protestant community is subjective but could include the following. (Not everyone would agree with this list of Protestant "saints," and the list includes no living people.)

Czar Nicholas II . . . . In 2000, the Russian Orthodox declared the last czar a saint and martyr. Nicholas and the Romanov family were executed by revolutionaries in 1918.

❈ PROTESTANT "SAINTS" OF ❈
THE TWENTIETH CENTURY—CONT.

George Fox and .... Two of the four chaplains who gave their life jackets to
Clark Poling   others when their troop ship, the *Dorchester*, was torpe-
                          doed in 1943

The ten Booms   A Dutch family who hid Jewish people in their home dur-
                          ing the Nazi era. They were arrested in 1944. Casper, the
                          father, died in prison; and Betsie, a daughter, died in the
                          Ravensbruck concentration camp. Her sister Corrie
                          (1892–1983) was released and emigrated to the United
                          States, where she became influential for evangelism
                          through her writings. Willem, a brother, was arrested for
                          working with the Dutch underground and died shortly
                          after the end of World War II. Christaan, a nephew, died
                          in prison for working with the underground.

Dietrich Bonhoeffer .... German theologian executed by the Nazis
(1906–1945)

Amy Carmichael ...... Native of Ireland, sent by a Church of England missionary
(1867–1951)   society to India, where she served fifty-six years without
                          a furlough

Jim Elliot .... American missionary slain by Ecuadorian Indians
(1927–1956)

Albert Schweitzer ...... Theologian and musician who gave up a successful
(1875–1965)   European career to serve as a medical missionary in
                          Africa

Martin Luther King .... Baptist minister who led the civil-rights movement from a
(1929–1968)   Christian perspective and was assassinated

Janani Luwum .... Anglican archbishop of Uganda, who with many other
(1922–1977)   Christians withstood the dictator Idi Amin and was
                          executed

Richard Wurmbrand .... Romanian pastor and convert from Judaism, who was
(1909–2001)   tortured and imprisoned by the Communist govern-
                          ment; then after his release he led the effort in America
                          to publicize the plight of Christians in the Soviet bloc

❧ HERETICS AND THEIR HERESIES ❧

These are some of the views the majority of the Christian church judged heretical through history, even though the church did not expressly condemn all of them as such.

Movement	Major Figure	Major Idea
Montanism elite	Montanus (second century AD)	True Christians are Spirit-filled ascetics awaiting the imminent return of Christ. Tertullian (160–220), the first Christian theologian to write in Latin, was a Montanist.
Manicheism	Mani (216–276)	This was not a Christian heresy but a Gnostic sect based on the conflict between light and darkness. Jesus is the releaser of the Light imprisoned in matter.
Adoptianism	Paul of Samosata (third century AD)	Jesus was energized by the Spirit at baptism and called to be the Son of God, and in this sense only he is God. Also called Adoptianist Monarchianism.
Sabellianism	Sabellius (third century AD)	God reveals himself at different times in different modes: Father, Son, and Spirit; he cannot be all three and still be one. Also called Modalistic Monarchianism and Patripassianism; forerunner of Unitarianism.
Arianism	Arius (250–336)	The Son is subordinate to the Father; being "begotten," he had a beginning and is not coeternal with the Father.
Donatism	Donatus (died 355)	The church must be holy: those who renounce the faith under persecution cannot administer the sacraments, and converts from the Catholic Church must be rebaptized.
Apollinarianism	Apollinarius (310–390)	Christ had one will, that of the divine Word; he was fully God but not fully human.

❈ HERETICS AND THEIR HERESIES—CONT. ❈

Movement	Major Figure	Major Idea
Pelagianism	Pelagius (383–410)	People are responsible for their deeds, not predestined to them, and must take the first steps toward their own salvation.
Eutychianism	Eutyches (378–454)	Christ had only one nature, the divine. This view is called Monophysitism, and it is the doctrine of several ancient churches still in existence.
Monothelitism	Pope Honorius I (died 638)	Christ has a divine and human nature but only one "energy" or will; several figures were involved in this ongoing controversy that was more political than theological.
Socinianism	Fausto Sozzini (1539–1604)	Scripture is to be studied rationally; Christ is human, not divine. Forerunner of Unitarianism.

❈ OTHER "GODS" MENTIONED IN THE BIBLE ❈

This is a selection from the approximately fifty false gods mentioned in Scripture.

"God"	Nationality	Selected Reference	Comments
Amon	Egyptian	Jeremiah 46:25	National god of Egypt
Artemis (Diana)	Lydian	Acts 19:35	Fertility goddess
Astarte (Ishtar, Ashtoreth)	Phoenician, Canaanite	1 Kings 11:5	Goddess of evening star (Venus)
Ba'al	Canaanite	1 Kings 19:18	Means "Master, Husband"; chief god of Canaanites, paired with Ashtoreth
Ba'al-Zebul (Ba'al-Zebub)	Philistine (Ekron)	2 Kings 1:2	Name later applied to Satan (Matt. 10:25)

❀ OTHER "GODS" MENTIONED IN THE BIBLE—CONT. ❀

"God"	Nationality	Selected Reference	Comments
Bel (Marduk)	Babylonian	Isaiah 46:1	National sun god
Castor and Pollux	Greek, Roman	Acts 28:11	Twins, patron gods of sailors
Chemosh	Moabite	Numbers 21:29	Worshiped with child sacrifice
Dagon	Philistine	Judges 16:23–24	Known also in Babylonia and Canaan
Hadad	Syrian	1 Kings 15:18	Another name for Ba'al and Rimmon; worshiped throughout ancient Near East
Hermes (Mercury)	Greek	Acts 14:12	God of eloquence, good luck, divine messenger
Lilith	Semitic	Isaiah 34:14 (NRSV)	A night demon or hag
Marduk (Merodach)	Babylonian	Jeremiah 50:2	Chief god of Babylon
Moloch (Molech, Milcom)	Ammonite	2 Kings 23:10	Worshiped with human sacrifice
Nergal	Mesopotamian	2 Kings 17:30	Lord of the underworld
Queen of Heaven	Assyrian	Jeremiah 7:18	Goddess of fertility, known as Astarte or Ishtar
Rimmon	Syria	2 Kings 5:18	God of storm, equivalent to Hadad and Ba'al
Zeus (Jupiter)	Greek, Roman	Acts 14:12	Head of the Greek and Roman gods

❋ 107 "SEVENS" FOUND IN THE BIBLE ❋

Here are 107 things in the Bible said to come in groups of seven.

1. Days of creation

2. Days between Noah's dove releases

3. People spared in the flood besides Noah (2 Pet. 2:5)

4. Lambs Abraham sent to Abimelech

5. Years Jacob served Laban for Leah and Rachel

6. Times Jacob bowed to Esau

7. Fat and thin cattle in Joseph's dream

8. Ears of good and blighted corn

9. Years of plenty and famine

10. Days Joseph's family mourned for Jacob

11. Daughters of Reuel

12. Days of the Feast of Unleavened Bread

13. Lamps on the lamp- stand (menorah)

14. Days to make atone- ment

15. Times to sprinkle blood for atonement

16. Times to anoint the altar to consecrate it

17. Days Aaron is to stay in the tent for his consecration

18. Days a woman is to be unclean after bear- ing a male child

19. Days a leprous per- son is to be confined

20. Days a cleansed leper is to stay outside his tent

21. Days a newborn ani- mal must live before it can be offered

22. Weeks between Passover and Pentecost

23. Lambs sacrificed on Pentecost

24. Days to live in shel- ters during the Feast of Tabernacles

25. "Weeks of years" between jubilee years

26. Altars and sacrificial animals Balaam told Balak to provide

27. Nations Israel is to displace in Canaan

28. Years between release of debts

29. Days the Israelites marched around Jericho

30. Times they marched the seventh day

31. Priests with horns who led them

32. Years Israel served Midian

33. Years Ibzan judged Israel

34. Locks of Samson's hair

35. Months the Philistines kept the ark

36. Days Saul was to wait for Samuel at Gilgal

37. Sons of Jesse that Samuel didn't choose as king

38. Days the people of

❊ 107 "SEVENS" FOUND IN THE BIBLE—CONT. ❊

Jabesh-Gilead fasted after Saul's death

39. Sons and grandsons of Saul hanged by the Gibeonites

40. Years David ruled in Hebron

41. Years it took Solomon to build the temple

42. Days of feasting when the temple was dedicated

43. Days Zimri reigned as king of Israel

44. Times Elijah told his servant to look for rain clouds

45. Days the kings of Judah, Israel, and Edom marched to meet the Syrians

46. Times the Shunammite's son sneezed when returning to life

47. Times Naaman dipped in the Jordan

48. Years of famine during Elisha's time

49. Age of Jehoash when he began to reign

50. Sons of Elioenai

51. Kinsmen of Joel, chief of the Gaddites

52. Counselors of Artaxerxes

53. Days of feasting when Ezra read the law in the Water Gate

54. Days of feasting given by Ahasuerus

55. Eunuchs of Ahasuerus

56. Princes of Persia and Media

57. Maids given to Esther in Ahasuerus's harem

58. Sons of Job

59. Days and nights Job's friends sat with him without speaking

60. Bulls and rams Job was told to offer for his friends

61. Times the best silver was purified

62. Times during the day the psalmist praises the Lord

63. Things that are an abomination to the Lord

64. Pillars of wisdom

65. Times a righteous man falls and rises

66. Wise men a sluggard thinks he is wiser than

67. Abominations in the heart of the hateful

68. Women who will cling to one man in the day of the Lord's judgment

69. Channels into which the Lord will divide the River

70. Aspects of the Spirit of the Lord (Isa. 11:2)

71. Men of the king of Judah's council taken to Babylon

72. Days Ezekiel sat by the river Chebar before the word of the Lord came to him

73. Years it will take Israel to burn the weapons of Gog and Magog

74. Months it will require

❋ 107 "SEVENS" FOUND IN THE BIBLE—CONT. ❋

to bury the dead of Gog and Magog

75. Steps up to the East Gate in Ezekiel's vision of the restored temple

76. Cubits in height for the inner room of the temple

77. Days to make atonement for the altar

78. Days a person is defiled after touching a dead family member

79. Times hotter than usual that Nebuchadnezzar had the furnace heated

80. Time periods through which Nebuchadnezzar is to be like an animal

81. Weeks from the proclamation to rebuild Jerusalem till the coming of the anointed one

82. Shepherds to be raised up against the Assyrian

83. Facets of the stone set before the high priest Joshua

84. Eyes of the Lord ranging through the earth

85. Evil spirits brought back by the one cast out

86. Loaves of the boy with the loaves and fish

87. Baskets taken up after the feeding of the four thousand

88. Times Peter wondered whether he should forgive

89. Sadducee brothers who died after being married successively to the same woman

90. Demons cast out of Mary Magdalene

91. Years Anna had lived with her husband before he died

92. Times a day Jesus' disciples are to forgive a brother's sin

93. Men appointed to serve in the early church (deacons)

94. Sons of the priest Sceva

95. Days Paul stayed in Troas

96. Days Paul stayed in Tyre before going to Jerusalem

97. Days of Paul's vow of purification

98. Days Paul and Luke stayed in Puteoli before going to Rome

99. Churches of the Revelation

100. Golden lampstands

101. Stars

102. Spirits of God

103. Horns and eyes

104. Thunders

105. Seals

106. Heads of the beast

107. Bowls of wrath

❊ SIX LATIN PHRASES YOU NEED TO KNOW ❊

Sola fide, sola gratia, sola Scriptura ......"Faith alone, grace alone, Scripture alone," the watchwords of the Protestant Reformation

Ecce homo ...."Behold the man," the words of Pilate in John 19:5. The traditional site in Jerusalem is called the *Ecce Homo Arch.*

In hoc signo vinces ...."In this sign you will conquer," words the Roman emperor Constantine reportedly saw in the sky, together with a cross, which led to his conversion to Christianity

Soli Deo gloria ...."To God alone be the glory"; some Christian composers would write these words on their manuscripts

Fides quaerens intellectum ...."Faith in search of understanding." The phrase goes back to the work of Thomas Aquinas, the greatest medieval Catholic theologian; it refers to the idea that, while working from a nonnegotiable commitment of faith, we still seek to understand reality and truth through all avenues of inquiry.

Ex nihilo ...."From nothing," the thought that a new reality has come about having no previous form of existence; it is applied to God's creation of the universe

❊ OBSCURE CHRISTIAN "ISMS" ❊

Annihilationism ....The view that those who are not "saved" are not eternally punished, but simply cease to exist

Antidisestablishmentarianism ....The movement opposing those who advocated withdrawing state sponsorship from the Church of England

❄ OBSCURE CHRISTIAN "ISMS"—CONT. ❄

Antinomianism . . . . The view that Christians are free from any obligation to hold to a moral law

Dispensationalism . . . . A system in which Bible history is divided into periods during which God relates in a different way to the course of events. A cornerstone of the system is the idea that the age of the church is an interruption in God's plan for Israel, which will resume after the church is removed.

Docetism . . . . A semi-Christian form of Gnosticism (see below) holding that Christ, a spiritual being, appeared only to experience physical existence and death

Dualism . . . . A philosophy holding that the spiritual and material, or good and evil, are separate realities with opposing origins; contrasted with monism

Erastianism . . . . The doctrine that the civil authorities or legislators of a state are empowered to make decisions about the state's established religion, even if they are not adherents of it

Exemplarism . . . . The view that Christ's death atones for sin by setting a moral example that encourages repentance

Fideism . . . . The doctrine that the knowledge of divine matters can be attained only by faith, not the intellect

Gnosticism . . . . Derived from the Greek word for knowledge, this term describes a tendency that took many forms but essentially refers to a system in which salvation comes from receiving knowledge of matters hidden from others. Gnosticism sharply distinguishes the superior spiritual from the inferior material.

✸ OBSCURE CHRISTIAN "ISMS"—CONT. ✸

Iconoclasm . . . . The movement against the veneration of images of the divine, and the effort to destroy these images

Infralapsarianism . . . . A form of the doctrine of predestination that holds that God's decrees as to who would be the "elect" occurred after the fall of man; contrasted with supralapsarianism

Latitudinarianism . . . . A policy of retaining conventional church practices while deemphasizing matters of dogma, church organization, or worship issues. Today it might be called "cutting people some slack."

Modernism . . . . The adoption of a "modern" perspective on questions of truth, including a critical approach to the Bible, an emphasis on Christian life and society rather than doctrine, and the view that today's church is evolving into a reality not dependent on its ancient origins

Monism . . . . A philosophy that tries to explain everything that exists in terms of a single reality; contrasted with dualism or pluralism

Nominalism . . . . The philosophy that abstract categories of things, or "universals," are only names (*nomina*), and the reality is in the things themselves; contrasted with realism

Paedobaptism . . . . The practice of baptizing children as well as adults

Pluralism . . . . Similar to dualism, but not limited to two realities

Realism . . . . The philosophy that abstract categories of things, or "universals," are just as real (*res*, "thing") as the particular things in which they are embodied; contrasted with nominalism

❈ OBSCURE CHRISTIAN "ISMS"—CONT. ❈

Sabbatarianism	The practice of observing the Lord's Day (Sunday) in the manner of the Sabbath day of rest, or of adopting the seventh day (Saturday) as the Christian day of worship and rest
Supralapsarianism	A form of the doctrine of predestination that holds that God's decrees as to who would be the "elect" occurred before the fall of man; contrasted with infralapsarianism
Ultramontanism	The tendency in Catholicism to centralize all authority in the pope and the papal *curia*, or Roman congregations (dicasteries or departments)

❈ UNUSUAL ANIMALS OF THE BIBLE ❈

Behemoth (Job 40:15)	The word *behemoth* is a plural form of the word meaning "cattle." It seems to designate any large animal that lives in marshes. Some interpreters have suggested it refers to the hippopotamus, which means literally in Greek "river horse."
Coney (Prov. 30:26 NIV)	Also translated "rock badger," the Hebrew word designates an animal about the size of a rabbit that does not burrow but lives in rocky areas. It is not a badger, and some authorities prefer the term *coney*, an old word for "rabbit."
Hoopoe (Lev. 11:19)	A crested bird with a long, slender bill, with a habit of searching for grubs and insects in manure piles; therefore considered unclean
Kite (Lev. 11:14)	A scavenger and bird of prey of the hawk family
Leviathan (Job 41:1)	Used to designate a primeval sea monster defeated by Yahweh (Ps. 74:14); the term in Job seems to refer to any large sea creature, such as a whale.

❋ UNUSUAL ANIMALS OF THE BIBLE—CONT. ❋

Ossifrage (Deut. 14:12 KJV) ..... Also translated "vulture," the Hebrew word may designate the lammergeier, or bearded vulture, largest of the vulture family. The term *ossifrage* means "bone-breaker," from the bird's habit of dropping bones or tortoises on rocks to break them.

Phoenix (1 Clement 25–26) ..... Not mentioned in the Bible, but in this writing from the *Apostolic Fathers*, the phoenix is a legendary bird that lives five hundred years, then dies. Its "worm" feeds on the carcass of the dead bird, which it embalms and then flies to the altar of the sun in Heliopolis, Egypt. Clement used the phoenix as a symbol of the Resurrection. In the Bible, Phoenix is the name of a harbor town in Crete (Acts 27:12).

Pygarg (Deut. 14:5 KJV) .... The King James Version's term for the white-rumped antelope; the Revised Standard Version calls it the "ibex."

Satyr (Isa. 13:21) .... In Greek mythology, the satyr is a creature composed of a man and a goat, supposed to inhabit wastelands and ruins. In the Bible, the word seems to refer to demons or is a figurative way of saying that a place will become desolate. Some authorities think it could mean the baboon.

Unicorn (Num. 23:22 KJV) ...... The King James Version's term for the wild ox, probably referring to a species now extinct. The idea of "one horn" is derived from the Greek Old Testament, where a word was used that may have originally designated the rhinoceros.

Water hen (Lev. 11:18) .... The meaning of the Hebrew word is uncertain but is thought to refer to one of two hundred species of the rail family that inhabit marshes or ponds. Some authorities think the word refers to an owl.

Talking animals .... The serpent in the Garden of Eden spoke with Eve (Gen. 3:1–5). Balaam's donkey carried on a conversation with its master (Num. 22:28–30). The four "living creatures" spoke and sang praise in the Revelation to John.

❊ COMMON ENGLISH PHRASES ❊
TAKEN FROM THE BIBLE

Flesh and bone . . . . Genesis 2:23

Helpmate . . . . Genesis 2:18,
misunderstanding the King James:
"I will make him an help meet [i.e., fitting] for him."

My brother's keeper . . . . Genesis 4:9

Land flowing with milk and honey . . . . Exodus 3:8

An eye for an eye . . . . Leviticus 24:20; Matthew 5:38

The apple of his eye . . . . Deuteronomy 32:10

Rod of iron . . . . Psalm 2:9

My cup runneth over . . . . Psalm 23:5 KJV

No balm in Gilead . . . . Jeremiah 8:22

Handwriting on the wall . . . . Daniel 5:25

The salt of the earth . . . . Matthew 5:13

No one can serve two masters . . . . Matthew 6:24

Straight and narrow . . . . Matthew 7:13–14

Wolf in sheep's clothing . . . . Matthew 7:15

The blind leading the blind . . . . Matthew 15:14

Blood money . . . . Matthew 27:5–6

Physician, heal yourself . . . . Luke 4:23

Eat, drink, and be merry . . . . Luke 12:19

The truth shall make you free . . . . John 8:32

Declared *anathema* . . . . 1 Corinthians 16:22 KJV

Fallen from grace . . . . Galatians 5:4

The root of all evil . . . . 1 Timothy 6:10

SUBJECT INDEX

ABOUT THE AUTHOR

T. J. McTavish is an amateur church historian, has the world's largest collection of bobble-head dolls, and is currently at work on his first novel, *Left Behind . . . but At Least I'm Purpose Driven.*

ACKNOWLEDGMENTS

Apart from my brilliant editor at W Publishing Group, who for some reason asked to remain nameless, there is another whom I would be sorely remiss were I not to thank him from the bottom of my heart: Dr. Richard Leonard. Without Richard none of this would have been possible.